A Civilization of Love

The Catholic Vision for Human Society

William Newton

GRACEWING

First published in 2011
by
Gracewing
2, Southern Avenue
Leominster
Herefordshire HR6 0QF
www.gracewing.co.uk

All rights reserved. No part of this publication may be used, reproduced, stored in any retrieval system, or transmitted in any form, or by any means, electronic, mechanical, photocopying, recording or otherwise, without the written permission of the publisher.

© William Newton 2011

The right of William Newton to be identified as the author of this work has been asserted in accordance with the Copyright, Designs and Patents Act 1988.

ISBN 978 085244 761 1

On the cover: Albrecht Dürer, *The Adoration of the Holy Trinity* (1511).

For Elisabeth

Acknowledgments

I wish to express my gratitude to various people who helped me in the writing of this book. First of all, my thanks must go to all the students of the International Theological Institute who attended my classes on Catholic social teaching. From our discussions and from their insights I have learnt so much. I would also like to thank Miss Alison Bright and Miss Selene Viens for their diligent help in preparing the text for publication. Lastly, my deepest gratitude is reserved for my dear wife Claire, whose support and love are the foundation of all my work.

Contents

Contents..v

Abbreviations..ix

Introduction..xi

1. What is Catholic Social Teaching?..........................1

The nature of Catholic Social Doctrine?...........................1
Why is the Church interested in social issues?................4
The competence of the Church in social matters............6
What is the authority of social teaching?.........................7
Does social teaching change?...10
To whom is Catholic social teaching addressed?..........12
What documents make up Catholic social teaching?...13

2. Principles of the Church's Social Doctrine............19

Anthropological Foundations..19
    Man is created in the Image of God........................20
    Man is fallen...24
A triad of principles..26
    The Common Good...26
    The Universal Destination of Goods.......................29
    Private Property..30
    Private Property and the Universal Destination of Goods...32
    The Preferential Option for the Poor.......................34
    Subsidiarity..37

Solidarity..41
Fundamental Values of Social Life............................43
    Truth...44
    Freedom...45
    Justice...47
    Love..49

3. The Family as the Vital Cell of Society.................57

The family as a cell of society......................................57
The contribution of the family to the society..............61
Forming a community of persons................................62
Serving life by procreation and education..................63
Political activity for the sake of the family..................68
The State at the service of the family...........................72
Recognition and protection of the family as built on marriage..72
The family and economic life..78

4. Human Work...85

The dignity of human work..85
Work as a duty and as a right.......................................88
The objective and subjective dimensions of work.....90
The relationship of labour and capital........................91
The rights of workers...95
The right to a fair wage..96
The right to form trade unions.....................................98
The right to strike...100

5. Economic Life..105

The purpose of the economy and human development....106
What ethics has to do with economics......................108

Contents

Why Catholic social teaching favours the market economy..113
The role of the State vis-à-vis the economy......................120
The moral obligation of the consumer.............................122
Globalization..124

6. The Political Community...133

The foundation and purpose of the political community......134
Political authority..136
Political authority and the moral order............................141
Self-defence, civil resistance, and rebellion......................142
Cooperating with evil..145
Political authority and punishment of criminals..............148
Forms of government..151
Democracy...155
The relationship of Church and State.............................161
Religious Freedom..167

7. Human Rights..175

The basis, characteristics, and aim of human rights........176
The relationship between rights and duties....................178
Human rights and the common good.............................180

8. The International Community.................................183

The purpose of the International Community.................185
The structure of the International Community................186
The current state of the International Community..........190
The International Community and development............195

9. Peace..201

The relationship of peace to justice and charity..............204

War and the failure of peace..206
Terrorism..212

10. The Environment..217
The Hermeneutic of Stewardship..217
The demographic question...223
Population and development...224
Population and the environment...227
The environment, the State, and the market system.........228

11. Liberation...231
A sign of the times: aspiration for liberty..........................231
Individualism..234
Liberation Theology...236

Conclusion...243

Bibliography..249

Index 253

Abbreviations

CCC   *Catechism of the Catholic Church*

CIC   *Code of Canon Law* (1983)

CSDC   *Compendium of the Social Doctrine of the Church*

Introduction

It has been said that Catholic social teaching is the Church's best kept secret.[1] If this is true, this is certainly not the intention of the Church. In fact, the tradition of addressing papal encyclicals to 'all men of good will,' and not just the bishops, priests, and the lay faithful, was started by Pope John XXIII when he wrote his social encyclical *Pacem in Terris* (1963), precisely because the Church wants Her social teaching to be common knowledge. Accordingly, social teaching should be among the most known of all the teachings of the Church. Today, one can sometimes have the impression that all of the Church's teaching is Her best kept secret; but it is my experience that among all Her treasures Her social teaching is, in fact, the most scarcely known even among those who are quite informed on other matters of faith. This being so, my objective here is to give a concise, clear, and accurate presentation of Catholic social teaching.

Having said what my goal is, let me say what it is not! My goal is not to replace the reading of the original texts of social teaching, namely the social encyclicals themselves, since there is no substitute for reading these primary texts. Such a return to the sources is undoubtedly something requiring considerable mental exertion because the encyclicals are detailed, sometimes technical, and almost always long; nonetheless, reading them is always well worth the effort. That said, it can be very helpful to accompany this by reading an overview of the major themes of social teaching, and this is the aim of my book.

Of course, many books on Catholic social teaching have already been written, and so one might ask why another is needed. My answer to that question is twofold: first, in teaching undergraduate courses on Catholic social teaching at the International Theological Institute in Austria, I became aware that there is a dearth of books in the English language which aim simply to present social teaching as it is given by the Church. Often, I found that books on social teaching had a polemic edge, sometimes even against the Church. Accordingly, they sometimes gave a slanted presentation of social teaching, emphasizing those aspects that are in accord with the author's own agenda, while ignoring, down-playing, or criticizing those elements that oppose their view of the world. More than anything, this is very frustrating for anyone who has the simple aim of understanding the Church's teaching. Accordingly, my goal here is not to be innovative or to give my vision of society, but simply and faithful to transmit and explain what the Church has said.

The other reason for another book on social teaching is that social teaching is a very dynamic area of theology. Since it is a commentary on social issues, and since modern societies are evolving at a rapid pace, social teaching is constantly developing. Books written ten or twenty years ago obviously can still be very useful, but they will almost inevitably be incomplete because in the intervening period new social issues have emerged and new documents have been promulgated. In the last decade, we have even had a new pope who brings his own considerable contribution to the social teaching of the Church, not least in his recent social encyclical *Caritas in Veritate*.

The presentation of social teaching in this book is thematic. After a consideration of some foundational issues, such as the purpose and scope of social teaching, and the major principles upon which it is founded, I consider nine major themes of social teaching. This structure is similar (though not identical) to the *Compendium of the Social Doctrine of the Church* (from now on called 'the Compendium') produced by the Pontifical Council for Justice and Peace in 2004. In some sense, this book can be read as a companion

Introduction

to the Compendium. The Compendium is a great gift to the Church. Social teaching has, understandably, been developed by popes addressing the concrete social issues of their time. Therefore, before the Compendium, there was no systematic presentation of social teaching from the Church.[2] The Compendium is an attempt to draw out from the many social encyclicals the major themes of social teaching and present them in a systematic way. However, the Compendium is long and detailed and, because of this, not easily accessible. Here I have attempted a more concise thematic presentation of social teaching that, I hope, is easier to access.

Granted that this book is a more concise presentation of social teaching, what real motivation is there to read any book on social teaching? I believe that now is the moment for social teaching to be widely disseminated, and I believe there is a new openness to what it has to say about society. One might say now is the *kairos* for social teaching! The reason is this: with the collapse of Communism over the last two decades, there remain in the modern world only two real alternatives being offered for the structuring of human society, at least in the Western world. On the one hand, there is Western materialistic consumerism, and on the other hand, there is Islam. From a Christian perspective, neither of these options is ideal because neither answers to the deepest truth about man. The only realistic alternative to these two is the vision of society offered by the Catholic Church and articulated by Catholic social teaching. If you are not happy with the thought of Western consumerism or Islam being the model of society for the next generation, then it is time you became a little more informed about Catholic social teaching!

* * *

The title of this book is *A Civilization of Love: The Catholic Vision for Human Society*. This phrase—'Civilization of Love'—was coined by Paul VI in his *Regina Coeli* address on Pentecost Sunday 1970. Speaking about the descent of the Holy Spirit on the community of the Apostles, he said that 'it is the civilization of love and of peace which Pentecost has inaugurated.' His point is that the descent of the Spirit was a seminal event not just for the Church but also for the secular world, because 'it gave rise to a new sociology: one which penetrates the values of the Spirit, which forms our hierarchy of values, and which confronts us with the truth, and with the ultimate destiny of humanity.'[3]

In the Holy Year of 1975, Pope Paul returned to this theme. The desire to build this civilization of love seems to have become, in his mind, a leitmotif for that Jubilee year. In his general audience of 31 December 1975, at the close of the Holy Year, he asked, 'what can be gained from that moment of spiritual richness and moral commitment, which the Holy Year by a sure logic directs us to and with a certain power inspires?' He went on to answer his own question by saying: 'Yes, this is what we want, especially in public affairs, as the result of the time of grace and goodwill that was the Holy Year ... [a] civilization of love!'

Neither the phrase nor the idea it enshrined died when Paul VI passed away on the Feast of the Transfiguration in 1976. His successor, John Paul II, took the phrase to heart, using it more than two hundred and thirty times in his addresses, homilies, letters, and encyclicals. It even appeared in his first public address after his election as Pope. In that address, John Paul II said that the very aim of his pontificate would be to build this 'civilization of love.'[4] The phrase later appeared in two of his great social encyclicals, namely *Sollicitudo Rei Socialis* and *Centesimus Annus*.[5]

But what exactly is the substance of this phrase—a civilization of love? It seems to be simply this: to build a society in which the twofold commandment to love God and love neighbour (Lk 10:27) permeates the actions and thoughts of its citizens and also the very fibre of its structures: a civilization where this twofold love is the soul of society. This, in the end, is the essence of the Catholic vision for human society.

That being the case, this book seeks to explore the individual elements of this vision as they have been articulated by the Church. The question, therefore, becomes: what does the call to love God and love neighbour mean when it comes to the economy, to the political community, to international relations, to the environment, and so on: what are the demands of a civilization of love in each of these aspects of human society? As we shall see, the vision of a civilization of love is truly comprehensive and touches every aspect of man's life in society.

Notes

[1] Edward P. Deberri, James E. Hug, Peter J. Henriot, and Michael J. Schultheis, *Catholic Social Teaching: Our Best Kept Secret* (New York: Orbis, 1992).

[2] Given that the Pontifical Council is constituted by the Pope, it has a clearly defined mandate to teach and promote the social teaching of the Church (cf. John Paul II, *Pastor Bonus*, 142-144).

[3] Paul VI, *Regina Coeli Address*, 17 May 1970.

[4] John Paul II, *Urbi et Orbi Address*, 17 October 1978.

[5] Cf. John Paul II, *Sollicitudo Rei Socialis*, 33; *Centesimus Annus*, 10.

1

What is Catholic Social Teaching?

The nature of Catholic Social Doctrine?

One of the clearest statements on the nature of Catholic social teaching is given by John Paul II in his second social encyclical, *Sollicitudo Rei Socialis* (1987). He states that it is

> [an] accurate formulation of the results of a careful reflection on the complex realities of human existence, in society and in the international order, in the light of faith and of the Church's tradition. Its main aim is to interpret these realities, determining their conformity with or divergence from the lines of the Gospel teaching on man and his vocation, a vocation which is at once earthly and transcendent; its aim is thus to guide Christian behaviour.[1]

Characteristically of John Paul II, this is a very precise and full definition. Several things are worth pointing out. Most importantly, the goal the Church has in mind in proposing Her social doctrine is the guidance of behaviour. Social teaching seeks to answer the question of how we should act as citizens of this world. Therefore, it is classified as a branch of moral theology: it is moral theology applied to social living.[2]

John Paul II also makes the important point that social teaching tends to be reflective rather than prescriptive. This means that it reads more like a commentary on the current social situation than like a blueprint for the perfect society. In this way, it is not an ideology that presents a detailed plan for the structure of society. Accordingly, it ought not to be considered as a 'middle way' between the ideologies of capitalism and Marxism.[3]

To say it is reflective also means that there can be a time-lag between the emergence of a particular social issue and a reflection on this by the Church. For example, the poor treatment of workers by capitalists had been going on for many years before Leo XIII penned the encyclical *Rerum Novarum* in 1891. Likewise, it is only in recent years that some detailed reflection on the environment has emerged, (cf. *Centesimus Annus* [1991] and *Caritas in Veritate* [2009]), even though the environment has been a social issue since the 1970s.

John Paul II observes that the reflection on the social situation is made 'in the light of faith and of the Church's tradition.' This points out that the principles of social doctrine are drawn first of all from revelation. For example, the dignity of man as created in the image of God, or the unity of the human race in Adam, or the gift of creation to all men, are principles that come to us by revelation, that is, principally through Sacred Scripture, and which have been treasured and deepened over the centuries by theological reflection.

Of course, the primacy of faith and revelation in no way excludes reason. There are many principles of social teaching that can also be reached by reason, such as the unity of the human race—since all men share the same nature—or the right to own property. Moreover, reason comes to the service of faith, allowing us to unpack what is contained in principles of social teaching given by faith. For example, reason is needed to work out the implications of saying that God gave creation to all men in general and not to any in particular. One conclusion it will reach is that all have the right to some share in the goods of the earth. Reason is particularly at the service of the social teaching in the disciplines of philosophical anthropology and political philosophy, since both disciplines can help social teaching articulate its distinctive vision of man and society.[4] Indeed, the Church does not reject any human science that can be at the service of a better understanding of man and society, such as sociology or psychology, but rather 'enters into dialogue with the various disciplines concerned with man. It assimilates what these disciplines have to contribute.'[5]

While social teaching takes revelation as its starting point, this does not compromise its universal appeal.[6] As we have just said, much of what it proclaims about man and society (such as the dignity and equality of each human being or the right to private property) are truths that can also be reached by reason. Furthermore, great effort is made in the presentation of social teaching to show how both its principles and conclusions are in accord with reason. Finally, and most importantly, revelation and reason have the same source, namely God, and so can never contradict each other. Consequently, even when social teaching is presenting the truth about society arrived at from revelation, it is presenting what is true and unopposed to reason. Therefore, it is intrinsically appealing to man who, as a rational creature, is made for the truth.

Catholic social teaching is made up of principles, values, and norms.[7] Principles are starting points from which conclusions can be drawn about whether a concrete social situation is good or bad. There are essentially four: the dignity of the human person, the common good, subsidiarity, and solidarity. Values are attitudes and ways of acting which society ought to realize and promote, such as truth, freedom, justice, and mercy. Norms are statements about what simply must be the case in a good society. They are 'benchmarks' against which a society can be judged, such as the universal right to life and freedom of religious expression, the right to own property and to found a family. We shall look at these in much more detail in the next chapter.

Why is the Church interested in social issues?

If we were to consider the nature and mission of the Church only superficially, it would seem that the Church ought not to take an interest in social issues. According to the Gospels, the mission Jesus assigned to his Church is first of all a supernatural mission, namely to preach the Gospel and save souls (Mt 28:19). By concerning Herself too much in social issues, it might be argued, She is in danger of losing sight of this mission. There is no denying that one of the unfortunate tendencies among Catholics today is to foreshorten the horizon of the Church's mission, as if Her mission was merely to make this world a better place. In light of this, social teaching can seem to be dangerous because it absorbs Christian energy in the here and now.

Despite this objection there are, of course, good reasons why the Church has an obligation to concern Herself intimately with social issues. First, Christ Himself was concerned about the physical as well as the spiritual well-being of those whom He walked amongst while He was on earth. For example, He healed their diseases and fed them (Mk 1:32–34; Mt 14:15–21). Just like Christ, the Church is concerned about what is good for man as a whole, and since man has a body as well as soul, and seeing as he is social by nature, the Church understandably is concerned about how society is run.

Second, the social environment has a significant influence on how individuals understand themselves and their vocation, and ultimately whether or not people are open to hear the Gospel and fulfil their vocation as sons of God.[8] This is the reason Christian parents are—or at least ought to be—concerned about the moral tenor of the society their children grow up in (including smaller 'societies' such as clubs, schools, and friends), since the society can have a profound influence on their children's moral and spiritual values. Societies that are sexually permissive, for example, or promote crass consumerism, communicate to their members a particular understanding of the meaning of life and what it means to be a human being. The Church, as the Mother of all men and women (since all are called in Christ to be Her children) is, in every age, understandably concerned about the type of society Her children are living in.[9]

The doctrine of Christ the King means that all reality, temporal and material as much as eternal and spiritual, is under the dominion of Christ, the Universal King.[10] Since, then, the whole world belongs to Christ, His loyal subjects (the faithful) ought to strive as much a possible that His 'will be done on earth as it is in heaven.' The natural law, which holds a central place in Catholic social teaching, is the personal expression of the will of God. By reminding the world of this law and by seeking to make it a guiding principle of society, the Church is promoting the Kingdom of God. Seen in this light, the Church is not stepping outside Her supernatural mission when She proposes Her social teaching, since the goal of this teaching is to raise temporal affairs to a higher, and ultimately divine, standard.

Lastly, we believe in a God who 'became flesh and dwelt amongst us' (Jn 1:14). In the same way, our faith must be incarnated in concrete human actions. The Church, therefore, has something to say about personal morality—such as sexual behaviour, telling the truth, stealing—and likewise about social morality. Christ's 'new' commandment of love (Jn 13:34) has social ramifications and, in the end, this is what social teaching is: the working out of the implications of the commandment to love our neighbour as ourselves. Morality, of course, has got itself a bad name in our time; but whether it is in fashion or not, Jesus reminds us that we will be judged on what we have done or not done 'to the least of these brothers of mine' (Mt 25:40).

For all these reasons, Catholic social teaching cannot be a marginal concern of the Church and of Christians or seen as 'tacked on' to Her mission as something peripheral. Since social teaching is a presentation of the social implications of the Gospel, the Church has a duty to proclaim it: 'woe to me if I do not preach the Gospel' (1 Co 9:16)! Of course, with the duty comes the right: the Church also has a right to make Her social teaching known.

Nonetheless, the proclamation and implementation of social teaching is not the final goal of the mission of the Church. It is one component of the Church's evangelical mission, along with other aspects such as ecumenical and interreligious dialogue, catechesis, and witness. Always, the cutting edge of this mission is proclamation understood as an invitation extended to non-believers to enter into a personal relationship with Jesus Christ in the Church.[11] Social doctrine finds its proper place as ordered to this special and final goal.[12]

The competence of the Church in social matters

Vatican II's Pastoral Constitution on the Church in the World, *Gaudium et Spes*, speaks about 'the legitimate autonomy of earthly affairs.'[13] This implies that the Church does not claim a detailed technical competence in social matters.[14] For example, the Church is not an expert in the science of economics, so She does not pretend to know the best way to ensure full employment. However, She does propose at least two general principles in regard to the question of full employment. First, that full employment is a mandatory objective of any government and, second, that it is not the role of the State itself to create jobs, but to foster private initiative by which jobs are created. The point here is that the social teaching restricts itself to outlining the principles for a just society; it does not enter into details of how this is to be achieved. Others are better able to do this and there are often various acceptable solutions. It is because the Church restricts Herself to proposing principles in social issues (such as economics) that there can be legitimate disagreements even among Catholics on the best concrete solutions.

That said, the Church does claim expertise in two areas. In his encyclical *Populorum Progressio* (1967), Pope Paul VI calls the Church 'an expert in humanity'.[15] By this, he meant that She knows what man is and She knows his destiny. The Constitution *Gaudium et Spes* tells us 'that only in the mystery of the incarnate Word does the mystery of man take on light,' and that only Christ, God and man, 'fully reveals man to Himself.'[16] This means that the Church, because She knows Christ, has access to the deepest truths about man; and only a thorough understanding of man can be the basis for constructing a social order that is worthy of man.

Furthermore, how to order a society correctly is a moral question, not just a technical one, since it involves more than simply finding the most efficient economic and political structures and mechanisms.[17] It requires that these structures bring about justice and that they respect, nay promote, human dignity. So, first of all we need to know what justice is, and what it is not. Would such and such a structure be fair? Does this way of arranging things promote human dignity or not? These are the fundamental questions, and they are questions about morality. As the authentic interpreter of natural law—as an expert in morality—the Church has something very important to offer to society in this respect.

What is the authority of social teaching?

A question that is often asked about Catholic social teaching—and indeed today about any teaching coming from the Church—is the question of Her authority. The first point to make is that the Church has the authority to determine definitively (infallibly) not just truths of faith but also moral truth. Vatican II states that the Church has authority to teach in the name of Christ the truths of faith 'and every thing that serves to make the People of God live their lives in holiness.'[18] That is to say, She can definitively teach not only about dogmas such as the Trinity, the resurrection, and heaven, but also about what is morally good and what is morally bad. In *Veritatis Splendor*, John Paul II warns against a modern mistake of separating faith and morals, as if one could be spiritual without being moral.[19] This power of the Church (to teach authoritatively on morals as well as faith) is a gift to us from Christ, and we ought to be profoundly grateful for it, because it helps us to become more fully human.

As part of the moral teaching of the Church, social teaching in general has the same authority as the Magisterium's teaching on personal morality, such as sexual behaviour, stealing, lying, and so on. In judging the weight of individual teachings on, say, economics or politics, it is not enough to consider only the type of document in which the teaching is found, be it an encyclical, or an Apostolic Letter, or merely a speech. Most of Catholic social teaching is contained in Papal encyclicals, but this alone does not determine the authority of the teaching. It is more important to consider how things are expressed in the document. The questions we must ask include: Is the statement solemnly expressed? Is it repeating something taught consistently by the Church from the earliest times? Is it repeating something of natural law? Is the intention to define, or merely to propose and exhort? These are the factors that determine the authority of any magisterial teaching.

Much of social teaching consists of the application of established principles of morality, especially principles of natural law, to various social situations. Principles of natural law, such as those encoded in the Ten Commandments, are true for everyone in every age. They are infallibly true. Conclusions drawn from these principles that have been consistently taught throughout the ages, such as the right to own property and the prohibition on abortion, are said to be part of the Church's ordinary and universal Magisterium. They are also infallibly true.[20] Even when this is not the case and there is no intention to define something infallibly, there is still the obligation (on the side of the faithful) to religious submission of mind and will, so-called religious assent (*obsequium religiosum*).[21] This implies a disposition on the part of the believer to accept the teaching as true and shape his life according to it, while remaining open to the fact that the Church might modify this teaching in the future.[22]

To make all this more concrete, let us consider some examples, all things that we shall consider in more detail later. According to social teaching, it is for the parents to determine the size of their family. The State errs when it takes over this decision. This right of the parents is part of natural law. It has also been repeated many times by various popes, in encyclicals, letters, and speeches. In each case they are not really defining a truth, but are rather reminding us what is part of natural law and thus universal, perennial, and binding. On the other hand, social teaching tacitly accepts the right of nations to have nuclear weapons, at least while there is no mechanism to remove all these weapons from the face to the earth. While the right to self-defence is part of natural law, having this or that weapon is not so clearly a right. So, given the nature of this matter and the manner in which the Church has expressed Herself, we seem to have before us an authoritative but not infallible statement of truth. Therefore, the Church could reconsider this matter and declare that nuclear weapons do not constitute part of a nation's right to self-defence.

Let us remind ourselves of the important difference between dissent and questioning. Dissent is a bold and public statement that the Church is wrong about some issue and that other Catholics have a right (and perhaps even an obligation) to disregard this teaching. Questioning has an altogether different attitude and reflects an altogether different disposition. It, too, can be public, but it stops short of claiming the Church is definitely wrong and that others can disregard Her. Rather, it points out the difficulties or unresolved issues in a given teaching and seeks, in collaboration with the Church and in a spirit of charity and humility, to find a solution.

Does social teaching change?

Social doctrine, unlike speculative truths of the faith such as the Blessed Trinity and the Incarnation, has something contingent, or changeable, about it. The Trinity is eternally the same ('the same today, yesterday, and forever' [Heb 13:8]), but social teaching is about concrete historical situations which are constantly in a state of flux. So for example, Leo XIII's Encyclical *Rerum Novarum* addresses the plight of the worker at the end of the nineteenth century, a situation that had not existed one hundred years before and that no longer exists today, at least in the Western world. John Paul II notes that social teaching is 'subject to the necessary and opportune adaptations suggested by the changes in historical conditions and by the unceasing flow of the events which are the setting of the life of people and society.'[23]

In studying social teaching, it is very important to distinguish between principles and the application of these principles in the historical situation of the time. The principles, such as the dignity of man, the common good, solidarity, and the right to property, are perennial; but their application to historical concrete situations is specific and yields unique conclusions. An encyclical like *Rerum Novarum* is important not only because of what is has to say about a specific situation, namely the oppression of the working class at the end of the nineteenth century, but also (and moreover) because of the principles it highlighted. For example, in defending the worker, Leo XIII defended the worker's right to acquire private property and rejected a solution which put all property into the hands of the State, since this would pervert the role of the State and enslave citizens.[24] This same principle, thirty years later, would be the centrepiece of the Church's rebuttal of Marxism,[25] and seventy years later part of Her commentary on the welfare state.[26] The very same principle is applied in different concrete situations to reap different (though not contradictory) conclusions.

There is something constant: the principle, and something new: the conclusion (Mt 13:52). A celebrated case in point is the Church's assessment of capital punishment. Most recent statements on this view favourably the fact that many States no longer use this form of punishment.[27] At first sight, this might appear as a change in the Church's position, since in the past She clearly held capital punishment as a normal part of the State's power in the realm of law and order.[28] The truth is that what has changed is not a principle of social ethics but a concrete situation. The principle of protecting society against dangerous criminals remains; but now this can normally be achieved by secure incarceration (rather than execution). Accordingly, the application of the same principle—the right of the society to protect itself—yields, in the modern age, a different conclusion.

There can also be a development in social doctrine when the implications inherent in principle are more clearly perceived.[29] For example, the dignity of the human conscious has received greater attention in the past half-century, and because of this the Church has been more vocal in Her call for religious freedom.[30] Also, since social doctrine is about human action, new possibilities can arise to which the old principles must be applied for the first time. For example, the principle that a nation can use force in self-defence is perennial, but the question as to whether it can use nuclear or chemical weapons in so doing, is new. The point is: social teaching is about the interaction of moral principles with concrete situations, and in every case it is very helpful to make the distinction between the two.

Finally, a word about the use of language is needed. It is better to speak about the renewal of social teaching rather than a change in social teaching. The latter way of speaking has precisely the danger of being misunderstood to mean a change in principles. The word renewal implies that something has indeed changed, but that what is essential has remained the same. We might speak of an old building being renewed (or renovated). In such a case the foundations of the building remain, while what is built upon these foundations, the exterior, is (sometimes significantly) modified.[31]

To whom is Catholic social teaching addressed?

It has already been noted that, in the modern era, the popes have addressed their social encyclicals to 'all men of good will.' This makes perfect sense seeing as the issues they discuss pertain to all people and not just to bishops, priests, or even just Catholics in general. Nonetheless, in a particular way, social teaching is proposed to the laity of the Church because, in the words of *Lumen Gentium*, 'the laity, by their very vocation, seek the kingdom of God by engaging in temporal affairs and by ordering them according to the plan of God.'[32] Re-echoing this in *Christifideles Laici*, John Paul II states that: 'the vocation of the lay faithful to holiness implies that life according to the Spirit expresses itself in a particular way in their involvement in temporal affairs and in their participation in earthly activities.'[33]

Since it is they and not the priests who are in a position to change social realities at the grassroots, the laity are charged with the task of ordering the societies they live in so that they conform to the value of the Gospel: the laity 'are called in a special way to make the Church present and operative where only through them can she become the salt of the earth.'[34] Canon Law states that:

> [E]ach lay person in accord with his or her condition is bound by a special duty to imbue and perfect the order of temporal affairs with the spirit of the gospel; they thus give witness to Christ in a special way in carrying out those affairs and in exercising secular duties.[35]

Since the Second Vatican Council, many ministries within the Church have been opened up to the lay faithful, such as being Extraordinary Ministers of Holy Communion and Lectors at Mass. This is undoubtedly good, but it would be a great shame if this were to blunt the fundamental mission of the laity. Their ecclesial mission is primarily *ad extra*, rather than *ad intra*: it is evangelisation, of which, as we have seen, the implementation of social teaching is one component.[36]

What documents make up Catholic social teaching?

Before speaking about the documents that make up Catholic social teaching, it is worth considering who authored them. Of course, since most of Catholic social teaching has come to us by way of papal encyclicals, the proximate authors are the popes and whoever assisted them. However, since social teaching is the application of the Gospel and moral principles to concrete situations, the lay faithful (who live and work in the world) are indirectly also in some sense the authors![37] It is clear, especially in the writings of Pius XI and Pius XII, that Catholic lay movements such as Catholic Action had a real influence on social teaching. In *Quadragesimo Anno*, Pius XI speaks of 'our beloved sons engaged in Catholic Action,' who 'with a singular zeal are undertaking with Us the solution of the social problems in so far as by virtue of her divine institution this is proper to and devolves upon the Church.'[38] Of course, even today, the Holy Father will draw extensively on the experience of various lay experts in formulating new social teaching in areas such as globalization and the environment.

There is no definitive list of documents that make up the corpus of social teaching, but there is a general consensus. Leo XIII's encyclical *Rerum Novarum* is the landmark document, giving to the Church, in the words of John Paul II, 'citizen status' in public life.[39] The major anniversaries of this document have been commemorated by other social encyclicals, such as Pius XI's *Quadragesimo Anno* (1931), Paul

VI's *Octogesima Adveniens* (1971), and John Paul II's *Centesimus Annus* (1991). *Rerum Novarum* itself was preceded by other encyclicals of Pope Leo XIII that ought to be considered as having some relationship to social teaching, such as *Diuturnum Illud* (1881), *Immortale Dei* (1885), and *Libertas Praestantissimum* (1888), which all consider political life. Pope Pius IX's *Quanta Cura* (1864) and Gregory XVI's *Mirari Vos* (1832) also made contributions to social teaching on the correct relationship between the Church and the State. Prior even to this, there are occasional interventions of Popes in regard to social issues, for example, Benedict XIV's condemnation of usury and dishonest profit in *Vix Pervenit* (1745) and Eugene IV's condemnation of slavery in *Sicut Dudum* (1435). Of course, all the way back to Apostolic times there has been reflection within the Church on social issues: St Thomas Aquinas himself wrote on these issues (*De Regimine Principum*, 1267). Even the Letters of St Paul and St Peter have something to say about living in society (Rm 13:1–2; 1 P 2:13–14), and Jesus Himself speaks about temporal authority as given by God (Jn 19:11).[40]

While, then, there is no definitive list or canon of social teaching documents, the following documents are fairly universally accepted as part of the corpus of Catholic social teaching:

Leo XIII	*Diuturnum Illud* (1881)
Leo XIII	*Immortale Dei* (1885)
Leo XIII	*Libertas Praestantissimum* (1888)
Leo XIII	*Rerum Novarum* (1891)
Pius XI	*Quadragesimo Anno* (1931)
Pius XI	*Mit Brennender Sorge* (1937)
Pius XI	*Divini Redemptoris* (1938)
Pius XII	*True and False Democracy*, Radio Broadcast (1944)
John XXIII	*Mater et Magistra* (1961)
John XXIII	*Pacem in Terris* (1963)
Vatican II	*Gaudium et Spes* (1965)
Vatican II	*Dignitatis Humanae* (1965)
Paul VI	*Populorum Progressio* (1967)

Paul VI	*Octogesima Adveniens* (1971)
Synod of Bishops	*Iustitia in Mundo* (1971)
John Paul II	*Laborem Exercens* (1981)
John Paul II	*Sollicitudo Rei Socialis* (1987)
John Paul II	*Centesimus Annus* (1991)
Benedict XVI	*Caritas in Veritate* (2009)

I have not included here any documents from individual bishops, other than the Bishop of Rome, or from regional Bishops' Conferences, since they cannot claim to teach for the Universal Church. Yet, among many documents from different Bishops' Conferences around the world, several documents in particular are worth noting. The Bishops' Conference of Latin America (Consejo Episcopal Latinoamericano, CELAM) have penned several documents of interest to social teaching, notably the documents consequent of their meetings in Medellin (1968) and Puebla (1979). The most significant contribution from the North American Bishops' Conference is *Economic Justice for All* (1986). The Bishops' Conference of England and Wales has issued a handful of documents with social content. The most significant are *The Common Good and the Catholic Church's Social Teaching* (1996) and *Vote for the Common Good* (2001).

The Congregation for the Doctrine of the Faith has also produced several documents of great interest, notably: Instruction on certain aspects of the 'Theology of Liberation' (*Libertatis nuntius*, 1984), Instruction on Christian freedom and liberation (*Libertatis conscientia*, 1986), and Doctrinal Note on some questions regarding the participation of Catholics in political life (2003). Of course, the Pontifical Council of Justice and Peace has, in addition to the Compendium, made many statements on social teaching, often given in addresses by the President of the Council. One particularly useful document is *The Social Agenda* (2000). This is a collection of excerpts from different magisterial documents on social teaching. Finally, the Pontifical Council for the Family, because of its concern for marriage and family life, has produced various documents that touch upon social issues, such as the *Declaration on the Decrease of Fertility in the World* (1998), *The Family and Human Rights* (1999), and *Family, Marriage and 'De Facto' Unions* (2000).

Notes

1. John Paul II, *Sollicitudo Rei Socialis*, 41.
2. *Ibid.*; *CSDC*, 72.
3. John Paul II, *Sollicitudo Rei Socialis*, 41.
4. *CSDC*, 76-8.
5. John Paul II, *Centesimus Annus*, 59.
6. *CSDC*, 75.
7. *CSDC*, 81.
8. *CSDC*, 62.
9. *Ibid.*
10. The doctrine of Christ the King was proclaimed by Pius XI in 1925 in the face of the totalitarian claims of atheistic Communism, which gave no place to God in society (Pius XI, *Quas Primas*).
11. John Paul II, *Redemptoris Missio*, 44 and *Ecclesia in America*, 66; cf. Pontifical Council for Interreligious Dialogue, *Dialogue and Proclamation*, 10.
12. *CSDC*, 67.
13. Vatican II, *Gaudium et Spes*, 36.
14. *CSDC*, 64.
15. Paul VI, Encyclical Letter *Populorum Progressio*, 13; *CSDC*, 61.
16. Vatican II, *Gaudium et Spes*, 22.
17. *CSDC*, 70; cf. Benedict XVI, *Caritas in Veritate*, 14.
18. Vatican II, *Dei Verbum*, 8.
19. John Paul II, *Veritatis Splendor*, 4.3, 26.2.
20. Doctrine is taught definitively (and so infallibly) either by the extraordinary Magisterium—an Ecumenical Council or a declaration from the Pope *ex cathedra*—or by the ordinary and universal Magisterium—the teaching of the Pope in union with the Bishops when they are not gathered together in a Council. The

perennial and consistent teaching of the Church on faith and morals is included under the latter. For this distinction see Vatican II, *Lumen Gentium*, 25 and Congregation for the Doctrine of the Faith, *Concerning the Teaching Contained in Ordinatio Sacerdotalis Responsum ad Dubium*. The *ordinary and universal Magisterium* must be distinguished from the *ordinary Magisterium* which applies to the teaching given by the Bishop of Rome or by another Bishop outside of these special circumstances. In that case, the teaching is not definitive but authoritative.

[21] Vatican II, *Lumen Gentium*, 25.

[22] For a thorough discussion of these issues, see William May, 'The Church as Moral Teacher' in *An Introduction to Moral Theology*, (Huntington, IN: Our Sunday Visitor Publishing, 2003), pp. 245–265.

[23] John Paul II, *Sollicitudo Rei Socialis*, 3.

[24] Leo XIII, *Rerum Novarum*, 3–15.

[25] Pius XI, *Quadragesimo Anno*, 111–126.

[26] John XXIII, *Mater et Magistra*, 104–121.

[27] John Paul II, *Evangelium Vitae*, 27.

[28] 'The secular power can without mortal sin carry out a sentence of death, provided it proceeds in imposing the penalty not from hatred but with judgment, not carelessly but with due solicitude' (Innocent III, *Profession of Faith Prescribed for Durand of Osca and his Waldensian Companions*).

[29] *CSDC*, 85.

[30] Cf. Pius IX, *Quanta Cura* and Vatican II, *Dignitatis Humanae*.

[31] For a penetrating discussion of the difference between renewal and change, see Benedict XVI, *Christmas Greetings to the Members of the Roman Curia and Prelature* (22 December 2005).

[32] Vatican II, *Lumen Gentium*, 31.

[33] John Paul II, *Christifideles Laici*, 17.

[34] Vatican II, *Lumen Gentium*, 33.

[35] *CIC* 225 §2.

[36] Cf. Russell Shaw, *Ministry or Apostolate?* (Huntington, IN: Our Sunday Visitor, 2002); Avery Cardinal Dulles, *The Mission of the Laity*, L. J. McGinley Lecture, Fordham University, 29 March 2006.

[37] *CSDC*, 79.

[38] Pius XI, *Quadragesimo Anno*, 138.

[39] John Paul II, *Centesimus Annus*, 5.
[40] For a detailed presentation of this pre-history of Catholic Social Doctrine, see Rodger Charles, *Christian Social Witness and Teaching*. Volume 1: *Catholic Tradition from Genesis to Centesimus Annus* (Gracewing: Leominster, 1998).

2

Principles of the Church's Social Doctrine

Catholic social teaching is founded upon one mega-principle, three foundational principles, and four values. If these are thoroughly understood, then one has gone a long way towards understanding social teaching and has in one's hand the key to 'unlocking' all the magisterial documents. This chapter is dedicated to explaining these seminal ideas.

Anthropological Foundations

The first principle of Catholic social doctrine—the 'mega-principle'—is the truth about the human person and his consequent dignity.[1] This principle is concisely presented by Pope John XXIII when he states that the good of man is the goal of the whole social order and that man himself has a goal that is supernatural, namely communion with God. He says:

> This teaching [social doctrine] rests on one basic principle: individual human beings are the foundation, the cause and the end of every social institution. That is necessarily so, for men are by nature social beings. This fact must be recognized, as also the fact that they are raised in the plan of Providence to an order of reality which is above nature.[2]

Moral theology is built upon anthropology and it is as sound as its anthropological foundations. This is as much as to say that before we can say how a person ought or ought not to act, we need to know what a man is and in what his destiny consists. Likewise, before we judge whether a society is rightly ordered, we need to know what the purpose of society is, and, since it can have no other goal than the benefit of its members, we come back to the same question: what is man? If we think that man is only an animal, then we will think acting like an animal is perfectly appropriate. Personal morality will follow on from this. For example, monogamy will be considered unnatural, and society will be structured on the basis of the survival of the fittest, as it is in the animal world. If we think man is only a body (pure matter) and has no transcendent dimension (no soul), then gross consumerism or Marxism will appear as entirely suitable ways to structure society. Consequently, what is needed before we can have a sound social doctrine is what John Paul II called an 'adequate anthropology.'[3] This anthropology must be a full description of man. Both theology and philosophy have something to offer here.

The two fundamental truths about man opened up to us by theology are, first, that man is created in the image and likeness of God and, second, that man is fallen and prone to sin. These are the deepest truths about man and they are only fully appreciated by the Christian faith. It is because of this that the Church can claim to be an 'expert in humanity.'[4]

Man is created in the Image of God

To say that man is created in the image and likeness of God is to say much. It implies that man in some sense transcends this world. It means that he is by his nature in relation to God, and has God as his final goal in life, and can only understand himself adequately as such. It implies that he is made for love and made for the truth, since God is love and truth. It implies that he is superior to all other creatures and, like God, has dominion—or stewardship—over them. It implies that he is rational and free and capable of self determination. It implies that man is made for communion or, in the language of social teaching, is a social creature to which solidarity (friendship with other citizens) is natural. It implies an equality among all human beings and between men and women, since all are created in God's image and, therefore, aside from the many difference that individuals might have in regard to talents, strengths, and even fortune, there remains this fundamental equality. All these truths are contained in this doctrine of the *imago Dei* and are profoundly significant for Catholic social teaching.

Let us consider these truths in a little more detail and see exactly how they are significant for social teaching. Here we need only take a first look, since what we have to say here is more fully unfolded throughout the entire book.

First, the doctrine of man created in the image of God points to the fact that human beings are made with a capacity for God (*capax Dei*), and that the final end or purpose of life is communion with God. As we shall see, while the goal of political and economic life is not directly to bring about this communion—that is the goal of the Church—this truth about man's destiny must be the horizon of all political and economic activity.

Second, society is the out-working of the social nature of man, a creature created in the image of a God who is Himself a communion of Persons. The social nature of man implies that man is from within himself unfailingly inclined to live in society—in communion with others—and that this is the usual way for every man to achieve his perfection as a human being. Society is a communion of persons—a community. A community is a group of people bound together by the pursuit of goals that can only be had by a common effort and which are a real benefit for all members of the group (such goals are called common goods). In this way, the *Catechism of the Catholic Church* (from now on referred to as 'the Catechism') defines society as 'a group of persons bound together organically by a principle of unity that goes beyond each one of them.'[5] Actually, society is a conglomeration of smaller communities. Some are natural, especially the family, and some are voluntary (the result of agreements) such as trade unions and sports clubs.

Individualism does not correspond to the truth about man as a social creature. Rather, it arises from a selfishness that is the result of our fallen nature. On the other hand, collectivism is also an inadequate model for the structure of human society, since it leads to the loss of personal identity and is, therefore, contrary to human dignity. As we shall presently see, only a correct understanding of the notion of the common good can hold the middle ground between the extremes of individualism and collectivism.

Third, creation in the image of God implies that each human being, created in the image of a personal God, is a person. Included in the notion of personhood, and intimately and indissolubly connected with it, is the dignity of the human being. We shall discuss the idea of human dignity further in the chapter on human rights (chapter seven); here, it would be important to note that human beings are not constituted persons (and hence have innate dignity) because of anything they do—such as think, be conscious, or exercise freedom. When these activities are missing, as in the case of children or the mentally disabled, such individuals are still persons. As the Compendium points out, personhood is the foundation of these activities but personhood is not constituted by them.[6]

Fourth, since every human being is created in the image of God, this doctrine gives a solid foundation to the essential equality that exists between all human beings, and by extension between all nations. In particular, it affirms the essential equality between men and women. Founded in the doctrine of the image of God, the equality of all persons is powerfully reaffirmed by the realization that God became man and died for all men and nations, without exception (1 Tm 2:4). It is, however, important to remember that equality does not mean 'sameness.' Authentic equality is not opposed to diversity, just as in God there is unity in diversity of Persons. This is an especially important point to remember when we consider the equality that exists between the sexes. Men and women are different physically and psychologically. This difference has often been the cause of tension between the sexes, but revelation indicates that it is a difference of complementarity (Gn 2:18). Men and women bring to each other, and therefore to society, different gifts that fit together and enhance each other. Ultimately, their differences are an opportunity, not for strife, but for collaboration and communion.[7]

Fifth, when God reveals His intention to create man in His own image, He then proceeds to form man from the dust of the earth by breathing 'the breath of life' into Him (Gn 2:7). In this mysterious language of the Book of Genesis, we understand an important truth about man: he is both material and spiritual. Of course, this truth about man is not exclusive to theology. The history of philosophy has been dominated by the discussion of the relationship between the body and the soul! This goes to show that, as we have already said, philosophy, as well as theology, has a contribution to make to an adequate understanding of man. In describing the relationship of the material and spiritual in man, the Catechism tells us that:

> [T]he unity of soul and body is so profound that one has to consider the soul to be the 'form' of the body: i.e., it is because of its spiritual soul that the body made of matter becomes a living, human body; spirit and matter, in man, are not two natures united, but rather their union forms a single nature.[8]

This precise description of the relationship between the material and spiritual dimensions of man holds the middle ground between two errors: a spiritualization of man that ignores his physical needs and even despises the body, and a materialization of man which degrades him because it conceives him as a mere body, considering as important in life only what is material.

A sixth important anthropological truth contained in the doctrine of the image of God is that human beings are free in a way that other animals are not. Organizing society in such a way that this freedom is respected and enhanced is, accordingly, important.

Here I have briefly outlined six consequences for social teaching given the starting point of man created in the image of God. This is meant to be illustrative rather than exhaustive. The point is to show how central this vision of man is to social teaching. Throughout the book we shall return continually to this starting point, since it is the most important truth about man and, therefore, the indispensable starting point for judging whether social realities are right or wrong.

Man is fallen

To say that man has fallen and is prone to sin is to be utterly realistic. Man is not as he ought to be and hence society is often not as it ought to be. All the divisions and injustices present in society are ultimately traced back to the reality of sin. Without a proper understanding of sin, it is impossible to understand society, so the Catechism rightly points out that 'ignorance of the fact that man has a wounded nature inclined to evil gives rise to serious errors in the areas of education, politics, social action, and morals.'[9]

Social teaching recognizes several categories of sin: personal sin, social sin and, so-called structures of sin. The idea of 'social sin' points to the fact that personal sins—sins of individuals—hurt not just the sinner, but other people and society in general. At one level this is obvious. Theft, for example, clearly hurts the one whose belongings are taken and, more generally, undermines solidarity and trust in society. However, it is not only sins against justice that harm society. Since each person stands to society like a part to the whole, and since the sickness of one bodily member is negative for the whole body, so even sins that appear to harm just the individual sinner have negative repercussions on the whole society. This can be understood if we take the example of pornography. Looking at pornography seems to be a private matter. However, this assessment ignores the intimate connection between the different virtues in a man. Pornography undermines the virtue of temperance — self control — and this attitude or disposition is needed if we are going to act both courageously and justly in society. The person who is self-centred, by being intemperate or unchaste, finds it very hard to make the sacrifices needed to give other people what is owed to them, that is to say, he finds it hard to act bravely and justly. Over and above such an explanation of how personal sin is also social sin, the profound and admittedly mysterious solidarity that exists between human beings leads to the conclusion that personal sin, even intensely private sin, lowers the moral and spiritual temperature of the whole society. John Paul II expresses this when he says: 'to speak of social sin means in the first place to recognize that, by virtue of human solidarity which is as mysterious and intangible as it is real and concrete, each individual's sin in some way affects others.'[10]

Structures of sin are cultural attitudes, laws, or political and economic structures that are evil because they influence people and encourage them to act badly.[11] Examples would include such things as anti-life laws and mentalities, institutionalized unjust discrimination, perhaps against women or certain ethnic groups (such as in the system of apartheid), and structures that perpetuate unfair trade. What is very important to remember here, however, is that structures of sin are always the result of personal sin. It is a mistake to divorce structures of sin from individual responsibility or, even worse, to claim that there is no such thing as personal sin (and immorality) but only structures that are sinful. In *Sollicitudo Rei Socialis*, John Paul II reminds us that '"structures of sin" ... are rooted in personal sin, and thus always linked to the concrete acts of individuals who introduce these structures, consolidate them and make them difficult to remove.'[12] Despite focusing on the reality of sin, Catholic social teaching is not at all pessimistic. In fact, if anything it could be accused of being overly optimistic; but this is not a human optimism. It is evangelical hope based on the belief that Christ has definitively conquered the power of sin in this world.

The most important corollary of the truth that all social strife is ultimately the result of sin is that there can be no lasting solution to social problems unless sin is dealt with. Therefore, and this is a point of cardinal importance that we shall return to at the end of this book, social reformation presupposes moral and spiritual reformation.

A triad of principles

Taking as its foundation an 'adequate anthropology,' Catholic social teaching has three other fundamental principles. These are the common good, subsidiarity, and solidarity.[13] They are applicable to all spheres of social doctrine, whether economics, politics, international community, or the environment. They are also interrelated and so form a package, as it were, since solidarity aims at achieving the common good, and subsidiarity is the outworking of solidarity, as we shall see.[14] These principles, along with the adequate anthropology, allow us to judge whether a society is well ordered and to propose the outline to solutions when there is disorder,[15] since a sound society will demonstrate solidarity and subsidiarity and in the first place the attainment of the common good.

The Common Good

The notion of the common good is built upon the idea that there are things all humans need to live a properly human life that cannot be obtained alone, but only by collaborating with others. These things are called common goods because they are good for all and they are had only by common effort. The attainment of the common good is the ultimate reason for society and for the political community. The raison d'être of leadership and authority is the attainment of the common good of the community, whether the community be a family or a state, or something in between. The common good of a nation can be multifaceted. For example, there is prosperity, peace, health, education, and civic fellowship. These are all things that make life more human and that are attained only in collaboration. For example, education is something that marks humans out from other animals. It makes human life more human, so to speak. It is also something that is achieved by teaching, reading, and discussion: all things that presuppose the involvement of others, a common effort. Education is, therefore, a common good. Health is also a common good in the sense that it is good to be healthy and in the sense that health is usually better achieved and maintained by working together to produce healthy food, healthy living conditions, and health-restoring medicine. It is different, however, from education in the sense that health is not a goal in itself but a stepping stone to other goals in life, whereas learning can be a goal in its own right. Fellowship is also a common good in this way. We do not rightly seek communion with other for any further purpose. If we do, then it is likely that our motivations are a little dubious, since we are seeking to use others and our acquaintance with them. Fellowship is also a perfect common good because when one person has it this does not deprive anyone else of the possibility of also sharing in it. Other goods are less perfectly common because, while they are theoretically open to all, the actual use by one person precludes or limits use by another. Public transport systems are common goods in this sense. Everyone can use them, but the more people there are using them at one time, the less benefit each receives; this is called the rush hour!

Sometimes, private and common goods can be in conflict with each other. In order to build a hospital with the goal of promoting health, a government may force a landowner to sell some of his land to the State. Again, when we pay taxes we are all 'sacrificing' something of our private good for a greater common good. However, the conflict ought to be seen for what it is. Those who give up their private good are not deprived from participating in the common good. The landowner may benefit greatly from the hospital if he becomes sick, and the taxpayer reaps many benefits from the taxes he pays.

There are two common errors in thinking about the common good. On the one hand, it is wrong to think of the common good as the sum total of everyone's private goods. If this is taken to be the common good, society degenerates into crass individualism and the government becomes merely a referee adjudicating conflicts between different groups with the aim of creating a society in which the only goal is private gain. This is the error of laissez-faire capitalism. On the other hand, there is the danger of making the State, and not the citizens, the subject of the common good. The danger is then that what is good for the State is set against what is good for the citizens, or a given groups of citizens, and human rights are violated under the pretext of the common good. This is the error of Communism and other totalitarian regimes, where people who stood up for basic rights, such as religious liberty, were branded 'enemies of the State'. The now classic definition of the common good of society is given by the Fathers of Vatican II in *Gaudium et Spes*. This steers a middle path between the two errors mentioned above. The common good is understood as 'the sum total of social conditions which allow people, either as groups or as individuals, to reach their fulfilment.'[16]

A final point: while the political community has as its goal the temporal common good, it must remember that each citizen has communion with God as his final purpose in life. This is to say that each human being has a common good beyond the confines of this world, namely God Himself. This Common Good is not the immediate concern of the government but, since the State's immediate concern is man who has this transcendent goal, it must be its horizon:

> [T]he action of the State [is not limited] to the pursuit of public prosperity during this life only, which is but the proximate object of political societies ... [b]ut as the present order of things is temporary and subordinated to the conquest of man's supreme and absolute welfare, it follows that the civil power must not only place no obstacle in the way of this conquest, but must aid us in effecting it.[17]

The Universal Destination of Goods

In Catholic social teaching, the principle of the Universal Destination of Goods is a particularly important application of the principle of the common good. This principle states that God gave the created world to all of mankind and not to any individual in particular. This means that creation is a common good to which all ought to have access.[18] The Fathers of Vatican II tell us that 'God destined the earth and all it contains for all men and all peoples so that all created things would be shared fairly by all mankind under the guidance of justice tempered by charity.'[19] This principle is so important that in *Laborem Exercens* John Paul II can call it the 'first principle of the whole ethical and social order.'[20]

The practical implication of this 'universal destination' is a right: every person has a right to all they need for a full human development. This is the implicit intention of God in creation. This right is natural, which means it comes with human nature and not from the positive law of the community; it is certainly not conferred by the State. Furthermore, in the words of Pope Paul VI, 'all other rights [in the economic realm], whatever they are, including property rights and the right of free trade, must be subordinated to this norm; they must not hinder it, but must rather expedite its application.'[21] This means that the right to the material goods needed for a life worthy of man is prior to any right to private property, or any other human regulation of created goods.

We should note, however, that the principle of the Universal Destination of Goods does not necessarily lead to the conclusion that there should be an equable distribution of created goods. While men are all essentially equal simply because they are human, in many other aspects there is natural inequality among men, for example in intelligence, strength, beauty, virtue, industriousness, and even luck! These lead to variations in prosperity between persons and, clearly, Scripture tolerates this. This fact, however, should not lead to less concern for the poor, or toleration of the *status quo*; it is always valid to ask whether the current distribution of goods is just, let alone loving.

Private Property

The right to private property is a constant principle of Catholic social teaching. It is hard to think of a principle that has been more consistently and vigorous defended by the Church over the course of the twentieth century, in the face of collectivistic ideologies, especially Marxism. It was defended first of all in *Rerum Novarum*, not as a defence of the rich, but because Leo XIII saw that if the right to private property was removed, the poor worker would lose his only means of bettering his material situation; he would be the first to suffer. Pope Leo explains:

> Socialists, therefore, by endeavouring to transfer the possessions of individuals to the community at large, strike at the interests of every wage-earner, since they would deprive him of the liberty of disposing of his wages, and thereby of all hope and possibility of increasing his resources and of bettering his condition in life.

But this very practical reason is not the foundation of the right to private property.[22] Indeed, in *Rerum Novarum*, Leo XIII points out that a right to private ownership is part of natural law.[23] It is part of natural law, since property is normally necessary for the perfection of human life. Unlike wild animals, humans cannot gain on a day to day basis all they need to live a fully human life; and unlike domesticated animals, they are not meant to docilely receive everything from a master; they are called to provide for themselves. Accordingly, ownership of such things as are needed for a fully human life—such as land, stores of food, clothing, housing, tools, and so on—is a natural right for man. This is especially true since the offspring of human beings, unlike many other creatures, require years of nurturing before they are able to survive and flourish on their own. Accordingly, their parents need to hold securely what is needed for their highly dependant offspring.

Furthermore, by owning things man has the opportunity to be creative and productive, and this is fitting for him as a rational creature.[24] When a married couple owns a house, they tend to develop it and make more of a home of it than when they merely rent it from someone else. The ingenuity and creativity that opens up in situations of ownership is behind Pope John XXIII's defence of private property in the face of the post-war welfare States. In *Mater et Magistra*, he notes that even if these welfare states do provide all the material things needed for a good standard of living, this cannot remove the right to private ownership nor, moreover, the duty to promote private ownership, since only ownership can promote creativity and vitality in the economic life of a society.[25]

Again, experience shows that in the absence of private ownership things are not looked after properly and there are many conflicts over their use. This is contrary to the peace and prosperity of the whole society. In this way, private ownership can be beneficial to the common good.

Finally, the alternative to private ownership is usually State ownership; but this normally leads to a gross distortion in the function of the State.[26] It requires that the State becomes too involved in the details of individuals' lives (determining the kind of work they do and what kind of housing they have, and so on). The State is then set on the path to totalitarianism, understood in the strict sense of having total control over all aspects of human life. Pope John XXIII noted that:

> [H]istory and experience testify that in those political regimes which do not recognize the rights of private ownership of goods, productive included, the exercise of freedom in almost every other direction is suppressed or stifled. This suggests, surely, that the exercise of freedom finds its guarantee and incentive in the right of ownership.[27]

Furthermore, in such situations the State is more than a nanny, it is a parent; and this undermines the authority and dignity of real parents. In a word, the family is harmed when private property is not allowed (this is the experience of Communism) and this is the most devastating thing that can happen in any society because the family, as we shall soon see, is the first living cell of any society.

Private Property and the Universal Destination of Goods

For a correct understanding of private property, its relationship to the principle of the universal destination of goods must be carefully articulated. The key point is that the Universal Destination of Goods is not in conflict with private property, quite the contrary! In the normal scheme of things, private property is the best way to realize God's intention in the Universal Destination of Goods, namely that all would have an adequate share in the blessings of creation. By private ownership—widely diffused—individuals concretely share in the blessings of the material world. In this way, the right to own things can be at the service of the Universal Destination of Goods. Throughout the twentieth century, the Church was an unflinching champion of ownership of private property, especially in opposition to Communism. Yet, as John Paul II explains, the Church:

> always understood this right [to private property] within the broader context of the right common to all to use the goods of the whole of creation: the right to private property is subordinated to the right to common use, to the fact that goods are meant for everyone.[28]

The subordination of the right to private property to the Universal Destination of Goods has several concrete implications. First, in some circumstances, the right to private ownership can be revoked by those who are in charge of the common good, for the sake of the common good. This happens in the case of nationalization, when a certain sector (such as the supply of water) is deemed so important for the common good that the State takes it out of private control. Second, at a personal level, if a man is in dire need and another has more than he needs, the poor man can take what he needs from the richer man without being guilty of stealing. Third, the principle of the Universal Destination of Goods is the foundation of the so-called 'social function' of private property. While all the goods an individual owns are really his—meaning not only that he has the right to use them, but also he has the right to dispose of them (e.g. sell them and bequeath them)—he is obliged to use these goods for the common good. Vatican II says every man 'should regard the external things that he legitimately possesses not only as his own but also as common in the sense that they should be able to benefit not only him but also others.'[29] Similarly, in *Rerum Novarum*, Leo XIII had stated:

> [I]f the question be asked: How must one's possessions be used?—the Church replies without hesitation in the words of the same holy Doctor [St. Thomas Aquinas]: 'Man should not consider his material possessions as his own, but as common to all, so as to share them without hesitation when others are in need'.[30]

The social dimension of property makes particular demands on our superfluous belongings. These are goods that a man has over and above what he needs for maintaining a decent standard of living for himself and his dependants.

The social dimension of ownership applies not only to material goods but also to spiritual goods such as know-how, inventions, and ideas. These also can, in some sense, be owned, as we see from the fact that inventions can be patented and discoveries protected by intellectual property rights. Speaking of such goods, John Paul II noted that, 'In our time, in particular, there exists another form of ownership which is becoming no less important than land: the possession of know-how, technology, and skill. The wealth of the industrialized nations is based much more on this kind of ownership than on natural resources.'[31] But these new forms of goods (and hence new forms of ownership) are a product of human intelligence and, therefore, rely upon an endowment given to individuals and groups by God; hence, they also come under the principle of the Universal Destination of Goods.[32] Normally, they additionally rely upon the inheritance of other people's research, often over many years, decades, or even centuries. What comes from God (and from the efforts of many) should be a blessing to many. For example, a remedy to a formerly incurable disease (such as AIDS) cannot be owned in such a way that the maximum profit is squeezed out of its production and sale. This property—this know-how—comes with the obligation to maximize not profit but its utility to those suffering from this disease.

The Preferential Option for the Poor

In Catholic social teaching, the principle of the preferential option for the poor is often discussed in the light of the Universal Destination of Goods, because the poor are those who lack sufficient access to the created goods of the world.[33] This preferential option means that those in charge of the common good, the governors of society, are called upon to give special attention to those who do not have access to material goods needed for a human standard of living. It is not opposed to the value of equality, because the rich can normally look after themselves while the poor cannot, as Pope Leo XIII points out:

> [W]hen there is question of defending the rights of individuals, the poor and badly off have a claim to special consideration. The richer class have many ways of shielding themselves, and stand less in need of help from the State; whereas the mass of the poor have no resources of their own to fall back upon, and must chiefly depend upon the assistance of the State.[34]

A similar idea is offered by Pope John XXIII seventy years later in *Pacem in Terris*, when he says:

> [C]onsiderations of justice and equity can at times demand that those in power pay more attention to the weaker members of society, since these are at a disadvantage when it comes to defending their own rights and asserting their legitimate interests.[35]

While the phrase 'preferential option for the poor' may be of recent coinage, perhaps even owing its popularity to Liberation Theology, the idea is present from the beginning of social teaching as we can see from these words of Leo XIII above. Indeed, John Paul II claims that it is one of the key ideas of *Rerum Novarum*.[36] Of course, ultimately the idea that special attention should be given to the poor is a basic Christian attitude, learned from the way God Himself deals with mankind. For this reason, John Paul II points out how this 'option for the poor' is an attitude requisite of everyone and not just of leaders of nations. He offers the following description:

> This is an option, or a special form of primacy in the exercise of Christian charity, to which the whole tradition of the Church bears witness. It affects the life of each Christian inasmuch as he or she seeks to imitate the life of Christ, but it applies equally to our social responsibilities and hence to our manner of

living, and to the logical decisions to be made concerning the ownership and use of goods.[37]

Another important point needs to be made: the preferential option for the poor ought never to become an option against the rich. This has been a danger in Liberation Theology when the Marxist idea of class struggle has been uncritically imported into Catholic social thought.[38] We shall discuss this in more detail later.

A question related to the preferential option for the poor is the question of the redistribution of wealth, and especially of land. At the heart of this question is how we are to judge when an individual or group own too much. To answer this, we must make a distinction between necessary goods and superfluous goods. Necessary goods are those that a person needs for himself and his dependents to live a human way according to his place in society. This can include some provision for the future, taking into account what would normally be needed (but not extraordinary and unforeseeable needs). All belongings beyond this are superfluous goods. It is not against justice to own such superfluous goods but, as we have seen, along with the ownership of them comes a duty to use them for the benefit of others.

Having made these distinctions we are in a position to make two simple statements on the question of redistribution of wealth. Here we shall focus directly on the question of the ownership of agricultural land. This is because this issue is of most pressing concern (especially in Latin America) and so we have some clear statements of the Magisterium on it.[39] But what will be said about land can apply more generally to other forms of wealth. The basic principle is that when ownership undermines the intention of God in the Universal Destination of Goods, then there is something wrong with ownership in that society and changes need to be made. Two cases can occur.

First, someone might own superfluous land but not sufficiently communicate its benefit to others, for example they under utilize it and prohibit poor farmers from using it. When this arises, it might be right for the State to appropriate the land (giving due compensation to the owner) and give it to the poor farmers. The situation of misuse must be quite serious. Pius XI points out that normally, while respect for ownership pertains to commutative justice and so can be regulated by law, it is hard to regulate the proper use of goods since correct use of things has more to do with the virtue of liberality, which is not so easy to encode in law.[40] For example, while a law can be easily framed to protect my right to own my car, it is not practical to have a law regulating the use I make of it, whether I use it enough for he common good or not! Only when there is gross misuse of property can the State step in.

The second case is when ownership is so concentrated that many people have no hope of owning land, even if the use made of the land by the few owners is ordered more or less to the benefit of others. Since ownership is a principle means to escape poverty, such concentration of ownership locks vast numbers of people into a life of poverty, depriving them of the opportunity of bettering themselves and attaining real security for their families. Accordingly, the situation might arise where the State must ensure that ownership of land in a society is readjusted, promoting a wider base of ownership.

Subsidiarity

The principle of subsidiarity corresponds to a vision of society as something more than a collection of individuals all under the power of the State. In contrast to such an atomized concept of society, Catholic social teaching understands society in a more communitarian way, ultimately as a conglomeration of smaller communities; the most fundamental and the most natural of these, of course, is the family. Accordingly, in the final analysis, the essential matrix of society is its families in communion with each other. Out of this matrix other groupings emerge, based on ethic identity and economic initiatives, as well as cultural and leisure interests.[41] These groups are numerous and diverse, but to give some examples in the British society, there are Geordies (people from the Northeast), Afro-Caribbean communities, private schools, professional institutes (like the Institute of Chartered Accountants), residents' associations, choirs, and tennis clubs. A society is vibrant when its families and such intermediate grouping flourish, and the principle of subsidiarity seeks to support this vitality.

The principle of subsidiarity is most clearly defined by Pius XI in *Quadragesimo Anno*. There, he states:

> Just as it is gravely wrong to take from individuals what they can accomplish by their own initiative and industry and give it to the community, so also it is an injustice and at the same time a grave evil and disturbance of right order to assign to a greater and higher association what lesser and subordinate organizations can do. For every social activity ought of its very nature to furnish help to the members of the body social, and never destroy and absorb them.[42]

Stated positively, the principle of subsidiarity says that higher groups, and especially the State, must assist lower groups to help themselves. In fact, this is the meaning of *subsidium* in Latin: it means 'help.' Stated negatively, the principle implies that the higher groups (especially the State) must not encroach on the lower with regard to what they can do for themselves. Take for example education: if lower groups such as families or groups of families can adequately educate their children (and desire to undertake this task), then the State must not prohibit this, rather it is obliged to help them to fulfil this task themselves—perhaps even financially by allocation of public funds.

There are several phenomena that are opposed to the principle of subsidiarity. From the side of the State there is the danger of an over-bearing welfare state, sometimes called 'the nanny state.' It is over-bearing when it reduces personal initiative; for example giving unemployment allowances that discourage individuals from searching for jobs or creating them. Closely tied to the phenomenon of the welfare state is the danger of excessive bureaucracy that overly controls private initiatives. Commenting on these two phenomena, John Paul II notes that:

> By intervening directly and depriving society of its responsibility, the Social Assistance State leads to a loss of human energies and an inordinate increase of public agencies, which are dominated more by bureaucratic ways of thinking than by concern for serving their clients.[43]

Finally, there is a danger that can come from the market economic system itself. This is the problem of economic monopoly, understood as the concentration of the means of production in the hands of few, something that undermines economic subsidiarity.[44] All three reduce the scope for personal initiative which, as an expression of human freedom, is a manifestation of the truth about man as created in the image of God. In this way, we see how the principle of subsidiarity is founded on the truth about man.

In the light of the principle of subsidiarity, the normal role of the State is to encourage personal initiative. It is called upon to create the atmosphere or conditions in which this flourishes. In this regard, a major task will be overseeing the redistribution of public money aimed at just this goal.

There are circumstances, however, when more dramatic, incisive, and invasive intervention is required on the part of the State. Because the principle of subsidiarity must be applied in its dynamic relationship with the other principles of social doctrine, especially the principle of the common good, when the common good is threatened it may sometimes be necessary for the State to temporarily take more control; for example to 'artificially' stimulate the economy when private initiative fails. This is not the suspension of the principle of subsidiarity but its application in a situation where the lower level group cannot fulfil its normal function. Also, the State has the duty to balance the demands of different groups, which at times may mean intervention to restore gross imbalances, as in the case of monopolies. Sometimes the need might arise for the State to arbitrate between lower level groupings. Such might be the case when employers and employees in a given industry cannot come to agreement over a just wage.[45] Such interventions ought to be exceptional and temporary, always aimed at re-establishing the conditions where the lower level associations are 'back on their feet' and taking active care of themselves. All this points to the fact that the State must perform a delicate and dynamic balancing act:

> Experience has shown that where personal initiative is lacking, political tyranny ensues and, in addition, economic stagnation in the production of a wide range of consumer goods and of services of the material and spiritual order ... [w]here, on the other hand, the good offices of the State are lacking or deficient, incurable disorder ensues: in particular, the unscrupulous exploitation of the weak by the strong.[46]

Since the State has this balancing act to perform, it should not be judged too harshly when it occasionally fails a little in this difficult task.

Closely allied to the principle of subsidiarity (one might say the 'flipside') is the principle of participation; since subsidiarity of a political, economic, or cultural flavour promotes the participation of individuals in the life of the society. Participation is a right, but also a duty, since, according to the principle of solidarity, all are called to contribute to the common good. As we shall see later, because democracy fosters political participation, this is one reason why the Church thinks well of it.[47]

Solidarity

The principle of solidarity is closely tied to that of the common good. It states that there is an obligation on each member of a society to strive to include all other citizens in the common good, meaning that they ought to consider the good of others in someway as their own. In this sense, solidarity is the same as 'civic friendship,' and to that extent closely related to charity.[48]

In truth—and this distinguishes it from subsidiarity—it is as much a virtue as a principle. This means that it is (or ought to be) a personal attitude and inclination that influences the social behaviour of each citizen. In *Sollicitudo Rei Socialis*, John Paul II describes it as:

> [not a] feeling of vague compassion or shallow distress at the misfortunes of so many people, both near and far. On the contrary, it is a firm and persevering determination to commit oneself to the common good. That is to say to the good of all and of each individual, because we are all really responsible for all. [49]

Pope Benedict XVI succinctly summarizes this when he says that 'solidarity is first and foremost a sense of responsibility on the part of everyone with regard to everyone.'[50]

Solidarity is particularly opposed by the 'structures of sin' that we have already discussed, since they represent a partisan view of society where one group seeks to promote itself at the expense of another, or individuals are set against each other in relationships of competition rather than collaboration. In their place, a society should seek to construct structures of solidarity. However, this is easier said than done because, since solidarity is a virtue and not just a principle, the State has much less influence over solidarity than it does over subsidiarity. The latter can, in some sense, be created by juridical structures (laws and rights). This is true of solidarity to a much more limited extent: organizations such as 'Neighbourhood Watch' can be created to foster solidarity among residents in the face of the threat of burglars, and it is possible to legislate to encourage fair trading practices and responsible disposal of refuse. But, as a social virtue akin to friendship, solidarity can, for the most part, only be encouraged, and the conditions for its flourishing ensured, since you cannot make laws making people friends!

The principle of solidarity must always respect the principle of subsidiarity. If by solidarity one group in society comes to the aid of another, it ought to do so in a way that helps the weaker and smaller group to help themselves. Likewise, the principle of subsidiarity pays deference to solidarity. In pursing their own interests and goals, each group ought to acknowledge the rights of other groups and the importance of the common good of the whole society. A healthy society is built on all three principles. As Pope Benedict XVI pointed out in *Caritas in Veritate*:

> The principle of subsidiarity must remain closely linked to the principle of solidarity and vice versa, since the former without the latter gives way to social privatism, while the latter without the former gives way to paternalist social assistance that is demeaning to those in need.[51]

Faith adds a profound depth to the virtue of solidarity. It becomes a Christian virtue that turns our neighbour into our brother because he too is loved by Christ and, therefore, all the more worthy of our total commitment:

> In the light of faith, solidarity seeks to go beyond itself, to take on the specifically Christian dimensions of total gratuity, forgiveness and reconciliation. One's neighbour is then not only a human being with his or her own rights and a fundamental equality with everyone else, but becomes the living image of God the Father, redeemed by the blood of Jesus Christ and placed under the permanent action of the Holy Spirit.[52]

In recent years, both John Paul II and Benedict XVI have noted that the most important factor in whether globaliza-

Principles of the Church's Social Doctrine

tion will be a positive or negative experience, especially for the poor, is whether or not solidarity will itself be globalized; meaning, whether each will seek to include all others in the economic benefits that until now have come only to a privileged minority of the world's citizens.[53] Pope Benedict asks: 'as society becomes ever more globalized, it makes us neighbours but does not make us brothers?'[54]

Fundamental Values of Social Life

Complementing these first principles of social teaching, there are four foundational values. These are enumerated by John XXIII in his encyclical *Pacem in Terris*. In that document, he states that, since society is a community of persons, 'we must think of human society as being primarily a spiritual reality.'[55] He then proceeds to proposes four values on which this 'spiritual reality,' a community of persons, must be built. These are truth, justice, love, and freedom.[56]

These values are spiritual goods that flourish in a well-ordered society: we call them values because we appreciate these goods: 'we value them.' Moreover, they are spiritual goods that will flourish if the principles of social doctrine are applied. For example, if subsidiarity is practiced, there is freedom for personal initiative and the truth about man as a rational creature is respected. If solidarity is practiced, there is justice, since everyone is included in the common good, and this is a manifestation of a love of neighbour. In this sense, the values are the goals at which the principles aim, just as in the same way a family might have as a value deep communion between family members, and so has a principle of family life that one meal a day is had as a family.

Being spiritual goods, however, there is a limit to what the State can do to make these values loved and respected in society; even if the principles of social teaching were implemented according to the letter, it is only when these principles are deeply embraced by citizens and lived according to their spirit that these values animate a society, that is, become the soul of society. Another way of expressing this is that these values have a corresponding virtue—a moral disposition.[57] The State can only encourage its citizens to acquire and use these virtues; it cannot make its citizens virtuous.[58]

Truth

Truth can be defined as conformity to reality, because when you know the truth about something or some situation, you know what it really is; and, of course, without this it is inconceivable that we can make good decisions about how to structure and run a society. Most importantly, as we have already discussed, we need to know who man is and in what his destiny consists: in short, we need to know the truth about man. This is the starting point that determines everything.

In the modern world there is a very serious crisis of truth called relativism. Throughout history there have been, of course, constant disagreements (often violent) about this or that truth—for example whether slavery is immoral or not—with one group seeing things one way, while another sees things differently; but relativism is much more serious than this because relativism denies the possibility of knowing the truth at all! This is sometimes motivated by what we have just said, namely the confrontation that can arise in a pluralistic society over different visions of reality. In the light of possible (or even probable) confrontation, relativism can seem like a good (even the mandatory) foundation for building a modern pluralistic society.

In fact, relativism curtails the search for truth and leads to an impoverished vision of human life and society; all that remains are elements acceptable to all: a society of the lowest common denominator. For example, it tends to a materialistic vision of society because every side can agree that man has material needs, but all do not agree that he has spiritual needs, and so these are ignored. Worse still, it tends to evolve into a secular intolerance for those who profess to know the truth, excluding them from any in influence in decision-making.[59] More will be said about this later.

The two great allies of relativism and, therefore, enemies of truth are cowardliness and laziness, since it takes courage and not a little energy to confront reality and conform to it. Truth is often demanding, since in its light we discover that we must make the not inconsiderable effort to change our behaviour. Courage is also needed to enter into dialogue and perhaps confrontation with others in society who have a different vision of reality. Accordingly, searching for the truth takes real effort and perseverance; we must constantly be on guard against laziness.

Freedom

Freedom is a fundamental value because it conforms to the truth of man created in the image of God, a creature capable of self-determination. A society that respects this value accordingly treats its members not as babies or animals, but as responsible adults. It calls them to responsible living commensurate with their dignity as human persons. Since there is a separate chapter later in the book on 'Liberation,' we shall only lightly touch on matters here.

The correct articulation of the relationship between truth and freedom is particularly important. There is a modern notion of freedom that makes it an absolute value, divorced from truth. Moreover, in an environment where truth is relative, it becomes a freedom to create truth according to personal preference, rather than freedom to conform one's actions to reality, that is, to the truth. John Paul II claims that the divorce of freedom from truth is the error of the modern age.[60] In *Centesimus Annus* he talks about 'an understanding of human freedom which detaches it from obedience to the truth, and consequently from the duty to respect the rights of others.'[61] He then goes on to trace out the dramatic fallout from this divorce in the twentieth century:

> The essence of freedom then becomes self-love carried to the point of contempt for God and neighbour, a self-love which leads to an unbridled affirmation of self-interest and which refuses to be limited by any demand of justice. This very error had extreme consequences in the tragic series of wars which ravaged Europe and the world between 1914 and 1945. Some of these resulted from militarism and exaggerated nationalism, and from related forms of totalitarianism; some derived from the class struggle; still others were civil wars or wars of an ideological nature.[62]

In the same encyclical, John Paul II notes that already at the end of the nineteenth century Pope Leo XIII had pointed out—especially in his encyclical on civic freedom, *Libertas Praestantissimum*—that the divorce of freedom from truth was the chief error of the modern age. This divorce is also effectively the backdrop of Pope Leo's landmark social encyclical, *Rerum Novarum*. The question at hand in that encyclical is the implicit claim of the capitalists to absolute freedom in economic matters, divorced from the truth of the dignity of the worker as a human being.

The relationship between truth and freedom lead us necessarily to address the notion of the natural law, because it leads us to ask the question about how truth is able to mould and form our freedom, and where this truth comes from. By natural law we understand the moral code written in the heart of each man and woman simply because they have a human nature and intelligence: it is the law that comes with human nature (in this way it is something different from the laws of nature). More than this, it a participation in God's own law—His Eternal Law—because it reveals to us the moral implication of being a part of His creation, a creation that arises from His eternal divine decree.

Contained in the idea of natural law is the fact that the truth that is meant to guide human freedom comes both from God and from us. It comes from God as its first source and so like Him is unchangeable. It comes from us in a secondary way since, gifted by God with human intelligence, we have knowledge of this law within ourselves.

In his encyclical *Veritatis Splendor*, John Paul II calls the natural law a 'participated theonomy.'[63] By this he wants to exclude two extremes in the understanding of moral law. First autonomy, the idea that the moral law is made up by man, and second, a heteronomy, as if the moral law decreed by God imposed on man 'norms unrelated to his good,' opposed to human reason and essentially unknown to him. The phrase 'participated theonomy' communicates that the law comes from God but that every human being shares in it, both because he is able to know the law and because, leading him to happiness, it is for his good rather than for God's!

The most basic precepts of the natural law are found in the Decalogue given by God to Moses; but, as we have said, they can be known even without revelation.[64] However, bad moral formation is able to obscure even these truths to some degree. It is for this reason that God has revealed what unaided reason could otherwise know.

Given the phenomena of globalization, the idea of the natural law is of great contemporary significance. Only a universal law, written in the hearts of every man, can underpin and regulate the relationship between all the peoples and nations of the world.[65]

Justice

Justice is a virtue that disposes us to give others what is due to them, so obviously this value, or virtue, will be at the centre of social living and, accordingly, at the centre of society and social teaching. There are three dimensions of justice: commutative justice regulates the relationship between two citizens (or two groups where one is not subordinated to the other); distributive justice disposes the person in charge of the common good to give to each member of a community or society what he needs; finally, general justice disposes the citizen to pay his dues to the community and society in which he lives.

In social teaching it is not uncommon to come across the term 'social justice.' This can sometimes be used in a rather loose way to mean simply bringing about a society that promotes justice at every level. More precisely, there is a definition of social justice given by Pius XI in *Divini Redemptoris*. There he says:

> In reality, besides commutative justice, there is also social justice with its own set obligations, from which neither employers nor workingmen can escape. Now it is of the very essence of social justice to demand from each individual all that is necessary for the common good. But just as in the living organism it is impossible to provide for the good of the whole unless each single part and each individual member is given what it needs for the exercise of its proper functions, so it is impossible to care for the social organism and the good of society as a unit unless each single part and each individual member - that is to say, each individual man in the dignity of his human personality - is supplied with all that is necessary for the exercise of his social functions.[66]

The point here is that social justice is essentially a form of general justice in that it places the demand on all members of society to make their contribution to the common good of society. But, since this can only be achieved if society gives to each individual what he needs to realize his unique contribution (distributive justice), social justice is a 'two-way street' so to speak.

The truly just person gives each man his due not with reluctance or to keep the peace but inspired by the dignity of each human person. After all, it is because they are human beings that something is owed to them. In this way, it becomes clear that true justice presupposes an (at least implicit) appreciation of the truth about the human person. Once again, we can see the connection with the first principle of social teaching—the dignity of the human person. In fact, there is an urgent need to move away for a contractual vision of justice, that sees it as an attitude of 'you scratch my back and I'll scratch yours,' to a vision that embraces the spirit of justice: the affirmation of the other person as a human being.

Love

Catholic social teaching offers a vision of human society as 'a civilization of love.'[67] Love or charity is the master virtue (the so-called mother of the virtues) because without love all other social virtues are lifeless and eventually wither away. To love is 'to will the good of another' as if it were one's own good, and only this can animate a society in such a way as to make it fully human; just as only this virtue can make a family a true family. Again, this cannot be legislated for or manufactured by social structures alone: it requires grace and conversion.

The social demands of love include personal and concrete acts of kindness to our neighbours and to those whom, given our individual situations, are part of our lives. But beyond this, love ought to inspire us to seek to change society, where necessary, so that the obstacles that impede the well-being of our neighbour might be removed. This is to say, charity includes (and should inspire) social action on behalf of the poor and needy. The Compendium points to these two dimensions of love when it says:

> It is undoubtedly an act of love, the work of mercy by which one responds here and now to a real and impelling need of one's neighbour, but it is an equally indispensable act of love to strive to organize and structure society so that one's neighbour will not find himself in poverty.[68]

The social teaching of John Paul II pays particular attention to the interaction of justice and love understood as mercy. In his encyclical on God the Father, *Dives in Misericordia* (which contains an element of his social teaching and might be classified as partially a social encyclical) he says that:

> In every sphere of interpersonal relationships justice must, so to speak, be 'corrected' to a considerable extent by that love which, as St. Paul proclaims, 'is patient and kind' or, in other words, possesses the characteristics of that merciful love which is so much of the essence of the Gospel and Christianity.[69]

The point is that in building a civilization worthy of man, a civilization of love, justice alone is never enough; for various reasons it must be enlivened by and subordinated to charity. First, in regard to material belongs, if everyone in the developed world were to have only what is strictly just, that is, if everyone were moderate in their ownership of property and personal consumption, there would still be millions in poorer countries who would not have what is necessary for a properly human way of life. In this sense, our generosity towards the poor must go beyond justice and be inspired by a charity that moves us to self-sacrifice. Second, justice can easily degenerate into a selfish assertion of one's own rights or, worse, a downward spiral of recrimination and resentment, as one group seeks justice against the wrong-doing of another. On this, John Paul II notes that:

> The experience of the past and of our own time demonstrates that justice alone is not enough, that it can even lead to the negation and destruction of itself ... It has been precisely historical experience that, among other things, has led to the formulation of the saying: *summum ius, summa iniuria*.[70]

In these situations only love, in the form of mercy, can find a way out. A good example of this is the way South Africa emerged from Apartheid. Rather than prosecuting those who had committed often serious crimes (when the white population controlled the country), it was decided to seek the truth about these crimes but not to impose penalties, in the belief that punishing these criminals would be detrimental to the unity of the society. In this extraordinary social situation, mercy modified the usual demands of justice.

Other examples, where social teaching calls for justice to be corrected by mercy, include fair trade and Third World debt. Fair trade between rich and poor countries can require the rich country to give the poor country special terms of trade, thereby giving up its own economic 'right' to a purely reciprocal market access (to the market of the poor country). The cancellation or significant reduction in the repayment of debt owed by poor countries can be a 'required' act of mercy on the part of rich lenders. In so doing, they lay down their right to be repaid according to the original terms of the loan.

Finally, in his encyclical *Caritas in Veritate*, Benedict XVI reminds us that a connection also exists between charity and truth. He points out that charity without truth is mere sentiment and can often lead to actions that are harmful and contrary to the good of mankind.[71] An example would be the promotion of euthanasia which is sometimes based upon a mistaken compassion divorced from the truth of the innate dignity of the human person.[72] On the other hand, truth without charity is likely to be harsh and inhuman, ready perhaps to perceive a problem but without the energy to help solve it. Benedict goes as far as to say that without charity the complete truth cannot even be had. He notes that moral knowledge is never just a matter for the intellect; it also depends on love because only love can set the right moral objectives; in the case of society, the fully human development of all.[73] Benedict says, therefore, that social teaching is *caritas in veritate in re sociali* (charity in truth in social matters).[74] Ultimately, then, what is needed if mankind is to find the correct solutions to the pressing social issues of our time is charity in truth, which goes under the name of wisdom. Vatican II reminded us that:

> Our era needs such wisdom more than bygone ages
> if the discoveries made by man are to be further

humanized. For the future of the world stands in peril unless wiser men are forthcoming.[75]

Notes

[1] Since the dignity of the human person is a general anthropological truth, it is, perhaps, more precise to say that this truth is an inheritance received by social teaching, while the other three principles—common good, subsidiarity, and solidarity—are proper to social teaching itself.

[2] John XXIII, *Mater et Magistra*, 219.

[3] John Paul II, General Audience (10 October 1979); John Paul II, General Audience (9 January 1980).

[4] Paul VI, *Populorum Progressio*, 13.

[5] CCC, 1880.

[6] CSDC, 131.

[7] Cf. Congregation for the Doctrine of the Faith, *Letter to the Bishops of the Catholic Church on the Collaboration of Men and Women in the Church and in the World.*

[8] CCC, 365; cf. Council of Vienne (1312), Constitution *Fidei Catholicae* in Denzinger 902 (481).

[9] CCC, 407.

[10] John Paul II, *Reconciliatio et Paenitentia*, 16.

[11] CSDC, 119.

[12] John Paul II, *Sollicitudo Rei Socialis*, 36; cf. John Paul II, *Reconciliatio et Paenitentia*, 16.

[13] CSDC, 160.

[14] CSDC, 161.

[15] CSDC, 162.

[16] Vatican II, *Gaudium et Spes*, 26.

[17] Pius X, *Vehementer Nos*, 3.

[18] CSDC, 171.

[19] Vatican II, *Gaudium et Spes*, 69.

[20] John Paul II, *Laborem Exercens*, 19.

21 Paul VI, *Populorum Progressio*, 22.
22 *CSDC*, 176.
23 Leo XIII, *Rerum Novarum*, 6.
24 In *Rerum Novarum*, Pope Leo even suggests that this creativity is a title to ownership, meaning it can give a person a right to own something; since by work man leaves 'the impress of his personality' upon things (such as land and materials) and, as it were, extends his personality into them, thereby incorporating them into himself (cf. Leo XIII, *Rerum Novarum*, 9).
25 John XXIII, *Mater et Magistra*, 109.
26 Leo XIII, *Rerum Novarum*, 14–15.
27 John XXIII, *Mater et Magistra*, 109.
28 John Paul II, *Laborem Exercens*, 14.
29 Vatican II, *Gaudium et Spes*, 69.
30 Leo XIII, *Rerum Novarum*, 22.
31 John Paul II, *Centesimus Annus*, 32.
32 *CSDC*, 179.
33 John Paul II, *Sollicitudo Rei Socialis*, 42.
34 Leo XIII, *Rerum Novarum*, 37.
35 John XXIII, *Pacem in Terris*, 56.
36 John Paul II, *Centesimus Annus*, 11.
37 John Paul II, *Sollicitudo Rei Socialis*, 42.
38 Cf. Congregation for the Doctrine of the Faith, Instruction on Certain Aspects of the 'Theology of Liberation' (*Libertas Nuntius*).
39 John Paul II, *Address to the Indios and Peasants of Mexico* (29 January 1979). Cf. Pontifical Council for Justice and Peace, *Towards a Better Distribution of Land* (§ 35–37).
40 Pius XI, *Quadragesimo Anno*, 47.
41 *CSDC*, 185.
42 Pius XI, *Quadragesimo Anno*, 23.
43 John Paul II, *Centesimus Annus*, 48.
44 *CSDC*, 187.
45 Cf. John XXIII, *Mater et Magistra*, 44: 'It is for individuals, therefore, to regulate their mutual relations where their work is concerned. If they cannot do so, or will not do so, then, and only

then, does "it fall back on the State to intervene in the division and distribution of work, and this must be according to the form and measure that the common good properly understood demands" (Pius XII, *Christmas Radio Broadcast*, 1941).'

46   John XXIII, *Mater et Magistra*, 57–58.

47   John Paul II, *Centesimus Annus*, 46.

48   *Ibid.*, 10. The term 'solidarity' is of quite recent vintage. The idea, but not the term, is found in *Rerum Novarum*; the term itself is first used by Pius XII in his Christmas Radio Broadcasts of 1941 and 1944, and more extensively by John XXIII in *Mater et Magistra* (see Pius XII, Christmas Radio Broadcast, 1941, *Internal Order of States and Peoples*, 31; Pius XII, Christmas Radio Broadcast, 1944, *True and False Democracy*, 25; John XXIII, *Mater et Magistra*, 23, 157, 190). The use of 'solidarity' rather than 'civic friendship' is perhaps an attempt to adapt the language of social teaching to the modern ear.

49   John Paul II, *Sollicitudo Rei Socialis*, 38; cf. *CSDC*, 193.

50   Benedict XVI, *Caritas in Veritate*, 38.

51   *Ibid.*, 58.

52   John Paul II, *Sollicitudo Rei Socialis*, 40.

53   *Ibid.*, 45; John Paul II, *Address on Globalization* (27 April 2001), 2; Benedict XVI, *Caritas in Veritate*, 19, 38.

54   Benedict XVI, *Caritas in Veritate*, 19.

55   John XXIII, *Pacem in Terris*, 36.

56   *Ibid.*, 35–37; cf. *CSDC*, 198.

57   *CSDC*, 197.

58   The distinction between principles and values seems to be partly a historical phenomenon. The principles were clarified earlier than the values, and because they tended to have a normative character—they set down norms for action—they have been called principles. The values, while implicit in earlier teaching, were first highlighted only later, in *Pacem in Terris*. The point is that the distinction is not absolutely rigorous. Some of the principles, especially solidarity, might also be considered as values. Solidarity, understood as civic friendship and closely related to charity, is a spiritual good that should flourish in a well-ordered society; it is also a virtue.

59   Congregation for the Doctrine of the Faith, *Doctrinal Notes on Some Questions Regarding the Participation of Catholics in Political Life*, 6.

60. John Paul II, *Veritatis Splendor*, 31.
61. John Paul II, *Centesimus Annus*, 17.
62. *Ibid.*
63. John Paul II, *Veritatis Splendor*, 41.
64. *CCC*, 1955.
65. *CSDC*, 141.
66. Pius XI, *Divini Redemptoris*, 51; cf. *CCC*, 1928.
67. Paul VI, *Regina Coeli Address* (17 May 1970). Cf. John Paul II, *Letter to Families* and *Sollicitudo Rei Socialis*, 33.
68. *CSDC*, 208.
69. John Paul II, *Dives in Misericordia*, 14.
70. *Ibid.*, 12.
71. Benedict XVI, *Caritas in Veritate*, 2.
72. John Paul II, *Evangelium Vitae*, 15.
73. Benedict XVI, *Caritas in Veritate*, 30.
74. *Ibid.*, 5.
75. Vatican II, *Gaudium et Spes*, 15.

3

The Family as the Vital Cell of Society

The family as a cell of society

In the words of *Apostolicam Actuositatem*, the document from the Second Vatican Council on the laity, the family is the 'first vital cell of society.'[1] To call the family a 'cell' is obviously an analogy. So the question before us, therefore, is what exactly does this imply? First, it is interesting to note that the family and not the individual is said to be the first cell of society. This way of seeing things can be contrasted with an individualistic outlook that gives no significant place to the family, conceiving of society as a myriad of individuals all directly under the authority of the State.[2] However, the Catholic position is clearly more realistic (more in tune with reality), since individuals come into society by being born into a family and are then made fit members of society through the family. From this we can see that the family holds the middle or central place in the structure of society—it is the pivot.

Removing this pivot of society risks unbalancing it in one of two ways: it leads to either individualism or collectivism.[3] It is sobering to note that the totalitarian Communist regimes of the twentieth century radically undermined the family and, at the beginning of the twenty-first century, the individualistic societies of the West are heading in the same direction. In our day, the Catholic family-centred vision of society is more and more coming into conflict with an atomized or individualistic vision. One major battle ground is parental authority over children. This has been compromised in some Western countries, for example, over the question of whether parents should be informed if their teenage daughter procures an abortion or with regard to the parents' right to determine the education of their children (for example, prohibiting parents from withdrawing their children from sex education classes that they deem inappropriate). The parents are bypassed because each child is thought to be first of all a citizen and only then, or only accidentally, a member of a family.

Both the family and the State are so-called natural societies—this means that they are societies intended by nature or, to put it another way, they fit with what it means to be human and flow from the natural inclinations in every human being. Human beings are naturally inclined to form male-female partnerships for the purpose of generating and rearing offspring. Then, also as a consequence of man's social nature, these families tend to band together to form tribes, then peoples, then nations. For this reason the State can be called natural, meaning something commensurate with human nature. Natural societies—the family and the State—are different from other societies such as sports clubs and businesses which are artificial societies, created by the will of some men.

The analogy of the family as the cell of society indicates that—while both the family and the State are natural—from one perspective the family is prior to the State; this is because the State is a conglomeration of families, as a body is a conglomeration of cells. A very important consequence of this is that family has rights prior to the State and which are not derived from the State by positive law.[4] This means that these rights are innate (in-born) and are part of natural law; they are not given to the family by the State. In his Apostolic Exhortation on the family, *Familiaris Consortio*, John Paul II gave an initial articulation to these rights and, in union with the 1980 Synod of Bishops, called for them to be studied and written up into a charter.[5] In 1983, the Vatican subsequently promulgated the *Charter of the Rights of the Family*. According to the preamble, 'the family, a natural society, exists prior to the State or any other community, and possesses inherent rights which are inalienable.'[6] Among the rights listed in the charter are the right to found a family, the right to bring up children according to the parents' religious beliefs and cultural values, the right to procreate and educate children, the right to family policies and an economic order that supports the family.[7]

The analogy of the family as the 'first vital cell of society' also obviously means to impress upon us that the health of the society is dependant on the health of its families, as a body is on the health of its cells. If the body allows its cells to become diseased, then it is the whole body that suffers. Pope John Paul II famously said that 'as the family goes so goes society' and that 'the future of humanity passes by way of the family.'[8] The Compendium tells us that 'without families that are strong in their communion and stable in their commitment peoples grow weak.'[9] All three statements reflect a foundational insight of Catholic social teaching.

The analogy of the family as the cell reminds us also of the fact that the family relates to society as a part to a whole. Now, it is a self evident truth that the whole is greater than the part, and in some sense the part is for the sake of the whole. But how are we to understand this aspect of the analogy, since it seems dangerously to subordinate the family to the State? Let us approach this by considering what might seem to be two contradictory statements on this matter. On the one hand, the Compendium tells us that, 'the family, then, does not exist for the society or the State, but society and the State exist for the family'[10] while Pius XI says:

> [T]he family is an imperfect society, since it has not in itself all the means for its own complete development; whereas civil society is a perfect society, having in itself all the means for its peculiar end, which is the temporal well-being of the community; and so, in this respect, that is, in view of the common

> good, it has pre-eminence over the family, which finds its own suitable temporal perfection precisely in civil society.[11]

The fact is that these two statements emphasize different but complementary truths. The family is naturally first, meaning that societies are only built up from families. It was not the case that first there was a society, and then people grouped into families, but rather first there were families and then these naturally grouped into societies. Pius XI prefaces the above statement as follows:

> In the first place comes the family, instituted directly by God for its peculiar purpose, the generation and formation of offspring; for this reason it has priority of nature and therefore of rights over civil society.[12]

However, families on their own cannot attain everything their members need for a full human development. In this sense, they are called 'imperfect societies.' It is only in collaboration with other families (and so ultimately the wider society) that these goods — such as education, material prosperity, and security — can be achieved. This is why Pius XI can say that society 'has pre-eminence over the family.' But, and this is very important, it has pre-eminence because the family 'finds its own suitable temporal perfection precisely in civil society.' So, it is not that society has pre-eminence over and against the good of the family, but only as providing what is good for the family. This is why the Compendium can say (without contradicting Pius XI) that the family 'does not exist for the society or the State, but society and the State exist for the family.'

Clearly, then, it would be wrong to interpret Pius XI's statement about the pre-eminence of the society as if the good of the society was something different from the good of the family. In this regard we should note that as an analogy, like all analogies, the idea of the family as a 'cell' should not be stretched too far. Cells in the human body are often sacrificed for the good of the whole, even whole limbs are sometimes amputated. Obviously, families are made up of persons and are not dispensable in this way. If the part is for the sake of the whole, in the case of the family it is a 'part' that must always 'participate' in the common good of the whole, of society.

Ultimately, then, from this analogy we see that there is a reciprocal relationship between the society or State and the family: the family contributes to society, and the State serves the family. The Charter mentioned above says that 'the family and society, which are mutually linked by vital and organic bonds, have a complementary function in the defence and advancement of the good of every person and of humanity.'[13] We might say that it is more than complementary; it is reciprocal. We should, therefore, now consider this reciprocal and complementary relationship in more detail.

The contribution of the family to the society

When Catholic social teaching addresses the role of the family in society, it often uses the phrase the 'social subjectivity of the family.'[14] By this it is pointing out that the family is an 'actor' in society; so the question becomes: how should the family act so as to fulfil its role and make a positive contribution to society?

It is instructive to note that the Church sees marriage as essentially turned out towards society. For a marriage to be valid, at least since the Council of Trent, it has to be contracted in the face of the Church—in the presence of representatives of the ecclesial community. There are also impediments that prevent marriage between close relations, so-called impediments of consanguinity. These are not, as is sometimes thought, aimed (principally) at preventing the genetic defects that are more common in offspring from closely related persons. Rather, these impediments recognize that marriage is meant to strengthen the fabric of society, and this is better achieved when most people marry outside of their immediate family.

Because the family is built upon the rock of marriage, the most fundamental way in which the family ought to serve the society is by the spouses fulfilling their primary tasks; and these, according to John Paul II's Apostolic Exhortation on the family, *Familiaris Consortio*, are three-fold:[15] first, forming a communion of persons;[16] second, serving life in the procreation and education of children;[17] and, third, involving themselves in political activity for the sake of family life.

Forming a community of persons

A communion of persons is a group of individuals who are bound together in a common love for each other and in the pursuit of a common goal. This is what marriage is meant to be and only from this core can the family flourish. This, then, is the primary task of each married couple: to persevere in loving each other and in developing their spousal communion. The children granted to the spouses are meant to spring from the communion and to enlarge and enrich it. When married people put their primary efforts into developing their spousal communion, they not only render an indispensable service to their children, but also to society. Society itself, as we have seen, is ultimately a spiritual reality—it is a kind of communion since it is a kind of community; but it will enjoy as much communion as is brought to it by its families. For this reason, the Compendium says that 'the family is present as the place where communion—that communion so necessary for a society that is increasingly individualistic—is brought about.'[18] The point is that communion cannot be imposed on a society from above, it can only radiate from below—from the family. This expansion of communion from spouses to families, and from families to society is expressed by John Paul II in his *Letter to Families*:

> 'Communion' has to do with the personal relationship between the 'I' and the 'thou'. 'Community' on the other hand, transcends this framework and moves

towards a 'society', a 'we'. The family, as a community of persons, is thus the first human 'society.'[19]

Of course, if families are to be effective sources of communion in society, they must themselves be vibrant communities. The hotter a fire, the more it is able to heat those who are further away! This requires that families spend time together, not just so-called 'quality time' but also 'quantity time,' since there is no such thing as the former without the latter. In his *Letter to Families*, John Paul II laments that, 'families today have too little "human" life.'[20] By this he means not just that families are often small, but that they do not develop a rich family life capable of keeping the family together and, moreover, of spreading its unifying influence into the society.

Various social realities more or less contradict this primary task of building and bringing communion. These are divorce, de facto unions (permanent cohabitation), and same-sex marriages. All these realities are defective in their conception of spousal communion, and so cannot contribute in the same way as marriage to the communion of society.[21]

In fulfilling its role of bringing communion to society, a very practical task of the family is hospitality, because hospitality is nothing other than inviting others to share in their family communion. This invitation ought to be extended especially towards those who are without this experience, those who are alone. In its most simple form it may include inviting people into the family home for a meal; in a more radical way it may be realized in adopting a child or an old person who has no family.[22]

Serving life by procreation and education

It is through the family that new members of the society are born, and this is an authentic service to society. This is not always appreciated in the Western world, where a consumerist mentality more readily sees the birth of a child as a threat to 'my share' of the limited goods of the earth. The child comes, it seems, to take and not to give; it is yet another mouth at the already overcrowded table of humanity. A conversion of perspective is needed if we are to see the truth that a child is a common good who comes to enrich society. In his *Letter to Families*, John Paul II places this challenge before us. What he says is so glorious, and the point so decisive, it seems worth quoting it in full:

> But is it really true that the new human being is a gift for his parents? A gift for society? Apparently nothing seems to indicate this. On occasions the birth of a child appears to be a simple statistical fact, registered like so many other data in demographic records. It is true that for the parents the birth of a child means more work, new financial burdens and further inconveniences, all of which can lead to the temptation not to want another birth. In some social and cultural contexts this temptation can become very strong. Does this mean that a child is not a gift? That it comes into the world only to take and not to give? These are some of the disturbing questions which men and women today find hard to escape. A child comes to take up room, when it seems that there is less and less room in the world. But is it really true that a child brings nothing to the family and society? Is not every child a 'particle' of that common good without which human communities break down and risk extinction? Could this ever really be denied? The child becomes a gift to its brothers, sisters, parents and entire family. Its life becomes a gift for the very people who were givers of life and who cannot help but feel its presence, its sharing in their life and its contribution to their common good and to that of the community of the family. This truth is obvious in its simplicity and profundity, whatever the complexity and even the possible pathology of the psychological make-up of certain persons. The common good of the whole of society dwells in man.[23]

Of course, it is not just a matter of physically producing new citizens! The task of the family, and the service rendered to society, is only fulfilled in the proper education of the children born; but it is precisely through the family—because it is a society—that children are trained in social virtues, by which they become good citizens. As the Catechism notes, 'the home is the natural environment for initiating a human being into solidarity and communal responsibilities,'[24] and as the Second Vatican Council's declaration on Christian Education says, 'the family is the first school of the social virtues that every society needs.'[25] As a society in miniature, all the principles of Catholic social teaching—the common good, subsidiarity, and solidarity—are at work in a healthy family: there is a familial common good which each member helps build and can enjoy, particularly the common good of family communion; there is subsidiarity, as the parents help the children to help themselves, particularly in the realm of learning; and there is solidarity where parents support the children and siblings help each other to achieve a fuller human development.

Of course, alongside these principles, the fundamental social values of truth, freedom, justice, and charity should also be part of the formation a child receives in the family. For example, the three forms of justice can be modelled within the society of the family. The parents must model distributive justice considering the particular needs of each child. In the numerous daily 'negotiations' in family life, the children must learn the lessons of commutative justice between each other, and what they owe to the whole family in general justice.

Special attention needs to be given to training in the authentic human freedom that we outlined above. The Catechism tells us that this comes from 'an apprenticeship in self-denial, sound judgment, and self-mastery,' all of which are 'the preconditions of all true freedom.'[26] Within this formation in freedom two areas need particular attention. First, singular attention must be given to the correct estimation of the value of material goods, emphasizing the superiority of spiritual goods such as truth, friendship, virtue and, of course, faith. This can only really be achieved by a materially austere upbringing.[27] The second area is human sexuality; of this we shall say something more below.

Of course, in all these different areas, the mode of education is as important as the 'information' transmitted by the parents. It is not so much the duty of parents to lecture their children in social virtues as to model them and create a family atmosphere in which they are subconsciously inhaled; for example, when it comes to forming their children in chastity, it indispensable that the parents themselves offer an authentic witness to this virtue.

Finally, it would be a mistake to think that the education of children is ordered only to taking up their duties in civil society, however important that is. Vatican II indicates that a holistic education is directed not just to this but also 'towards the formation of the human person in view of his final end and ... [towards] the duties of which he will, as an adult, have a share.'[28] Ultimately, then, it must include a formation that prepares each child to answer to the vocation God has for him or for her. The point is that education must have a religious dimension helping the child to deepen his relationship with God, since this is the final goal of human life. Also, parents are called upon to help their children discern their particular vocation, be it to marriage, priesthood, or consecrated life. Christian parents and families are part of the Church and so these parents must prepare their offspring to take their place also in this divine society and its mission to evangelisation.

Parents are the ones who give physical life to their children and so they are also called to give birth to their children spiritually through education. The Council Fathers tells us that 'since parents have given children their life, they are bound by the most serious obligation to educate their offspring and therefore must be recognized as the primary and principal educators.'[29] As rights and duties are correlative, accordingly, along with a duty to educate comes a right to educate. In *Familiaris Consortio*, John Paul II articulates the characteristics of this right. He says it is:

> [E]ssential, since it is connected with the transmission of human life; it is original and primary with regard to the educational role of others, on account of the uniqueness of the loving relationship between parents and children; and it is irreplaceable and inalienable, and therefore incapable of being entirely delegated to others or usurped by others.[30]

It is an essential right and duty because, as we have seen, it comes with the very nature of marriage as procreative. Second, it is a primary right and duty, meaning the parents must be the first educators. This is to say they must be the major formative influence on their children; not others: not their school teachers, not their peers, and not the media. They are responsible for directing the education of their children, even if others aid them and, therefore, to a great extent are responsible for how their children turn out. Third, it is an irreplaceable right and duty. The Council Fathers say that the parents' 'role in education is so important that only with difficulty can it be supplied where it is lacking.'[31] John Paul II is even more cautious. He says that 'their role as educators is so decisive that scarcely anything can compensate for their failure in it.'[32]

Lastly, it is an inalienable right and duty, meaning it cannot be wholly delegated. Of course, there is normally the need to draw on others to help educate children—especially in the modern world where there are so many fields of education to consider—but, as we have just said, the parents must stay in the driving seat of the whole formation process. They may delegate but they cannot abdicate.

In particular, the parents must take the major role in the education of morality, and particularly sexuality. These areas of formation cannot be wholly delegated.[33] The reason for this is because education in morality and especially sexuality goes to the heart of what it means to be a human being. A bad formation in these areas in particular represents an impoverished human formation.[34]

If the children are sent to school, the parents have the right to choose the school, and to withhold their child from attending classes that they have moral objections to, such as sex education classes or classes of religious instruction. Also, according to the principle of subsidiarity, the State ought to give financial help (from taxes) to parents to organize the education of their children, supporting them in the creation of schools:

> Whenever the State lays claim to an educational monopoly, it oversteps its rights and offends justice... [t]he State cannot without injustice merely tolerate so-called private schools. Such schools render a public service and therefore have a right to financial assistance.[35]

Political activity for the sake of the family

The final task for the married couple, the third contribution they make in society, is for families to become what John Paul II calls protagonists in family politics.[36] By this he means that families ought to strive to become an influential force in the political community. The particular goal of this political activity would be to safeguard the central place of marriage and the family in society. He notes that families can no longer rely on others to do this: families themselves need to bind together with other like-minded families and fight for a special recognition, protection, and promotion of marriage and family life by the government. If they do not, then they will inevitably fall victim of laws that devalue marriage and family life. As the cradle of human life, families also have a particular responsibility to up hold the sanctity of life in society and so ought to take a special interest and leading role in pro-life political activity.

The political influence of the family is obviously achieved primarily by lobbying political representatives. A more radical way—not explicitly considered by Catholic social teaching—might be to give all citizens of a country, including children, the vote (universal suffrage in the strict sense) but have the votes of minors cast by their parents. This would be one way to make families true heavyweights on the political scene.

Two related areas of political life, of which the Christian family cannot be unconcerned, are pro-life legislation and the rights of children. As the sanctuary of life, the family built on marriage is the ideal environment for welcoming new human life. This attitude of respect to new human life is, obviously, most radically opposed by the practice of abortion. In seeking to prevent or overturn abortion legislation, the Christian family should be conscious that it is rendering a true service not just to the unborn child, but also to society in general. Abortion, aside from contradicting the social value of justice, radically undermines solidarity in society. Since the relationship between a mother and child is the primordial relationship in society, if a mother can be persuaded to kill her unborn child, the foundation of solidarity in society is shaken to its core. What motivation can there be to have solidarity with the poor who live far from us both geographically and socially when the most basic and intimate solidarity is done away with? Benedict XVI makes this very point when (quoting from John Paul II's encyclical *Evangelium Vitae*) he says that:

> The Church forcefully maintains this link between life ethics and social ethics, fully aware that 'a society lacks solid foundations when, on the one hand, it asserts values such as the dignity of the person, justice and peace, but then, on the other hand, radically acts to the contrary by allowing or tolerating a variety of ways in which human life is devalued and violated, especially where it is weak or marginalized.'[37]

Some people claim that a pro-life society is opposed to democracy since, they say, it involves the imposition of the morality of one group on the whole of society. The truth is quite the contrary. The Compendium notes that abortion and anti-life legislation are what undermines democracy because they represent the dictatorship of the majority: by a majority decision the basic human rights of a minority, namely the unborn, are abolished.[38] Accordingly, to fight for a pro-life culture is to uphold goal of true democracy—the common good of every member of society—and to render a true and priceless service to society.

Paradoxically, while recent decades have witnessed the spread of legislation allowing abortion, there has been a growing concern to legislate for the rights of children already born. In some countries there are no or few rights afforded to a child prior to birth, but a whole host of rights moments later when the child is born! While condemning abortion, the Church warmly welcomes this new sensitivity to the rights of children, especially when it is aimed at helping children who, in many countries, suffer poverty, war, exploitation, and lack of educational opportunities.

The rights of children have found concrete expression in the United Nations' Convention on the Rights of the Child (1989), an international convention that sets out the social, economic, and cultural rights of children. The Convention reaffirmed the indispensable place of the family in ensuring the rights of children, since it says that the family is 'the natural environment for the growth and well-being of all its members, especially the child.' Elsewhere, the Convention even alludes to the rights of unborn children when it states that the child 'needs special safeguards and care, including appropriate legal protection before as well as after birth.'

Two areas of concern, however, (and these are particularly the areas in which families must be politically alert) was the absence of any mention in the Convention of marriage as the basis of the family and, in the implementation of the Convention, a tendency to pit the rights of the child against those of the parents.

Noting the absence of any special mention of marriage in the Convention, Benedict XVI emphasizes that 'it is precisely the family, founded on marriage between a man and a woman, which is the greatest help that can be given to children. They want to be loved by a mother and father who love each other.'[39] Accordingly, for governments to champion the rights of children and at the same time to do nothing to support marriage, or even to undermine it—as is the case when other forms of union are made equivalent to marriage—is to build up with one hand while tearing down with the other. In fact, according to social teaching, the first right of a child is to be born into marriage, since this is the ideal environment for them to flourish. John Paul II says that 'stress could thus be laid on the right of the child to be born in a real family, for it is essential that he should benefit from the beginning from the joint contribution of the father and the mother, united in an indissoluble marriage.'[40] Echoing this some years later, Cardinal Ratzinger said that 'it is through the secure and recognized relationship to his own parents that the child can discover his own identity and achieve his own proper human development.'[41]

We have already said something about the danger of bypassing the family and the consequent erosion of parental authority, an authority that, when exercised properly, is for the good of the children. Aware of this danger, and directly addressing the Convention, John Paul II reaffirms the prerogative of the parents to direct the moral and spiritual education of their children:

> The Holy See gladly acceded to and endorses the Convention on the understanding that goals, programs and actions stemming from it will respect the moral and religious convictions of those to whom they are directed, in particular the moral convictions of parents regarding the transmission of life, with no urging to resort to means which are morally unacceptable, as well as their freedom in relation to the religious life and education of their children.[42]

The State at the service of the family

Having laid out the contribution of the family to society, let us now consider the ways in which the State ought to be at the service of the family. This consideration must focus in particular on two areas: first, the legal recognition of the family as built on marriage, and; second, the correct relationship between the family and economic life.

Before we do this, it seems good to make two general remarks concerning this relationship of the State to the family. First, families benefit by being in society because by this membership they are able to attain many benefits that would elude them if they were alone, such as material prosperity, health, and education. Accordingly, families and, in particular, parents should look at society in a positive way, even if it is clear that modern society also has some elements that are threatening or damaging to the family. These are aberrations in society and not part of what society should be.

Second, the interaction between the State and the family ought always and in all things to be marked by the principle of subsidiarity.[43] As we have seen, the implication of this principle is that the State must never usurp the role of the family and do for families what they can do for themselves, for example organize the education of their children, find adequate housing and work, and sort out their healthcare needs. Moreover, subsidiarity means the State ought to help families, even financially, to help themselves in these and other areas. Only when there is a radical failure in the family—such as abuse, neglect, or abandonment—may the State rightfully take over from the parents.[44]

Recognition and protection of the family as built on marriage

The first duty of the State towards the family is very simple. It is to recognize it and, moreover, promote it as the first cell of society! More particularly, it must recognize the special character of marriage between one man and one woman as the foundation of the family.[45]

Of course, to promote marriage, the State must have a clear idea what it is. A very precise and thorough statement about the nature of marriage is given in Canon Law. There, leaving aside the possible sacramental dimension, marriage is described in the following terms:

> The matrimonial covenant, by which a man and a woman establish between themselves a partnership of the whole of life, is by its nature ordered toward the good of the spouses and the procreation and education of offspring.[46]

In addition, it says that 'the essential properties of marriage are unity and indissolubility.'[47]

The main points to note are: first, that the goal of marriage is described as the promotion of the well-being of the couple and the procreation and education of children; and second, that a matrimonial union can only be between one man and one woman, and so not between persons of the same-sex or between one man and many women (polygamy). The latter is excluded by the property of 'unity.' The property of 'indissolubility' means that the union lasts for a lifetime.

The State fails in its fundamental duty to the family when it gives legal recognition to other forms of union, namely de facto unions or same-sex unions—unions that do not have the character of marriage as outlined above—making them equal to marriage.[48] De facto unions are sometimes more colloquially called co-habitation. This term covers a variety of relationships between a man and a woman but is always characterized by the fact that 'they ignore, postpone, or even reject the conjugal commitment.'[49] This rejection of marriage can be permanent or temporary, conscious or un-reflected.

According to Catholic social teaching, the State renders an injustice to marriage when it gives to these other unions equal status, rights, or benefits as are given to marriage because these other unions do not contribute in the same way to the common good of society. They do not contribute by way of the procreation and education of children in an environment conducive to the wholesome development of a child, who is a future citizen. De facto unions lack the stability children require from their parents, while same-sex unions fail to provide the masculine and feminine contribution children need for a healthy personal development.

Many in modern society claim that the equality of these unions with marriage is a matter of justice, but they forget that justice has two faces. It is unjust to treat equal things differently and it is unjust to treat different things equally. De facto and same-sex unions are not socially equal to marriage because they do not make an equal contribution to society and, therefore, to treat them as such is unjust. This point is concisely made in a document recently published by the Pontifical Council of the Family entitled *Family, Marriage, and 'De Facto' Unions*:

> Equality before the law must respect the principle of justice which means treating equals equally, and what is different differently: i.e., to give each one his due in justice. This principle of justice would be violated if de facto unions were given a juridical treatment similar or equivalent to the family based on marriage. If the family based on marriage and de facto unions are neither similar nor equivalent in their duties, functions and services in society, then they cannot be similar or equivalent in their juridical status.[50]

De facto and same-sex unions are at best a-social, in the sense that they are not ordered to the common good of society but to the private good of the couple alone. This is very clear in de facto unions, since they are defined by a lack of a firm and public mutual commitment. This is in contrast to marriage, which only comes about by a public profession of commitment (one spouse to the other), precisely because it has always been recognized that by marrying couples take on a social function, namely procreating and educating children, future members of society. Being fundamentally choices made for private benefit, de facto unions do not warrant the public reward of social recognition or benefits.

Giving de facto unions and same-sex unions legal equivalence to marriage is not only an injustice because they do not contribute to the common good as marriage does, it also discredits marriage in the minds of citizens by bringing it down to the level of these other unions, just as allowing divorce makes every marriage appear to be a conditional and potentially temporary arrangement.[51] We ought to remember that 'civil laws are structuring principles of man's life in society, for good and for ill'[52] and that they 'play a very important and sometimes decisive role in influencing patterns of thought and behaviour.'[53] In the end, the legal recognition of these other unions would be a redefinition of marriage. That marriage would be considered as just one among several forms of personal union is very much opposed to the good of society because a healthy esteem of marriage is a condition for a society's future. For a political authority to act in such a way is for it to act against the common good and, therefore, outside its own authority: 'by putting homosexual unions on a legal plane analogous to that of marriage and the family, the State acts arbitrarily and in contradiction with its duties.'[54]

Obviously, from a Christian perspective such unions also involve behaviour that is immoral, namely fornication.[55] Could this be a reason for such unions to be criminalized? Several criteria must be considered. First, 'the scope of civil law is certainly more limited that that of the moral law,' because its goal is the just and peaceful coexistence of members of society.[56] John Paul II says that 'the real purpose of civil law is to guarantee an ordered social coexistence in true justice, so that all may "lead a quiet and peaceable life, godly and respectful in every way" (1 Tm 2:2).'[57] Accordingly, there are some actions that must be left to the judgment of the conscience and to God. So, for example, a civil law against the moral evil of masturbation would be inappropriate. This is not to say that masturbation is not wrong—it certainly is—but that it falls outside the scope of civil law. It is arguably true to say that co-habitation and same-sex unions are similarly private affairs and so outside civil law. This seems to be the approach taken in the document from the Pontifical Council for the Family on de facto unions. It states:

> Two or more persons may decide to live together, with or without a sexual dimension, but this cohabitation is not for that reason of public interest. The public authorities cannot get involved in this private choice. De facto unions are the result of private behaviour and should remain on the private level.[58]

In this document, the authors want to exclude State promotion of de facto unions—to this extent they call it a private affair. The corollary is that, being private, even though it is morally disordered, it would not fall under civil law—it would not be criminalized. De facto unions (and same-sex partnerships) are to be neither promoted nor suppressed.

However, as we have mentioned above, all sins ultimately have a social impact (even masturbation) to the extent that they weaken the moral fibre of members of society. De facto unions and same-sex marriages are particularly undermining, since the family is the primary cell of society and marriage is undermined by these irregular partnerships. To this extent, they might be seen as 'structures of sin.' In conclusion, I think it would be true to say that social teaching does not exclude the criminalization of these partnerships, but it suggests they stay outside of civil law.

The second point to consider is that even when some morally bad action has social significance, this immoral behaviour might be tolerated in society because its suppression could cause other great evils, or because tolerance would promote some greater common good. Pope Leo XIII makes this general point about toleration in *Libertas Praestantissimum*:

> [W]hile not conceding any right to anything save what is true and honest, she [the Church] does not forbid public authority to tolerate what is at variance with truth and justice, for the sake of avoiding some greater evil, or of obtaining or preserving some greater good.[59]

In regard to de facto and same-sex unions there might be a case for toleration because criminalization would likely be to the detriment of children that are the result of these unions. Or, we might argue that tolerance preserves some common good, namely the rightful limits of State interest in the private life of citizens. So, this behaviour and these unions might be tolerated but should never be promoted by the State. There is a clear difference between tolerating and promoting something; and decriminalizing something can be a toleration of it without active promotion of it:[60]

> Those who would move from tolerance to the legitimization of specific rights for cohabiting homosexual persons need to be reminded that the approval or legalization of evil is something far different from the toleration of evil.[61]

Toleration of evil does not necessarily oppose the sovereignty of God, which as we have seen extends to all reality, even temporal matters. God Himself tolerates the evil of our sin. He in no way promotes it, but allows it for a time and for good reason. To hinder every sin He would have to undermine the freedom He wills for us.[62]

To finish this section, let us be clear, we are making some objective statements about different states of life. This is not a judgment directly on individuals. While the Catholic Church considers fornication (including homosexual acts) sinful, and the homosexual tendencies disordered,[63] it demands that as persons those engaged in de facto unions and same-sex unions be respected.[64]

The family and economic life

More and more it seems that family life has to mould itself to the demands of the economy, especially in regard to changes in working practices. Both parents are 'forced' back to work while the children are still young, and fragile labour security undermines the parents' ability to plan for the future of their children. These realities often fracture family life, leading to a reduction in the quality and quantity of time the family spends together. In stark contrast, Catholic social teaching holds that the flourishing of family life should be a guiding principle for economic life. As John Paul II observes in *Laborem Exercens*, 'the family constitutes one of the most important terms of reference for shaping the social and ethical order of human work.'[65] The point is that economic life should be ordered to family life and not vice versa. This means that the economy and labour in a society should be tailored in such a way as to promote marriage and the founding of a family. If something needs to change, it is the demands of work, and not family life. It is the fundamental task of the State to ensure the right ordering of values in this regard.

In bringing about the right relationship of family life and work, the so-called 'family wage' is the most important principle or tool.[66] Most simply expressed, this principle states that 'the worker must be paid a wage sufficient to support him and his family.'[67] The wage should reflect not just the market value of what a worker produces but also the needs of the worker himself and of his dependants. Ideally, such a wage should create the conditions where only one parent needs to work outside the home (at least while the children are young).[68] It should allow for a decent standard of living and some savings and the acquisition of property, if the person is frugal. Pope Leo XIII expresses his hope that a 'workman's wages be sufficient to enable him comfortably to support himself, his wife, and his children' and that 'if he be a sensible man,' practicing thrift, 'he will not fail, by cutting down expenses, to put by some little savings and thus secure a modest source of income.'[69]

There are different ways to make the family wage a reality.[70] Of course, it could consist in a wage paid directly by the employer to the employee with the amount depending partly on the domestic needs of the employee. This way of administering the family wage seems unfair to the employer and would no doubt discourage companies from hiring people with families. Alternatively, the family wage might be implemented by the State redistribution of public money; giving benefits or tax relief to employees on the basis of their family situation.

Closely related to the principle of the family wage is the idea of remunerating mothers for their domestic work. Since they are forming and raising future citizens, their work makes a significant contribution to the common good of society. John Paul II notes that 'having to abandon these tasks [raising one's children] in order to take up paid work outside the home is wrong from the point of view of the good of society.'[71] Consequently, elsewhere he says that the domestic work of mothers 'should be acknowledged and deeply appreciated,' since:

> The 'toil' of a woman who, having given birth to a child, nourishes and cares for that child and devotes herself to its upbringing, particularly in the early years, is so great as to be comparable to any professional work. This ought to be clearly stated and upheld, no less than any other labour right.[72]

This recognition of motherhood should, he claims, be backed up financially. He goes as far as to suggest that motherhood 'should be recognized as giving the right to financial benefits at least equal to those of other kinds of work undertaken in order to support the family during such a delicate phase of its life.'[73]

In societies heavily influenced by individualism, the family wage can appear to some as wrongfully discriminatory and basically unfair. Since, they might argue, every person should get the same wage for the same job. In response, a strong defence for the family wage can be given from natural law. Commutative justice means that a man ought to receive recompense equivalent to the value of his labour; but his labour is the means that nature gives him to live as a man: this is the intrinsic value of his labour. If a man has dependants, then to live as a man, he must provide for his dependants. Hence, in justice, a wage must be given that is equal to this intrinsic value.[74] Again, if a man is paid too little, he will not marry and if married, not have children—but both these are contrary to the good of society. The children of today are the workers of tomorrow and their work will benefit not just their parents but everyone in society. Therefore, social justice demands the family wage. Let everyone remember that the work he does presupposes the support of society. No one can ultimately claim that the fruits of his work are the result of his efforts alone; there is an inheritance to acknowledge.[75] Without the support of society, manifest in things like education, healthcare, infrastructure, and so on, everyone would still be a subsistence farmer or hunter gatherer! Therefore, in work, there is a social dimension to consider and this includes that the wages paid be not only for the benefit of the individual but also for the society as well.

Notes

1. Vatican II, *Apostolicam Actuositatem*, 11; *CSDC*, 211.
2. *CSDC*, 254.
3. *CSDC*, 213.
4. *CSDC*, 211, 214.
5. John Paul II, *Familiaris Consortio*, 46.
6. Pontifical Council for the Family, *Charter of the Rights of the Family*, Preamble art. D.
7. Pontifical Council for the Family, *Charter of the Rights of the Family*; cf. John Paul II, *Familiaris Consortio*, 47.
8. John Paul II, *Familiaris Consortio*, 86.

9   *CSDC*, 213.
10 *CSDC*, 214.
11 Pius XI, *Divini Illius Magistri*, 12.
12 *Ibid.*, 12.
13 Pontifical Council for the Family, *Charter of the Rights of the Family*, Preamble art. G.
14 John Paul II, *Letter to Families*, 17; *CSDC*, 230.
15 John Paul II, *Familiaris Consortio*, 17. John Paul II states that the fourth task of the Christian family is participation in the mission of the Church. This is not discussed here because it falls outside the realm of social teaching.
16 *CSDC*, 221–229.
17 *CSDC*, 230–243.
18 *CSDC*, 221.
19 John Paul II, *Letter to Families (Gratissimam Sane)*, 7.
20 *Ibid.*, 10.
21 John Paul II, *Familiaris Consortio*, 44.
22 *CSDC*, 246.
23 John Paul II, *Letter to Families (Gratissimam Sane)*, 11; cf. *CSDC*, 230.
24 *CCC*, 2224.
25 Vatican II, *Declaration on Christian Education (Gravissimum Educationis)*, 3.
26 *CCC*, 2223.
27 John Paul II, *Familiaris Consortio*, 37.
28 Vatican II, *Declaration on Christian Education (Gravissimum Educationis)*, 1.
29 *Ibid.*, 3.
30 John Paul II, *Familiaris Consortio*, 36.
31 Vatican II, *Declaration on Christian Education (Gravissimum Educationis)*, 3.
32 John Paul II, *Familiaris Consortio*, 36.
33 Pontifical Council for the Family, *The Truth and Meaning of Human Sexuality*, 41–43.
34 John Paul II, *Familiaris Consortio*, 37.

35 Congregation for the Doctrine of the Faith, *Instruction on Christian Freedom and Liberation (Libertatis Conscientia)*, 94.

36 John Paul II, *Familiaris Consortio*, 44.

37 Benedict XVI, *Caritas in Veritate*, 15.

38 *CSDC*, 233.

39 Benedict XVI, *Address to Pontifical Council for the Family* (8 February 2010).

40 John Paul II, *Address to the Committee of European Journalists for the Rights of the Child* (13 January 1979).

41 Congregation for the Doctrine of the Faith, *Donum Vitae* II, A, 1; cf. *CSDC*, 235.

42 John Paul II, *Letter Of The His Holiness John Paul II To The Secretary General Of The United Nations Organization On The Occasion Of The World Summit For Children* (22 September 1990).

43 *CSDC*, 214.

44 *CCC*, 2209.

45 *CSDC*, 253.

46 *CIC*, 1055.

47 *CIC*, 1057.

48 *CSDC*, 227–228.

49 Pontifical Council for the Family, *Family, Marriage, and 'De Facto' Unions*, 2.

50 *Ibid.*, 10.

51 *CSDC*, 227.

52 Congregation for the Doctrine of the Faith, *Considerations Regarding Proposals To Give Legal Recognition To Unions Between Homosexual Persons*, 6.

53 John Paul II, *Evangelium Vitae*, 90.

54 Congregation for the Doctrine of the Faith, *Considerations Regarding Proposals To Give Legal Recognition To Unions Between Homosexual Persons*, 8.

55 Aside from the issue of immorality, both these forms of union undermine an individual's chances of attaining personal maturity and fulfilment. Maturity and fulfilment require definitive commitment and this is lacking in de facto unions. Addressing the issue of same-sex unions, John Paul II says that it is 'only in the union of two

sexually different persons that the individual can achieve perfection in a synthesis of unity and mutual psychological completion' (John Paul II, *Address to the Tribunal of the Roman Rota* [21 January 1999], 5). We have not considered these issues here in detail because they pertain more to anthropology or general moral theology than to social teaching.

56 John Paul II, *Evangelium Vitae*, 71.

57 *Ibid.*

58 Pontifical Council for the Family, *Family, Marriage, and 'De Facto' Unions*, 11.

59 Leo XIII, *Libertas Praestantissimum*, 33.

60 *CSDC*, 229.

61 Congregation for the Doctrine of the Faith, *Considerations regarding Proposals to give Legal Recognition to Unions between Homosexual Persons*, 5.

62 St Thomas reminds us, 'God therefore neither wills evil to be done, nor wills it not to be done [else no one could sin], but wills to permit evil to be done; and this is a good' (*Summa Theologiae*, I, q.19 a.9 ad 3).

63 Congregation for the Doctrine of the Faith, *Persona Humana*, 8.

64 *CCC*, 2358.

65 John Paul II, *Laborem Exercens*, 10.

66 *CSDC*, 250.

67 Pius XI, *Quadragesimo Anno*, 71.

68 John Paul II, *Laborem Exercens*, 19.

69 Leo XIII, *Rerum Novarum*, 46.

70 John Paul II, *Laborem Exercens*, 19.

71 *Ibid.*

72 John Paul II, *Letter to Families (Gratissimam Sane)*, 17.

73 *Ibid.*

74 Leo XIII, *Rerum Novarum*, 44.

75 Pius XI, *Quadragesimo Anno*, 69.

4

Human Work

The topic of human work is right at the centre of social teaching. It is worth noting that Leo XIII's landmark encyclical *Rerum Novarum* has very much to do with human work, seeing as it was occasioned by the exploitation of workers at the end of the nineteenth century. Ninety years later, John Paul II wrote a whole encyclical, *Laborem Exercens*, on the subject of human work. He tells us the reason why he considered this subject worthy of such detailed attention. He says it was:

> In order to highlight—perhaps more than has been done before—the fact that human work is a key, probably the essential key, to the whole social question, if we try to see that question really from the point of view of man's good.[1]

How can he say that human work is the key to the social question, meaning the right ordering of society? How exactly is work at the heart of human society? These are the questions that confront us in this chapter.

The dignity of human work

We can learn much about the dignity of work by considering what the Bible has to say on the matter. We encounter the topic of human work already in the first chapter of the book of Genesis. Genesis, in the words of John Paul II, is 'the first "Gospel of work."'[2] There we read:

> So God created man in his own image, in the image of God he created him; male and female he created them. God blessed them and said to them, 'Be fruitful and increase in number; fill the earth and subdue it' (Gn 1:27–28).

First, it is worth noting that these words of Scripture give us a possible definition of work; something more difficult than at first it might seem! What, for example, distinguishes play from work? Work might be taken as all human activity — freely chosen activity — that contributes to the goal of subduing the earth, understood as bringing out of creation things that benefit man. John Paul II calls work an activity that 'presupposes a specific dominion by man over the earth and in its turn … confirms and develops this dominion.'[3]

Also according to these words from the book of Genesis, there is a close relationship between God creating man in His own image — in the image of God — and the command to work, expressed here as the command to 'subdue' the earth. In creating the universe, God is the first worker. Created in His image, man is necessarily called to work. In fact, by work, man shares in the creative work of God in the sense that he brings to greater perfection what God has given in creation. In his Apostolic Letter on keeping the Lord's Day holy, *Dies Domini*, John Paul II says that 'the "work" of God [creation] is in some ways an example for man, called not only to inhabit the cosmos, but also to "build" it and thus become God's "co-worker."'[4] For example, when a carpenter (to take a particularly God-like work!) makes a chair, he takes what God has given in creation, namely wood from a tree, and fashions it into something useful for himself or others. For this reason, the Christian vision of work is a wholly positive one. After the fall of Adam, God reveals that one punishment of this rebellion will be the toil of work. Yahweh says, 'cursed is the ground because of you; through painful toil you will eat of it all the days of your life' (Gn 3:17). But this cannot be interpreted as if work itself was a curse. We have already seen it was a commandment given to Adam before the fall: the punishment consists exclusively in the toil.

Also from the first chapter of the book of Genesis, the command for a Sabbath's rest is very important for a correct understanding of human work because it radically relativizes the importance of work.[5] Man must not become a slave to work, nor may he enslave others by it. Moreover, work is a means to a human life that has as its ultimate goal communion with God. Work should never become the goal of our lives, our god, something that is a real danger in a career orientated society. The Sabbath is also a bulwark against the temptation of thinking that by human work we can become self-sufficient, self-reliant. Certainly, we ought to work so we can live—to think that God will provide for us otherwise is likely to be presumption—but we can never have complete control over the success of our work. We are to be solicitous that we work well, but to hand over to God the bringing of this work to fruition. At the end of the week, the Sabbath rest is a statement of trust in God. The Christian, therefore, ought to hold a middle position between, on the one hand, placing the goal of one's life in work and, on the other, despising work and seeing it only as a necessary evil.

For most of his adult life, Jesus was a worker, and a manual worker at that. In antiquity, manual work was the work of slaves, but the Son of God—who assumed the 'form of a slave' (Ph 2:6)—was not ashamed to be a humble carpenter and thereby taught us about the dignity of work. The relative importance of work is also brought out in some of Jesus' words. He warns that it profits man nothing 'if he shall gain the whole world, and lose his own soul' (Mk 8:36) and that we are to 'seek first the Kingdom of God and its righteousness,' and not worry about our material needs since, in seeking the Kingdom, 'all these things shall be added unto you' (Mt 6:33). Finally, Jesus revealed to us the salvific significance of work. The Catechism tells us that work not only 'honours the Creator's gifts and the talents received from him,' but that 'it can also be redemptive.'[6] Or, in the words of the Compendium, human work is a 'participation not only in the act of creation but also in that of redemption.'[7] Jesus' work was to do His Father's will (Jn 17:4), a work brought to completion on the cross when He offered Himself up for our salvation. Our own work, especially the suffering and toil that are often involved, can also become salvific for us and for others when it is united with Him:

> By enduring the toil of work in union with Christ crucified for us, man in a way collaborates with the Son of God for the redemption of humanity. He shows himself a true disciple of Christ by carrying the cross in his turn every day in the activity that he is called upon to perform.[8]

Work as a duty and as a right

Because God has commanded man to work, and because work is the usual way in which a person can support himself and his dependents, man has a duty to work. St. Paul has harsh words for those in the community who are not fulfilling this duty and presumably living at the expense of others. He says that, 'if a man will not work, he shall not eat' (2 Th 3:10). The point is that there is a strong moral obligation to work, all the more so for those who have dependents. In addition, work is a platform for each to contribute to the common good of the society and to obtain resources with which he can undertake charitable works: St. Paul encourages all to work so 'that [he] may have something to share with those in need' (Ep 4:28).[9]

Being a duty, work is also a right (since rights and duties are correlative). However, this right is not binding on the society in quite the same way as the right to life or the right to religious freedom. The State is not obliged to simply create jobs regardless of whether there is a need for such work. Rather, as we shall see later in the chapter on economic life, the State ought to help create the economic conditions in which private initiatives flourish, thereby creating jobs.[10] In this way the government can be considered as an 'indirect' employer.[11]

An indirect employer is a person or institution that has a significant influence on the labour market.[12] Aside from the State, we can think of large companies (e.g. multinationals) that are able to influence such things as the price of raw materials and by this affect the state of whole economies and consequently employment opportunities and wage structures. These organizations, like the State, have a moral responsibility to act in a way that stimulates employment.

Unemployment, especially among young men, is very destabilizing for a society, as the English proverb warns: 'the Devil shall find work for idle hands.' In the words of John Paul II, unemployment is 'in all cases is an evil, and ... when it reaches a certain level, can become a real social disaster.'[13] There may not be an obligation on the part of the State to actually provide work for all, but, for the good of individuals and of society as a whole, full employment remains a mandatory objective for all governments.[14]

The right to work takes on a particular light in its relationship to the right to found a family, because without stable and adequate employment, a couple is likely to postpone having children. Then, once a family is founded, unemployment can be particularly devastating to family life. As we saw in chapter three, the health of family life ought to be a major principle in the formation of economic policy and this certainly includes employment policy, both for the State and for private business.

The good of family life also has implications for the right of women to work. Being equal in dignity to men, women have as much of a right to work as men do. Nonetheless, to realize this right several things are needed. First, women need full access to education and professional training.

Second, according to Catholic social teaching, it is not enough to have non-discriminatory employment legislation that 'levels the playing field', as it were, between men and women. Rather, the right of women to work must take into account the specific vocation of woman to motherhood and so must be realized in such a way that their special and irreplaceable vocation of motherhood is not compromised: 'true advancement ... requires that labour should be structured in such a way that women do not have to pay for their advancement by abandoning what is specific to them.'[15] The point is that it is as much discrimination of women to have a system of work that makes motherhood difficult or disadvantageous as it is to arbitrarily preclude women from various jobs or grades of employment.

The objective and subjective dimensions of work

The most important principle of social teaching in the area of human labour is the distinction between the objective and subjective dimensions of work. This distinction is discussed at length by John Paul II in his encyclical on human work, *Laborem Exercens*, which is by far and away the most important source of social teaching on the subject of human work.[16] The subjective dimension is the human person. If we say that we are now speaking about the subjective dimension of work, we mean that we are now focusing on the one who is working, a human person with innate dignity. The objective dimension is comprised of all the other components that go to make up a comprehensive description of work, such as the materials, the tools and technologies, the products, and the systems of organization. While a full description of human labour requires that both dimensions are taken into consideration, the subjective dimension always has precedence. This precedence is manifested particularly in two areas. First is the judgment of social teaching on the relationship between labour and capital. The second is the determination of a just wage, which will be discussed a little later under the more general heading of the rights of workers.

The relationship of labour and capital

Leo XIII's landmark encyclical *Rerum Novarum* comes to the defence of workers suffering under a system of liberal capitalism that effectively viewed workers as another form of capital alongside the means of production and raw materials. Accordingly, they could be treated in a similar way: the idea being to get the most out of them at the lowest possible cost. Furthermore, to the proponents of liberal capitalism, capital was the sole origin of value in anything produced. This meant that capitalists—those who owned the factories and machines—had the right to the overwhelming share of the profit in any enterprise. In reaction to this, Karl Marx claimed that the value of whatever is produced comes exclusively from the labour. This would mean that (if private ownership was allowed at all) the factory owner would have a right only to what was needed to buy raw materials and keep the factory operational.[17]

Social teaching takes a different approach than both liberal capitalism and Marxism, claiming that the relationship between capital and labour is neither exclusive nor antagonistic, but is complementary and cooperative: 'capital cannot do without labour, nor labour without capital.'[18] In this vein, in *Quadragesimo Anno*, Pius XI says that:

> [O]ne class is forbidden to exclude the other from sharing in the benefits. Hence the class of the wealthy violates this law [of the common good and right to a share in prosperity] no less, when, as if free from care on account of its wealth, it thinks it the right order of things for it to get everything and the worker nothing, than does the non-owning working class when ... it demands for itself everything as if produced by its own hands, and attacks and seeks to abolish, therefore, all property and returns or incomes, of whatever kind they are or whatever the function they perform in human society, that have

not been obtained by labour, and for no other reason save that they are of such a nature.[19]

While taking neither the side of liberal capitalism or Marxism, social teaching does give priority to labour in its complementary relationship with capital. This conclusion flows from the superiority of the subjective dimension of labour over the objective dimension. Ultimately, this is a technical way of expressing the simple truth that people are more important than things! Nonetheless, this priority of labour is also clearly part of the logic of production. This is explained by John Paul II when, fifty years after *Quadragesimo Anno*, he revisits the question of capital and labour in his encyclical *Laborem Exercens*. He argues that capital cannot have superiority because whatever is considered as capital finds its origin either in a gift from God, as in the case of natural resources—such as iron ore, oil, and water—or in the development of these resources into instruments of production—such as tools, machines, refined materials—which is the fruit of the labour of workers. This means that in any given activity the worker is ultimately dependent not directly on capital but on 'two [other] inheritances': either on the prior gift from God or the work of other workers.[20] The point is that if labour is dependent and subordinated to anything it is only to the gift of God in creation or another person's labour, but never to capital. Man puts capital to work and uses it; capital does not put man to work and use him.[21] This last conclusion should be distinguished from the possibility that a capitalist (or at least the employer) has a relationship of superiority to a labourer (employee). This is something different than the relationship of capital to labour as such, since in this former case we are speaking about the relationship of two parties within the category of work (labour).

On this last point then, there might appear to be some common ground between social teaching and Marxism, at least to the extent that both claim a superiority of labour over capital. Nonetheless, a serious difference remains because Marx was wrong to assert a natural antagonism between capital and labour. This antagonism is not in the logic of production itself but only in the disordered hearts of selfish men. Furthermore, John Paul II points out that Marxism as a form of materialism (dialectic materialism) tends in practice to replicate the error of liberal capitalism, since it judges the success of society in terms of material prosperity and not in the abundance of personal and spiritual goods. In theory, it champions labour over capital, but in practice, its own materialistic world view ends up subordinating the worker to material goals. John Paul II calls this the 'error of materialism' and defines it as 'a conviction of the primacy and superiority of the material, and directly or indirectly places the spiritual and the personal ... in a position of subordination to material reality.'[22]

In the modern day, there are two paradoxical tendencies in regard to the relationship between capital and labour. On the one hand, there is a growing appreciation of the value of labour, because of an awareness that human 'know-how' is becoming more and more the decisive factor in some sectors of the economy, especially in areas like computing, pharmaceuticals, and telecommunications. On the other hand, the advent of globalization and the search for cheaper methods of production opens up the danger of reverting to the situation criticized by *Rerum Novarum*, where unscrupulous capitalists drive down wages by seeking out the cheapest source of labour, this time in an international labour market.[23]

Social teaching proposes a good way to overcome, to some degree, the abiding tension between capital and labour. This is the participation of the workers in the ownership of the companies they work for. This brings about the real socialization of capital in a way that nationalization of companies does not. Nationalization—where ownership is transferred to the State—tends to result in a situation where no one effectively owns anything, or worse, it is practically a transfer of management from one small group of private individuals to another small group of bureaucrats. John Paul II notes that 'merely taking these means of production (capital) out of the hands of their private owners is not enough to ensure their satisfactory socialization.' He goes on to say that 'we can speak of socializing only ... when on the basis of his work each person is fully entitled to consider himself a part-owner of the great workbench at which he is working with every one else.'[24] The solution offered by social teaching is not the removal of private property but its extension. Therefore, a very practical way of realizing this socialization—aimed at diffusing the false antagonism between capital and labour— is for employees to receive as part of their wages shares in their own company.

In *Laborem Exercens*, John Paul II presents another, and more radical, proposal. He says:

> A way towards that goal could be found by associating labour with the ownership of capital, as far as possible, and by producing a wide range of intermediate bodies with economic, social and cultural purposes; they would be bodies enjoying real autonomy with regard to the public powers, pursuing their specific aims in honest collaboration with each other and in subordination to the demands of the common good.[25]

This seems to point back to the idea of Corporatism or Occupational Groupings first proposed by Pius XI in *Quadragesimo Anno* during the Great Depression of the 1920s.[26] According to that idea, sectors of industry, such as (for example) steel, coal, tourism, or financial services would be run by committees consisting of capitalists, managers, and workers, who together would seek the best human and economic solutions to the serious problems and tensions in that sector, regulating costs, wages, and professional practices in light of the good of that sector and of the common good of the whole economy. In this sense, the idea of Occupational Groupings represents an economic model between the centrally-planned State-run economies of Communism, and the highly individualistic model of liberal capitalism. Pius XI saw it as a major contribution to civil peace, particularly threatened during the Great Depression by the conflict between workers and capitalists:

> [A] complete cure will not come until this opposition has been abolished and well-ordered members of the social body—Industries and Professions—are constituted in which men may have their place, not according to the position each has in the labour market but according to the respective social functions which each performs. For under nature's guidance it comes to pass that just as those who are joined together by nearness of habitation establish towns, so those who follow the same industry or profession—whether in the economic or other field—form guilds or associations, so that many are wont to consider these self-governing organizations, if not essential, at least natural to civil society.[27]

Something similar to Occupation Groupings already exists in many countries with respect to certain professions, particularly doctors, lawyers, and accountants. These occupations often have professional bodies that regulate who can work in these fields, and are (in part) responsible for the training of members of that profession, setting standards, and even have disciplinary powers over their members.

The rights of workers

The first and most fundamental right of the worker is the right to work—this we have already discussed. After this, social teaching champions a range of other worker's rights, such as the right to rest, the right to working conditions that respect human dignity, and the right to help when unemployed or sick; but there are three rights of particular importance that we should discuss in more detail here. Along with the right to work, these three form the heart of labour laws in a just society. They are: the right to fair remuneration for work done, the right to strike, and the right to form workers' associations.

The right to a fair wage

Where a fair wage is lacking, there can be no question of an employer treating his workers well. John Paul II says that 'there is no more important way for securing a just relationship between the worker and the employer than that constituted by remuneration for work.'[28] But, he notes, a just wage is more significant than this. He says that 'the justice of a socioeconomic system and, in each case, its just functioning, deserve in the final analysis to be evaluated by the way in which man's work is properly remunerated in the system.'[29] This is a very bold statement, since it is claiming that a just wage is a litmus test not only for the relationship of employer and employee, but for the health of the whole society. This is so because the worker wage is the 'practical means whereby the vast majority of people can have access to those goods which are intended for common use.'[30] The point is that the Universal Destination of Goods—or more precisely the intention of God in creation that all human beings would have an adequate share of this common gift—is normally realized by means of the money a person receives for his work. To underpay a worker is to undermine his participation in the goods of the world, and to thwart the intention of God in creation! This is the ultimate reason that labour is the key to the social question, so much so that the Congregation for the Doctrine of the Faith proposes labour reform as the Church's solution to the social injustices that others say can only be solved by revolution.[31]

A wage is not just simply because the employer and the employee have agreed on it. Pope Leo XIII rejects the following idea:

> [T]he employer, when he pays what was agreed upon, has done his part and seemingly is not called upon to do anything beyond. The only way, it is said, in which injustice might occur would be if the master refused to pay the whole of the wages.[32]

He rejects this because he is aware that, especially in his day, there were situations in which workers were so desperate for work that they were forced to accept unfair conditions of remuneration.[33] Rather, the calculation of a just wage needs to take into consideration both objective and subjective criteria. Objectively, consideration must to be given to the value of the product that is produced, the financial state of the company, and the common good of society. The last two criteria given here recognize that the wage demand of workers ought not to damage the economic viability of the company, nor be unfair within the context of the whole society. For example, excessive wage demands can cause inflation, to the detriment of the whole society.

The subjective dimension of work turns our attention to the worker himself and determines that a just wage is that which allows the employee and his dependents to live not merely above the level of subsistence, but a dignified human existence.[34] The wage should allow for some savings and the acquisition of property, if the worker is frugal. Summarizing all these factors, John XXIII says that the just wage:

> [M]ust be determined in accordance with justice and equity; which means that workers must be paid a wage which allows them to live a truly human life and to fulfil their family obligations in a worthy manner. Other factors too enter into the assessment of a just wage: namely, the effective contribution which each individual makes to the economic effort, the financial state of the company for which he works, the requirements of the general good of the particular country—having regard especially to the repercussions on the overall employment of the

working force in the country as a whole—and finally the requirements of the common good of the universal family of nations of every kind, both large and small.³⁵

The right to form trade unions

Social teaching sees labour unions as an authentic expression of workers' solidarity, that is, the concerted effort to work together for their common good. In *Rerum Novarum*, Leo XIII mounts a powerful defence of labour unions in the face of those in authority who were seeking to outlaw them.³⁶ He points out that for the State to ban trade unions is utterly contradictory, since both the unions and the State are build upon the same foundation, namely the social nature of human beings. Therefore, for a State to ban workers' associations would be to undermine her own legitimacy:

> For, to enter into a 'society' of this kind [a trade union] is the natural right of man; and the State has for its office to protect natural rights, not to destroy them; and, if it forbid its citizens to form associations, it contradicts the very principle of its own existence, for both they and it exist in virtue of the like principle, namely, the natural tendency of man to dwell in society.³⁷

The proximate aim of a trade union is social justice for its members as workers, within the context of the common good of society. This means that the activity of the union has the goal of ensuring for each of its members, as a worker, his share in the prosperity of the society in such a way that it is not selfish but respects the common good. Concretely, this will mean things like ensuring that each worker receives a fair wage, good working conditions, access to professional training, and help when there is injury or sickness. Saying this help is for their members 'as workers' means to limit the remit of the union to those issues that touch directly upon human work. They are not normally responsible for others things that are part of the life of their members such as housing, or the schooling of children of workers.

In carrying out their work, while unions are focused specifically on the material well-being of their members, they, like the State, must keep in mind who their members are, namely human persons whose well-being cannot be reduced to material prosperity. Thinking particularly of Catholic trade unions, something that perhaps now rarely exist, Leo XIII makes this point in *Rerum Novarum* when he says, 'what advantage can it be to a working man to obtain by means of a society material well-being, if he endangers his soul for lack of spiritual food?'[38] This is reiterated by Pius XI when, in quoting Leo, he points out that the broader aim of unions must be that:

> 'the individual members of the association secure, so far as is possible, an increase in the goods of body, of soul, and of property,' yet it is clear that 'moral and religious perfection ought to be regarded as their principal goal, and that their social organization as such ought above all to be directed completely by this goal.'[39]

Leo XIII was not unaware of the revolutionary undertones in some on the unions of his day,[40] and says that the State does have the right 'to prevent those associations in which men join together for purposes which are evidently bad, unlawful, or dangerous to the State.'[41] Since the historical context in which trade unions emerged was the oppression of workers in the nineteenth century, it is also easy to fall into thinking of unions in terms of antagonism between classes; but unions must never become vehicles for class struggle.[42] As we have seen, social teaching traces the origin of unions back to a deeper source: to the social nature of men. By nature, therefore, far from being an instrument of class struggle, they ought to be a cause of solidarity in society and even facilitate cooperation between employers and employees. In the words of John Paul II, the struggle that unions are necessarily engaged in, 'should be seen as a normal endeavour "for" the just good ... but it is not a struggle "against" others.'[43] Of course, given the nature of their work, unions certainly can be involved in the political life of society. In championing the right of workers, they can legitimately seek to influence political decisions and laws in order to bring about social justice for their members. However, they ought not to act as political parties nor be too closely aligned, since, as we have seen, their remit is much more limited.[44] Political parties must have policies and programs on education, health, foreign affairs, and law and order, all things that are probably beyond the scope of concern for labour unions.

Finally, no one should be forced to join a union (the so-called 'closed shop') nor be excluded from work or even from benefits won by the union on behalf of workers because he is not a member. On the other hand, in the era of globalization, unions are also called upon to globalise their solidarity, moving beyond the concerns only of their members to include the plight of workers in poor countries that are often geographically distant.[45] This is a challenge, since foreign workers can easily be seen as a threat to the security of employment of native workers.

The right to strike

Finally, social teaching upholds the right of workers to strike—whether as part of a union or not—as a last resort, without suffering any penalty from the employer. John Paul II says that 'workers should be assured the right to strike, without being subjected to personal penal sanctions for taking part in a strike.' A strike is here understood as the peaceful action of the workers withholding their labour in order to apply pressure on the employer, the State, or even public opinion, in an attempt to better their working conditions.[46]

In addressing the plight of the exploited worker of his time, Leo XIII affirmed the right to strike in *Rerum*

Novarum.⁴⁷ In doing so, he also touches lightly upon the limit to this right. In his day, as in ours, strikes were easily hijacked by those with political agendas, thereby being drawn into the sphere of class struggle. For this reason, whenever social teaching mentions the right to strike there is also a mention of the appropriate exercise of this right and its due limit. The limit is threefold and is expressed in the Catechism as follows:

> Recourse to a strike is morally legitimate when it cannot be avoided, or at least when it is necessary to obtain a proportionate benefit. It becomes morally unacceptable when accompanied by violence, or when objectives are included that are not directly linked to working conditions or are contrary to the common good.⁴⁸

A similar sentiment is expressed by Paul VI in his Apostolic Letter, *Octogesima Adveniens*:

> Here and there the temptation can arise of profiting from a position of force to impose, particularly by strikes—the right to which as a final means of defence remains certainly recognized—conditions which are too burdensome for the overall economy and for the social body, or to desire to obtain in this way demands of a directly political nature. When it is a question of public service, required for the life of an entire nation, it is necessary to be able to assess the limit beyond which the harm caused to society becomes inadmissible.⁴⁹

From this we can see that the first thing to be excluded, in legitimately exercising the right to strike, is violence. Second, the strike cannot be to the detriment of the common good. This can happen in several ways. It might be that halting work is so detrimental to the common good that the strike cannot be allowed: for example, a strike by transport workers in the time of war, or a strike by doctors even in time of peace. In both cases, the government would probably be acting legitimately to outlaw such strikes. This is what Paul VI means in the above quote from *Octogesima Adveniens* when he mentions 'public service, required for the life of an entire nation.' John Paul II says that 'when essential community services are in question, they must in every case be ensured, if necessary by means of appropriate legislation.'[50] Moreover, strikes that paralyse the socioeconomic life of the country harm other workers, hindering them from earning a living. This is likely to be unjust. Another way a strike might be to the detriment of the common good is if the demands made by those striking are harmful to the common welfare, for example a demand for an excessive wage increase, one that would cause significant inflation, to the detriment of the whole society.

The third principle restraining the right to strike is that strikes ought not to be called for political reasons but in order to attain 'objectives [that] are ... directly linked to working conditions' of the members. It is clearly wrong, therefore, for a labour union to use strikes to destabilize a government simply because it does not suit its political preference. Here we are not talking about confronting a corrupt and violent regime as was done by the Polish trade union 'Solidarity' partly using the weapon of general strikes.

It is not always simple to draw a clear line between a legitimate goal ('directly linked to working conditions') and one that is of a 'directly political nature,' but clearly this line can and has, not infrequently, been crossed. For example, considering the situation in Great Britain, it is not a simple matter to judge whether the bitter miners' strike of the mid-1980s was of a 'directly political nature.' Was it seeking to bring down the Conservative government of the time? That suspicion is heightened by the affiliation of the labour unions in the United Kingdom to the Labour Party, but others could perhaps mount a good argument that it was a legitimate attempt to protect the jobs of miners threatened by government and coal management policies. Whatever the truth in this particular case, social teaching warns against the ever present danger of strikes becoming a weapon for class struggle.

Notes

1. John Paul II, *Laborem Exercens*, 4.
2. *Ibid.*, 25.
3. John Paul II, *Laborem Exercens*, 4.
4. John Paul II, *Dies Domini*, 10; *CSDC*, 262.
5. *CSDC*, 258.
6. *CCC*, 2427.
7. *CSDC*, 263.
8. John Paul II, *Laborem Exercens*, 27.
9. *CSDC*, 264, 274, 287.
10. *CSDC*, 291.
11. John Paul II, *Laborem Exercens*, 17.
12. *Ibid.*; cf. *CSDC*, 288.
13. John Paul II, *Laborem Exercens*, 18.
14. *CSDC*, 288.
15. *Ibid.*, 19; cf. *CSDC*, 295.
16. John Paul II, *Laborem Exercens*, 5–6.
17. In *Quadragesimo Anno*, Pius XI considers (and refutes) an opinion that claims that 'all products and profits, save only enough to repair and renew capital, belong by very right to the workers' (Pius XI, *Quadragesimo Anno*, 55).
18. Leo XIII, *Rerum Novarum*, 19; cf. *CSDC*, 277.
19. Pius XI, *Quadragesimo Anno*, 57.
20. John Paul II, *Laborem Exercens*, 12–13.
21. *Ibid.*, 13.
22. *Ibid.*
23. *CSDC*, 279.
24. John Paul II, *Laborem Exercens*, 14.
25. *Ibid.*
26. Pius XI, *Quadragesimo Anno*, 81–87; cf. Leo XIII, *Rerum Novarum*, 49: 'It is gratifying to know that there are actually in existence not a few associations ... of workmen and employers together, but it were greatly to be desired that they should become more numerous and more efficient.'
27. Pius XI, *Quadragesimo Anno*, 83.
28. John Paul II, *Laborem Exercens*, 19; cf. *CSDC*, 302.

29 John Paul II, *Laborem Exercens*, 19.
30 *Ibid.*
31 Congregation for the Doctrine of the Faith, Instruction on Christian Freedom and Liberation *(Libertatis Conscientia)*, 83.
32 Leo XIII, *Rerum Novarum*, 43.
33 *CSDC*, 302.
34 Subjective criteria might also include the work-related responsibilities of the worker and his length of service in the company.
35 John XXIII, *Mater et Magistra*, 71; cf. Vatican II, *Gaudium et Spes*, 67.
36 Leo XIII, *Rerum Novarum*, 49–57.
37 *Ibid.*, 51.
38 *Ibid.*, 57.
39 Pius XI, *Quadragesimo Anno*, 32.
40 Leo XIII, *Rerum Novarum*, 54.
41 *Ibid.*, 52.
42 *CSDC*, 306.
43 John Paul II, *Laborem Exercens*, 20.
44 *CSDC*, 307.
45 Benedict XVI, *Caritas in Veritate*, 64.
46 *CSDC*, 304.
47 Leo XIII, *Rerum Novarum*, 36.
48 *CCC*, 2435; Vatican II, *Gaudium et Spes*, 68.
49 Paul VI, *Octogesima Adveniens*, 14.
50 John Paul II, *Laborem Exercens*, 20.

5

Economic Life

Since, according to the account of creation in the book of Genesis, God Himself is the Creator of the material world and He Himself has declared that it is good (Gn 1:1–25), the Christian outlook on material things ought to be essentially positive. It was God who entrusted the material world to the care of man, and it is to be accepted at a gift from Him and as a blessing. Throughout the history of the Church, this position has again and again been defended against Gnostic heresies that despise matter and even reject the Old Testament because it portrays God as the Creator of the material world.

The Christian tradition balances this enthusiasm for created things with an attitude of caution. As a result of the Fall, humans have acquired a tendency to over-value material things, making them the final goal of life. Let us note: it is not that material things are bad (or have become bad) but rather that there is a corruption in us, which makes it hard for us to put material things in their proper place in the hierarchy of human goods. This disordered estimation and desire for material things can lead in two negative directions. First, it can hinder man from pursuing more important things in life, namely spiritual goods such as virtue and communion, ultimately deflecting him from his supreme good and goal of life, namely God. Second, an excessive love for material things can lead to selfishness and injustice toward others, depriving them of their rightful share in the blessing of creation.

Both of these attitudes towards material goods—the blessing and the caution—are clearly present in parables of Jesus. On the one hand, we have the parable of the talents (Mt 25:14–30), in which the servants who work industriously with the resources that the master gives them (and make a profit) are praised, while the servant who does not even try to develop the resources left to him is scolded. On the other hand, the farmer who builds a bigger barn simply so he can store up all his wealth for himself, and in so doing neglects his duty to others and his relationship to God, is condemned (Lk 12:13–21).

When social teaching turns its attention to economic life, it starts from this twofold Scriptural position. This position is fundamentally positive but always insistent that economic life must be contextualized and relativized. It is only one part of human life, and not the most important at that. In this chapter, our objective will be to understand this stance more clearly.

The purpose of the economy and human development

The proximate purpose of the economy is the creation and increase of wealth, understood as greater quantity and quality of material goods. The Compendium outlines that 'the economy has as its object the development of wealth and its progressive increase, not only in quantity but also in quality.'[1] When an economy is failing to do this (as is the case in many of the countries of Africa, for example) then we can honestly say that these economies are failing.

Social teaching, however, is clear that while increased quantity and quality of goods is the aim of economic development, it is by no means the full description of development itself. Economic development is only one part of development. Paul VI's *Populorum Progressio* and John Paul II's *Sollicitudo Rei Socialis* both strongly emphasis an integral development that aims at the whole good of the person and the good of every person. This is also perhaps the central theme of Benedict XVI's encyclical *Caritas in Veritate*. In that encyclical, Pope Benedict hails *Populorum Progressio* as the *Rerum Novarum* of the modern age precisely because it makes this point so clear: human development is much more than economic development.[2] Paul VI had noted that progress drives us to 'do more, know more and have more in order to be more.'[3] Authentic development, therefore, must be 'integral, that is, it has to promote the good of every man and of the whole man.'[4]

Applying such a broad idea of development, a society is developed when it abounds not just in material goods but also has an abundance of spiritual goods such as culture, morality, and ultimately religious practice. Such a society would also need to demonstrate that this development was universal or at least very widespread and, moreover, that it broadened its horizons beyond its own national boundaries in seeking a similar development internationally. A nation that grows in material wealth but cares little for the poor within its own society or in the world at large might indeed be said to be economically developing, but it is not morally developing and so simply not developing according to the criteria of Catholic social teaching. It is for this reason that social teaching claims that if all countries are not helped to develop economically, we cannot speak about the authentic development of any. In *Sollicitudo Rei Socialis*, John Paul II says:

> [I]t should be obvious that development either becomes shared in common by every part of the world or it undergoes a process of regression even in zones marked by constant progress. This tells us a great deal about the nature of authentic development: either all the nations of the world participate, or it will not be true development.[5]

What ethics has to do with economics

We have already said that the proximate goal of economic life is universal material prosperity, but this is clearly not the final goal of human life. Man's final goal is communion, with others and ultimately with God. In order that this proximate goal of economic life might harmonize with the final goal, economics must be subjected to control and direction. Economic life is only one part of human life and it needs to finds its correct place within the whole. The Compendium explains that:

> The economy, in fact, whether on a scientific or practical level, has not been entrusted with the purpose of fulfilling man or of bringing about proper human coexistence. Its task, rather, is partial: the production, distribution and consumption of material goods and services.[6]

Accordingly, social teaching rejects laissez-faire capitalism. This is an approach that would afford an absolute free rein to capitalists and entrepreneurs, and follows on from a political decision not to circumscribe their economic activity by any regulation whatsoever.

Of course economics, like all sciences, has its own principles and methods, and social teaching certainly respects these as part of the so-called 'right to full autonomy of earthly affairs.'[7] However, what economics does not have within itself is the ability to correctly place (and subordinate) itself within the hierarchy of human goods and goals. Some proponents of laissez-faire capitalism dispute this and speak about the 'invisible hand' that leads those who pursue private gain to benefit society at large unwittingly by the generation of great wealth that in some manner will 'trickle down' to others by means of employment or some other method. Adam Smith spoke about entrepreneurs who were 'led by an invisible hand to promote an end which was no part of [their] intention.'[8] The truth of this is debated, and anyway this applies only to the distribution of material wealth; it does not touch upon how economics could subordinate itself to the promotion of spiritual goods. This is not a criticism of economics but a simple acknowledgment of its limitation. The correct place can only be given to economics from without. This is the role of ethics and the contribution of Catholic social teaching. The point is concisely made by Pius XI in *Quadragesimo Anno*. After noting that, 'even though economics and moral science employs each its own principles in its own sphere,' it is, nevertheless, 'an error to say that the economic and moral orders are so distinct from and alien to each other that the former depends in no way on the latter.' It is an error because:

> [I]t is only the moral law which, just as it commands us to seek our supreme and last end in the whole scheme of our activity, so likewise commands us to seek directly in each kind of activity those purposes which we know that nature, or rather God the Author of nature, established for that kind of action, and in an orderly relationship to subordinate such immediate purposes to our supreme and last end.[9]

To clarify this, let us make a comparison. A car has thousands of parts that are carefully related to each other. This is the business of the car manufacturer or car mechanic. They know this aspect of the car best and can design, construct, and make repairs so the car runs better. But it is not the role of the car manufacturer or mechanic to say whether the speed limit on a given stretch of road ought to be 30 mph, 50 mph, or unlimited. Moreover, there is nothing in the configuration of the parts of the car or the science of car manufacturing that would indicate whether this part of the road ought to be a 30 zone, or a 50 zone. The smooth running of the car is for the good of the driver in a limited sense—it means that he will not break down and can get from A to B quickly. But the decision about speed limits need to be taken from a broader perspective that considers not just the mechanisms of the car but the greater good of the driver, of pedestrians, and of those who live in the neighbourhood. This might mean that there should be laws to prevent car manufacturers from even building cars that can excessively exceed the national speed limit; indeed in some countries devises are placed in large vehicles such as trucks and coaches to limit their speed.

In a similar way, the structures of an economy ought to be tailored to make the economy efficient in achieving its aim of making wealth, and the experts in this field (the economists) are the best people to work all of this out. Nevertheless, the economy has to serve the whole good of man and, therefore, must be guided in its operation by higher principles and a higher vision. Another way of saying the same thing is that what is economically possible is not by that fact right and good, and while economics might tell us what is possible it alone does not tells us if this is good. In his encyclical *Caritas in Veritate*, Benedict XVI lauds the emergence of ethical finance companies, ethical because they do not invest, for example, in businesses that abuse human rights or the environment; but, he points out, this ought not to be a specialized sector: the whole economy ought to be ethical![10]

Undoubtedly, there will be instances where the demands of morality must limit and restrict economic life in its attempt to harness it for the common good. For example, there is the situation of monopolies. Experience shows that unregulated economic activity can lead to monopolies, understood as a situation where the production and supply of some product or service is in the hands of very few or perhaps even one person or group. This is contrary to the common good, since it gives excessive power to this individual or individuals and allows them to dictate the price of their products; something that is always most detrimental to the poor in any society. This is exactly the situation that Pius XI noted in the capitalism of his day when he wrote that:

Economic Life

> This concentration of power and might, the characteristic mark, as it were, of contemporary economic life, is the fruit that the unlimited freedom of struggle among competitors has of its own nature produced, and which lets only the strongest survive.[11]

Accordingly, for the common good, a State can seek to prevent monopolies or break up those that have formed. This is a limitation placed by ethics on economic life in light of the wider good of society. Note also that this regulation is also for the protection of economic life itself, since monopolies born out of the market economy are the effective destruction of the market economy. Pius XI notes that 'free competition has destroyed itself; economic dictatorship has supplanted the free market.'[12]

Another example where economic life cannot be left to its own devises is the just wage. Since the tendency of economics is towards efficiency and profit (both good in themselves), a just wage is by no means ensured without some ethical regulation.[13] Advertising is another area where the market cannot be wholly self-regulating, since through advertising there is a temptation on the part of advertisers to generate false needs and consequently false demands. In this way, 'advertising also can be, and often is, a tool of the "phenomenon of consumerism."'[14] When this happens, the true goal of the economy is perverted. Other examples abound: care for the environment, wholesome working conditions, and a Sabbath's rest. All these things—which we take for granted as part of a well-ordered society—are not achieved by economics itself, but by the subjection of economic life to higher principles and goals.

In the examples given here, it is traditionally the State that has the task of ensuring the ethical regulation of economic life, principally by creating and enforcing appropriate laws. But this does not do away with the demand that businesses should be ethical from within, importing ethical criteria into their mode of operation. In fact, with the advent of globalization this is of growing importance because nation States have been weakened in their power over enterprises that transcend national boundaries.[15]

All of this might make us think that economics and ethics are in a constant state of tension or conflict. Since, as we have said, economics has its own principles and ethics has its own, does this mean that they are forever destined to clash and compete for supremacy? Are they fundamentally opposed to each other? The answer here must be certainly not! In fact, it is better to say, quite the contrary; since ethics helps economics to find its proper place within human society as a whole, ethics comes to the aid of economics and perfects it. Moreover, there are many areas in which ethics and economic principles coincide in profound agreement. An important case of this is the efficient use of material goods. This is both good economics and good morality, since waste is contrary to our 'office' as stewards. Another case of coincidence is the proper treatment of employees. Giving attention to employees and paying them well is not contrary to the aim of companies to increase wealth because employees who are well looked after are generally more productive.[16] In fact, it is a trait of the modern economic scene that a company's human resources is often recognized as the most important asset it has. Therefore, John Paul II notes that lack of care for employees, as well as being morally inadmissible, 'will eventually have negative repercussions on the firm's economic efficiency.'[17]

This principle—good morality is good economics—is clearly expressed in *Caritas in Veritate*:

> The great challenge before us, accentuated by the problems of development in this global era and made even more urgent by the economic and financial crisis, is to demonstrate, in thinking and behaviour, not only that traditional principles of social ethics like transparency, honesty and responsibility cannot be ignored or attenuated, but also that in commercial relationships the principle of gratuitousness and the logic of gift as an expression of fraternity can and must find their place within

normal economic activity. This is a human demand at the present time, but it is also demanded by economic logic.[18]

By saying that 'the principle of gratuitousness' is a 'demand of economic logic' he is saying that selfishness is bad economics. Here, Pope Benedict is thinking of things such as irresponsible lending and, what he calls, 'scandalous speculation' (both of which are bad morality) that had contributed to the bad economic situation that existed at the time *Caritas in Veritate* was promulgated.[19]

Ultimately, we must agree with Leo XIII when he argues that—in contrast to bad morality—infusing Christian morality into economic life will draw down upon it God's blessing. He says, 'Christian morality, when adequately and completely practiced, leads of itself to temporal prosperity, for it merits the blessing of that God who is the source of all blessings.'[20]

In summary, we can say that an economy is correctly working when it brings about an increase in wealth in such a way that it is directed to the whole development of man and of every man, and to ensure this economic life must be guided by sound moral principles.

Why Catholic social teaching favours the market economy

There is no doubt that social teaching favours a market-based economic system over a centrally planned one. A market system is one where the production of goods and provision of services are a response to demand from consumers, and where the pricing of these goods is determined by the relationship of supply to demand. In contrast, in a centrally planned system the demand for goods and services is decided upon not by the customer but by bureaucrats who then accordingly organize for the production of the goods and supply of these services and fix their prices. Over the course of the last century, Communism, of course, has been the most widely spread form of a centrally planned economy.

Catholic social teaching favours the market system for both economic and anthropological reasons. One economic reason is that market systems respond better to the actual needs of people, whereas a centrally planned system is reliant on the accuracy of the predicted or supposed needs. Furthermore, the market system also tends to make better use of resources because there is competition for these resources, which gives them value; in the words of John Paul II, 'on the level of individual nations and of international relations, the free market is the most efficient instrument for utilizing resources and effectively responding to needs.'[21] Finally, the market system has a track record of being able to bring about increased prosperity over sustained periods of time. This is to say that it better achieves the proximate goal of an economic system![22] The failure of Communism to do this is undoubtedly one of the main reasons for its collapse as an economic and political system.[23]

From an anthropological point of view, the market system fits best with the value of freedom, since it fosters personal initiative and creativity, both aspects of man created in the image of God. In contrast, central planning tends to dampen and even extinguish initiative, because it does not find a place for it, and it does not reward it. Even in market systems, excessive bureaucracy can have the same result. In both cases, a human right is being compromised, since the Catechism tells us that 'everyone has the right to economic initiative; everyone should make legitimate use of his talents to contribute to the abundance that will benefit all.'[24] In *Sollicitudo Rei Socialis*, John Paul II reflects on the situation of those (mostly Communist) countries that had suppressed private economic initiative in the name of equality. He notes that this equality in practice becomes universal servitude to the State and dramatically saps the vitality of society:

> [T]here arises, not so much a true equality as a 'levelling down.' In the place of creative initiative there appears passivity, dependence and submission to the bureaucratic apparatus which, as the only 'ordering' and 'decision-making' body if not also the 'owner' of the entire totality of goods and the means of production, puts everyone in a position of almost absolute dependence, which is similar to the traditional dependence of the worker-proletarian in capitalism. This provokes a sense of frustration or desperation and predisposes people to opt out of national life, impelling many to emigrate and also favouring a form of 'psychological' emigration.[25]

The fostering of personal initiative, then, has benefits for society that pass beyond the purely economic, since it brings vigour to society. Furthermore, it encourages collaboration among people, thereby strengthening the fabric of society.[26] Finally, while centrally planned economies were in some respect a reaction against gross injustices occurring in the laissez-faire capitalism of the nineteenth century, social teaching asserts that the market economy is ultimately the more just system: it protects the basic right to private property (whereas centrally planned economies almost inevitably require a high degree of nationalization) and it rewards hard work and initiative.[27]

In this regard, a word ought to be said about profit. In the words of John Paul II, 'the Church acknowledges the legitimate role of profit as an indication that a business is functioning well,'[28] since profit indicates that both human needs (consumer needs) have been met and that the system of production is efficient and well ordered. Clearly, however, profit cannot be the only measure indicating the health of a company. Other factors must be taken into consideration. Among these are the well-being of the employees and the contribution the company makes to the common good of society. In fact, these are more important and the search for profit should be at the service of these. Benedict XVI explains that when 'the sole criterion for action in business is thought to be the maximization of profit,' there is a 'confusion between ends and means.'[29] Profit must serve. It must serve the good of the company, including the employees, and it must serve the greater good of society. Again, it is not a matter of either/or—either profit or the well-being of the employees—but both. Profit can be harmonized with these higher goals.

***

Despite its very positive attitude towards the market economy, social teaching's affirmation is not unqualified. The main qualification is that the market cannot supply all human needs, not even all material needs. The market economy, as we have said, rests upon the mechanism of supply and demand which is itself built upon the purchasing power of the consumer. A demand is generated when the consumer has a need for something but also when he has the power to pay for it. But, there will always be some members of society who have fundamental human needs— say for food, healthcare, and shelter—but who do not have the necessary purchasing power, such as the sick, the elderly, and the poor in general.[30] If the market is the only mechanism for providing these human needs, then these people will more than likely not receive what they need for a human standard of living. We say 'only mechanism' because private enterprise will usually have a significant role in the provision of food, shelter, and healthcare in any society, and this is normal and very good. But it falls to society to make provision for those who cannot be helped by the market. Again, the objective is not to place these people in a position of perpetual reliance on the welfare state. On the contrary, as much as possible, they should be helped to take their place and make their contribution in the economic life of the society. John Paul II summarizes all of this when he says:

> [T]here are many human needs which find no place on the market. It is a strict duty of justice and truth not to allow fundamental human needs to remain unsatisfied, and not to allow those burdened by such needs to perish. It is also necessary to help these needy people to acquire expertise, to enter the circle of exchange, and to develop their skills in order to make the best use of their capacities and resources.[31]

So, clearly, the market cannot cater for the needs of all human beings all the time; nor of all human needs, since there are some cultural goods, namely the transcendental goods of truth, good, and beauty that cannot be wholly given over to the market. Imagine, for example, if the range of education in a society was restricted to only by those areas with 'commercial appeal.' The culture of the country would be dramatically impoverished. The same would be true of the arts. Morality also cannot be left up to the market, as if what is morally acceptable could be equated with what sells, but must follow objective standards. Herein lies the case for some degree of regulation of the mass media. The underlining point is that to imagine that the market alone can cater for all human needs and needs of society is to run 'the risk of an "idolatry" of the market, an idolatry which ignores the existence of goods which by their nature are not and cannot be mere commodities.'[32]

The protection of the environment is another significant area where the market alone is insufficient. Since the reduction or disposal of waste is often expensive and brings no immediate financial benefit to a company, there is usually little incentive for companies to be environmentally responsible. Consequently, the State must legislate and regulate this aspect of the economy. We shall return to all this later in a chapter dedicated to the environment.

Finally, social teaching sounds a caution about the working of financial markets, by which it means the trading of shares, the provision of loans, and exchange of currencies. Of course, social teaching affirms the fundamental legitimacy of these systems, noting that they under-gird the market economy, since without access to loans and the ability to invest there can be no economic development in market economies. The critique offered by social teaching is that there is a tendency to ignore the instrumental nature of these components of the economy. When this happens, the financial markets are viewed no longer as a means by which businesses have access to the resources they need to generate wealth, but are ends in themselves. They become sources of personal gain by financial speculation.[33] When this happens, the financial market runs the risk of having 'abandoned its original and essential role of serving the real economy and, ultimately, of contributing to the development of people and the human community.'[34]

Here we should also say something about whether money can be lent at interest. This is an important question given the central place credit has the modern market based economy. The answer to this question is yes, money can be lent at interest, if there is a just reason to demand back more than was lent. Understanding the Church's historical objection to usury, therefore, boils down to determining what are and what are not just reasons for demanding back more than was lent.[35] A just reason — a title, as it is called — would certainly include the case where the loaning party incurred expenses in administrating the loan. However, simply depriving oneself of the use of money by lending is not a just title since holding on to a sum of money is no guarantee of increasing its value. Loaning might even give the loaner added security, in which case the borrower is doing the lender a favour![36] Another just title might be if the loaning party incurred the risk of losing their money. In that case, a small amount of interest could cover this eventuality that, no doubt, occurs from time to time. Perhaps the most important title occurs when the loan contributes to the generation of wealth. In this regard, a distinction can be made between a loan made for the purchasing of consumer goods, where there is no increase of wealth in the society, and that made for productive purposes or through the purchasing of shares in a company. In the latter case, the lender (who may better be called an investor) enters into a relationship of collaboration with the borrower and justly shares somewhat in any profit that arises. This highlights the fact that the Church's teaching on usury is closely connected with her insistence that, as far as possible, labour and capital should be closely associated with each other. Given this underlying motivation, credit unions and building societies seem particularly suitable means for giving access to credit. In these organizations, the loaner (the provider of capital) and the borrower (the provider of labour) are most closely united.

Let us conclude this section by turning to the assessment made by John Paul II on the market economy in his encyclical *Centesimus Annus* in 1991, written only two years after the collapse of Communism in Europe. The central question of that encyclical is about the path these newly liberated countries should follow. Should they model themselves on the capitalism of Western Europe and North America? After admitting that the answer is 'obviously complex,' he states:

> If by 'capitalism' is meant an economic system which recognizes the fundamental and positive role of business, the market, private property and the resulting responsibility for the means of production, as well as free human creativity in the economic sector, then the answer is certainly in the affirmative ... [b]ut if by 'capitalism' is meant a system in which freedom in the economic sector is not circumscribed within a strong juridical framework which places it at the service of human freedom in its totality, and which sees it as a particular aspect of that freedom, the core of which is ethical and religious, then the reply is certainly negative.[37]

The role of the State vis-à-vis the economy

With regard to the role of the State vis-à-vis the economy, social teaching holds the middle ground between two extremes. As we have seen, on the one hand it rejects the idea of a centrally planned economy while on the other it rejects a laissez-faire model that would reduce the role of the State to simply keeping law and order. In *Centesimus Annus*, John Paul II notes that this position is clearly expressed by Leo XIII in *Rerum Novarum*, since in that encyclical Leo XIII rejects both the socialist solution of State ownership of the means of production and the then current state of affairs in which the capitalist could misuse workers with impunity:

> *Rerum Novarum* is opposed to State control of the means of production, which would reduce every citizen to being a 'cog' in the State machine. It is no less forceful in criticizing a concept of the State which completely excludes the economic sector from the State's range of interest and action.[38]

This middle way is achieved by the State adequately respecting the principles of subsidiarity and solidarity in what might be called a creative tension![39] The principle of subsidiarity means the State ought to create the condition for private initiative to flourish. The principle of solidarity means that the State must sometimes check the autonomy of private initiatives so that the common good is assured, with the particular aim of protecting the weak. Again, in *Centesimus Annus*, John Paul II considers the interplay of these two principles with respect to promoting full and fair employment in society:

> The State must contribute to the achievement of these goals [full and fair employment] both directly and indirectly. Indirectly and according to the principle of subsidiarity, by creating favourable conditions for the free exercise of economic activity, which will lead to abundant opportunities for

employment and sources of wealth. Directly and according to the principle of solidarity, by defending the weakest, by placing certain limits on the autonomy of the parties who determine working conditions, and by ensuring in every case the necessary minimum support for the unemployed worker.[40]

The general point is this: an excessive emphasis on subsidiarity tends to individualism, while an excessive emphasis on solidarity can degenerate into a 'welfare' or 'nanny' State.[41]

It is clear, therefore, that the State must perform a delicate balancing act between, on the one hand, holding back from intervening so that private initiative can blossom and, on the other hand, intervening to protect the weak. Given the difficulty in maintaining this equilibrium, especially since the economy is in a constant state of flux, it is not surprising or necessarily blameworthy that governments never perfectly realize this balance and sometimes over-step the mark in one direction or the other.

The principle way in which the State creates an atmosphere for private initiative to flourish (and thereby acts according to the principle of subsidiarity) is by ensuring what might be called a just economic security and stability 'so that those who work and produce can enjoy the fruits of their labours and thus feel encouraged to work efficiently and honestly.'[42] Without this stability, the incentive for people to invest time and energy in personal initiatives is undermined. This security is brought about by a juridical framework which protects, among other things, the right of private initiative and the right to private property, within the context of the common good. The State may also promote economic stability by various measures such as influencing savings and investment through interest rates, keeping the currency of the country stable, as well as building up and maintaining public services, such as education and the country's infrastructure, such as the transport system.[43]

Sometimes the State is forced to intervene more strongly in the economy in order to stimulate it or address serious obstacles to the realization of the common good, such as monopolies (which we have already discussed). In doing this, the State is respecting the principle of solidarity, since all have a right to share in the economic prosperity of the society. Tempered by the principle of subsidiarity, such intervention ought to be exceptional and strictly temporary:

> Such supplementary interventions, which are justified by urgent reasons touching the common good, must be as brief as possible, so as to avoid removing permanently from society and business systems the functions which are properly theirs, and so as to avoid enlarging excessively the sphere of State intervention to the detriment of both economic and civil freedom.[44]

There are certain sectors of the economy that provide goods which are utterly essential for human life, such as provision of water and energy, and which cannot be easily provided for in a system of competition. For example, it is only practical to have a single system of water pipes and sewage disposal in a given area. This means that competition, which would normally regulate and reduce the price of water and sewage provision, cannot operate. In such cases, the State might legitimately take over this sector or at least permanently involve itself in the regulation of prices.[45]

The moral obligation of the consumer

In a market economy, power ultimately lies with the consumer who, through his choices of what to buy, indirectly determines what is produced and, as importantly, how it is produced. Poor working conditions in factories of the Third World (factories that supply goods for the Western markets) are undoubtedly the direct responsibility of the factory owners and managers, but the consumer has an indirect responsibility here, since his decision to buy their products reinforces the unjust situation. Accordingly, social teaching affirms that decisions about purchasing, and likewise about investments and savings, are always moral decisions. In *Caritas in Veritate*, Benedict XVI, points out that 'purchasing is always a moral — and not simply economic — act. Hence, the consumer has a specific social responsibility, which goes hand-in-hand with the social responsibility of the enterprise.'[46]

The criteria in these decisions can never be only the question of cost, quality, or return, but it must also include the question of justice and solidarity.[47] Factors that might be considered include the working conditions of the employees of the producing company, the prices paid to the producers of the raw materials, the general ethical status of the company (whether they are involved in abortion, and so on), and the environmental impact of the production of the product. Again, in *Caritas in Veritate*, Benedict XVI notes that this consumer power is set to increase with the phenomenon of globalization, because the range of products available to the consumer is enlarged and competition between producers thereby more intense.[48] The point is that with this increase in power comes an increase in responsibility because, by choosing one product over another, the consumer can guide the production process. John Paul II speaks of creating a life-style in 'which the quest for truth, beauty, goodness and communion with others for the sake of common growth are the factors which determine consumer choices, savings and investments.'[49]

The choice is stark. Either consumers use their power to humanize the market, or they will succumb to consumerism. Consumerism is a materialistic ideology which promotes having over being and things over other people. Commenting on consumerism, John Paul II tells us that 'it is not wrong to want to live better,' but 'what is wrong is a style of life which is presumed to be better when it is directed towards "having" rather than "being," and which wants to have more, not in order to be more but in order to spend life in enjoyment as an end in itself.'[50] Consumerism is a pervasive ideology which, if not consciously checked, can seep into all aspects of human life. John Paul II notes that 'the market imposes its way of thinking and acting, and stamps its scale of values upon behaviour.'[51] Undoubtedly here he is thinking of the moral utilitarianism, since later he notes that 'we are seeing the emergence of patterns of ethical thinking which are by-products of globalization [of the market mentality] ... and which bear the stamp of utilitarianism.'[52] In this way, even marriage can be considered in a consumerist way so that the old partner is discarded for the latest model, and having children is seen unattractive because of the financial implications.

Globalization

The term of 'globalization' means the process of the unification of the world into a single society. This can mean an economic, a political, or a cultural unification, or indeed all three together, seeing as an economic unity tends to lead to a greater political unity and also tends to bring in its wake a transformation of culture.

Economic globalization, then, points to the reality of a single global economy. This is based on the liberalization of free trade on a worldwide scale, on the free movement of capital and labour, and on the migration of technology. In the words of John Paul II, it is 'the increasing elimination of barriers to the movement of people, capital, and goods,'[53] while the Compendium calls it 'a process that progressively integrates national economies at the level of the exchange of goods and services and of financial transactions.'[54] In practice it means that even the simplest household products, such as tables, pens, and clocks, are now commonly made in (often several) distant countries while the company that makes them is often located in yet another. Moreover, it means that just because this is so today does not guarantee that it will be next year, because the companies making

Economic Life

these products, in the search for cheaper production costs, may well relocate.

Globalization is a theme that has moved more and more to centre stage in the concerns of social teaching. *Caritas in Veritate* (2009), Pope Benedict's first social encyclical, gives some sustained attention to the phenomenon but, of course, it would be wrong to claim that this is the first time the Church has considered the question of globalization. The theme of the International Community, which is part of any consideration of political globalization, has been a constant concern since *Pacem in Terris* (1963) and *Gaudium et Spes* (1965). John Paul II also considered globalization several times.[55] Nonetheless, *Caritas in Veritate* is by far and away the most detailed and sustained consideration to date. That there was a time lag between the emergence of globalization and a detailed consideration of it is not surprising given that Catholic social teaching is reflective more than proscriptive.

There are some who think that globalization is a very positive development, while others seek to highlight its negative consequences. Others again, whether positive or negative, believe it is inevitable as the final stage of a natural development of economic evolution and to that extent both unstoppable and impossible to direct. Benedict XVI notes that 'sometimes globalization is viewed in fatalistic terms, as if the dynamics involved were the product of anonymous impersonal forces or structures independent of the human will.'[56]

The available statistics on the effect of globalization are ambiguous. Some formerly poor countries have undoubtedly benefited, especially China, where poverty has drastically fallen in the last twenty years. On the other hand, sub-Saharan Africa has seen no growth and even an increase in poverty. Undoubtedly, globalization has led to the relocation of manufacturing centres from rich countries to poorer ones, as companies seek to lower their manufacturing costs. In theory, then, more jobs are created in poorer nations. However, these jobs are by nature unstable. As they exist because they provide a cheaper way for a company to manufacture its goods, the fluid character of production means that they can just as easily vanish if the company finds another labour pool that is even cheaper or more convenient. Because of this, labour unions are weakened. A union that opposes a company might simply see the company relocate its production centre, to the great detriment of all its members. Another factor—noted by Pope Benedict in *Caritas in Veritate*—is that poorer countries have been 'downsizing [their] social security systems' so as to be more competitive in the global labour market (because the employer is not required to pay social security contributions for their workers). The net result is 'grave danger for the rights of workers, for fundamental human rights and for the solidarity associated with the traditional forms of the social State.'[57]

From statements like this, we sense an underlying sentiment of caution about the process of globalization. The assessment of the Compendium is one of serious concern that up to now globalization has not benefited the poorer countries:

> [T]here are indications aplenty that point to a trend of increasing inequalities, both between advanced countries and developing countries, and within industrialized countries. The growing economic wealth made possible by the processes described above [globalization] is accompanied by an increase in relative poverty.[58]

This caution, however, cannot be interpreted as a judgment that globalization is in itself a bad thing. John Paul II states that:

> [G]lobalization, a priori, is neither good nor bad. It will be what people make of it. No system is an end in itself, and it is necessary to insist that globalization, like any other system, must be at the service of

the human person; it must serve solidarity and the common good.⁵⁹

The point is that we must not be fatalistic about globalization: it can and must be guided. It is not an impersonal force but the result of human decisions. In the words of Pope Benedict:

> It has been the principal driving force behind the emergence from underdevelopment of whole regions, and in itself it represents a great opportunity. Nevertheless, without the guidance of charity in truth (*caritas in veritate*), this global force could cause unprecedented damage and create new divisions within the human family.⁶⁰

And elsewhere in the same encyclical, he says:

> The processes of globalization, suitably understood and directed, open up the unprecedented possibility of large-scale redistribution of wealth on a worldwide scale; if badly directed, however, they can lead to an increase in poverty and inequality, and could even trigger a global crisis.⁶¹

In order to guide it, at least three things are necessary. First, it must be admitted that individual States are increasingly incapable of ensuring the ethical regulation of economic life because the process of globalization has burst national boundaries. There is now a need for international authorities invested with real power to guide and regulate the process. Pope Benedict notes that not only must these authorities have 'real teeth' to ensure compliance of all parties, they must also ensure that the poorer nations would have a position of real equality. Otherwise, solutions 'risk being conditioned by the balance of power among the strongest nations.'⁶²

Second, Pope Benedict points out that the re-subordination of economics to morality is even more necessary in the age of globalization, due to the fact that the State has lost much of its power to legally curb the excesses of the market because companies now commonly operate on an international plane.[63] We can no longer rely on the State to impose a moral veneer on the market by the redistribution of wealth; rather, the market must be ethical from within.[64] This, as we shall point out later, requires a moral revolution in the hearts of those who have economic power and influence. In this way, globalization is proving what social teaching has been saying for a hundred years!

Third, John Paul II points out that up until now what is lacking in the process of globalization is the globalization of solidarity! He says that 'the challenge, in short, is to ensure a globalization in solidarity, a globalization without marginalization.'[65] Pope Benedict makes the same point when he notes that 'as society becomes ever more globalized, it makes us neighbours but does not make us brothers.'[66]

Finally, as we have already noted, the process of globalization is taking place in three highly interrelated dimensions: economic, political, and cultural. This means that economic globalization is often accompanied by the exportation of Western culture, but more alarmingly the crass elements of Western society, namely, consumerism, low moral standards, and an anti-life mentality.[67] Benedict XVI laments that 'frequent attempts are made to export this mentality to other States as if it were a form of cultural progress.'[68] This exportation of degenerate Western culture is a significant cause of tension between Western countries and militant Islam, since it represents a kind of cultural colonialism. John Paul II warns particularly against the exportation of Western atheism:

> Globalization must not be a new version of colonialism. It must respect the diversity of cultures which, within the universal harmony of peoples, are life's interpretive keys. In particular, it must not deprive the poor of what remains most precious to them, including their religious beliefs and practices, since genuine religious convictions are the clearest manifestation of human freedom.[69]

Economic Life

One of the main dangers of cultural globalization is, of course, moral relativism. Some see relativism as a necessary part of globalization, since the process draws together diverse cultures. Yet, in truth, quite the opposite of relativism is needed if different nations and peoples are going to live and work together harmoniously. A common code of ethics is needed. This, of course, can be found in a rediscovery of natural law (encoded in the Ten Commandments), the law written by God in human heart of every man and, therefore, pertinent to every culture:

> It is within man as such, within universal humanity sprung from the Creator's hand, that the norms of social life are to be sought. Such a search is indispensable if globalization is not to be just another name for the absolute relativization of values and the homogenization of life-styles and cultures. In all the variety of cultural forms, universal human values exist and they must be brought out and emphasized as the guiding force of all development and progress.[70]

Notes

[1] *CSDC*, 334.

[2] Benedict XVI, *Caritas in Veritate*, 8.

[3] Paul VI, *Populorum Progressio*, 6; cf. Benedict XVI, *Caritas in Veritate*, 18.

[4] Paul VI, *Populorum Progressio*, 14; cf. Benedict XVI, *Caritas in Veritate*, 18.

[5] John Paul II, *Sollicitudo Rei Socialis*, 17. Here, perhaps, John Paul II is saying even more than that development, in order to be authentic, must include a moral dimension of concern for the less fortunate. He appears to be arguing that even economic development requires that it become universal if it is to be sustained. This insight is perhaps being verified by the process of globalization. It might be argued that underdevelopment of whole regions of the world is a threat to the continued economic

development of already wealthy countries. To give two examples: it limits the expansion of the market of rich countries and it tends to draw jobs from the richer to the poorer countries, resulting in increased unemployment in the rich.

6   *CSDC*, 332.
7   Vatican II, *Gaudium et Spes*, 36.
8   Adam Smith, *The Wealth of Nations*, Book IV, Chapter II.
9   Pius XI, *Quadragesimo Anno*, 43.
10 Benedict XVI, *Caritas in Veritate*, 45–46.
11 Pius XI, *Quadragesimo Anno*, 107; cf. John Paul II, *Centesimus Annus*, 48.
12 Pius XI, *Quadragesimo Anno*, 109.
13 Leo XIII, *Rerum Novarum*, 43–44.
14 Pontifical Council for Social Communication, *Ethics in Advertising*, 10.
15 Benedict XVI, *Caritas in Veritate*, 37–39.
16 *CSDC*, 340.
17 John Paul II, *Centesimus Annus*, 35.
18 Benedict XVI, *Caritas in Veritate*, 36.
19 *Ibid.*, 65.
20 Leo XIII, *Rerum Novarum*, 28.
21 John Paul II, *Centesimus Annus*, 34.
22 *CSDC*, 347.
23 John Paul II, *Centesimus Annus*, 24.
24 *CCC*, 2429.
25 John Paul II, *Sollicitudo Rei Socialis*, 15.
26 *CSDC*, 338.
27 *CSDC*, 347.
28 John Paul II, *Centesimus Annus*, 35.
29 Benedict XVI, *Caritas in Veritate*, 71.
30 John Paul II, *Centesimus Annus*, 34; cf. *CSDC*, 349.
31 John Paul II, *Centesimus Annus*, 34.
32 *Ibid.*, 40.
33 Benedict XVI, *Caritas in Veritate*, 21, 36.

34 *CSDC*, 369.
35 Benedict XIV, *Vix Pervenit*.
36 This aspect of usury was condemned in a decree of the Holy Office, 4 March 1679 (*Denzinger*, 1191).
37 John Paul II, *Centesimus Annus*, 42.
38 *Ibid.*, 15.
39 *CSDC*, 351.
40 John Paul II, *Centesimus Annus*, 15.
41 Cf. Benedict XVI, *Caritas in Veritate*, 58.
42 John Paul II, *Centesimus Annus*, 48.
43 *CSDC*, 352.
44 John Paul II, *Centesimus Annus*, 48.
45 *CSDC*, 353.
46 Benedict XVI, *Caritas in Veritate*, 66.
47 *CSDC*, 359.
48 Benedict XVI, *Caritas in Veritate*, 66.
49 John Paul II, *Centesimus Annus*, 36.
50 *Ibid.*
51 John Paul II, *Address on Globalization to the Pontifical Academy of Social Sciences* (27 April 2001), 3.
52 *Ibid.*, 4.
53 *Ibid.*, 2.
54 *CSDC*, 361.
55 John Paul II, *Centesimus Annus*, 58; John Paul II, *Address on Globalization to the Pontifical Academy of Social Sciences* (27 April 2001).
56 Benedict XVI, *Caritas in Veritate*, 42.
57 *Ibid.*, 25.
58 *CSDC*, 362.
59 John Paul II, *Address on Globalization to the Pontifical Academy of Social Sciences* (27 April 2001), 2.
60 Benedict XVI, *Caritas in Veritate*, 33.
61 *Ibid.*, 42.
62 *Ibid.*, 67.

[63] *Ibid.*, 24.
[64] *Ibid.*, 39.
[65] John Paul II, *Message for 1998 World Day of Peace*, 3.
[66] Benedict XVI, *Caritas in Veritate*, 19.
[67] *CSDC*, 366.
[68] Benedict XVI, *Caritas in Veritate*, 28.
[69] John Paul II, *Address on Globalization to the Pontifical Academy of Social Sciences* (27 April 2001), 4.
[70] *Ibid.*

6

The Political Community

In the Old Testament, prior to Saul, Israel had no human king, but was led by God through prophets and judges. Later, the Israelites asked God for a king so that they could be like the other nations (1 S 8:4). Through Samuel, God gave them Saul and then David, and consequently a whole dynasty of kings. Appointed by God in this way, the role of the king was to uphold God's ways, especially establishing His rule of justice and concern for the poor. The prophets frequently remind the subsequent kings of their duty, and numerous failures, in this respect (1 K 21; Is 10:1–4; Am 2:6–8, 8:4–8; Mi 3:1–4).

In pronouncing that taxes ought to be paid to Caesar, Jesus shows His respect for political authority (Mk 12:13–17). Later, in front of Pilate, He affirms that authority comes from God (Jn 19:21). On the other hand, in stating 'Give to Caesar what is Caesar's, and to God what is God's' (Lk 20:25), He points out the limits of political authority. In addition, in warning His disciples not to 'lord it over' each other (Mt 20:25), He indicates that all authority is for service, just as He Himself, the King of the Universe, came 'not to be served but to serve' (Mt 20:28).

Like its Master, the attitude of the early Church to civil authority was twofold. On the one hand, we have clear statements in the New Testament concerning the rightful obedience of believers to political authority (Rm 13:7; 1 Tm 2:1–2; 1 P 2:17) and these from men who would ultimately be put to death by these same authorities. Also, just like in Christ's statements, there is a clear affirmation of the limit of temporal authority. The ultimate testimony to this is that of the martyrs of the earlier centuries, such as St Polycarp, who resisted the State and leaders when they overstepped their political authority and demanded things contrary to the faith, such as worship of the Emperor.[1] The same situation—the excessive demands of the political authorities—has arisen constantly throughout the history of the Church, such as during the reformation, and not least in our own times. We are reminded, for example, of the famous statement of St Thomas More about himself (spoken from the scaffold) that he was 'the king's good servant, but God's first.' As preparation for the Jubilee year of 2000, John Paul II set up a commission with the task of cataloguing the names of those who had died for their faith in the twentieth century. The commission collected the names and stories of 13,400 men and women, many of who had died as the result of political persecution, especially under Communism and National Socialism, neither of which respected religious freedom. In 1925, in the face of the totalitarian claims of atheistic Communism, Pius XI instituted the feast of Christ the Universal King, a reminder of the relative and subordinated character of political power.[2]

The foundation and purpose of the political community

The social nature of man is the foundation of the political community. Men naturally bind together in order to seek those things that enrich human life and can only be had together, what social teaching calls common goods:

> Men, families and the various groups which make up the civil community are aware that they cannot achieve a truly human life by their own unaided efforts. They see the need for a wider community, within which each one makes his specific contribution every day toward an ever broader realization of the common good.[3]

By this common endeavour, a people is formed who shares a common goal, a common life, and a common set of values. The political community grows out of this civil society, when the latter becomes large or complex and, therefore, requires a more formal arrangement. The rule of law and the existence of a potentially coercive authority then becomes necessary for the cohesion of the society. The point is that the political reality should, as far as possible, follow on from the social reality. Pius XII says the State, 'should, in practice, be the organic and organizing unity of a real people.'[4] Of course, some people (some group that forms a civil society) do not have a corresponding political reality, such as the Kurds, the Aboriginal Australians, and even, to a much lesser extent, the English, Scots, and Welsh. In such situations, some tension is always more or less likely.

The question of ethnic minorities is discussed by John XXIII in *Pacem in Terris*.[5] There he notes that there can be real and sometimes insurmountable problems in granting a minority their own State, such as when the minority is thinly dispersed throughout the whole majority population. If the question is asked as to whether every people can demand a corresponding political reality, namely a State, the answer is that, as we have seen, the raison d'être of the State is the common good. So, if the common good of a people would be jeopardized by being too small, as might be the case for Aboriginal Australians, then there would be a moral obligation to remain part of the larger group. This could also be the case if the rump state would be compromised were the smaller people to separate.[6]

When a minority cannot have its own State, then obviously it is essential that the rights and culture of the minority people is carefully respected by the majority and, according to the principle of subsidiarity, as much autonomy as possible is given to them. On the other hand, John XXIII tells us, the minority must cultivate appreciation for the benefits they receive from their association with the majority and certainly never resort to terrorism to assert their independence.[7]

Obviously, when the majority are aggressive towards the minority, self-defence (even armed) is not excluded.

The purpose of the political community, as we have said, is to attain the common good, by which each member of the community is able to attain more fully what is necessary for a wholesome human life. In addressing this, John XIII states that 'in our time the common good is chiefly guaranteed when the personal rights and duties are maintained.'[8] Human rights make the dignity of the human person concrete, and they act as principles by which the laws of the State can be constructed. When human rights are respected, both according to the letter and the spirit, then human beings have the opportunity to flourish.[9] However, we must not overlook that Pope John also speaks about duties. Without this, the language of human rights can turn into a selfish pursuit for development, and the common good is undermined. The question of human rights will be considered in more detail in a subsequent chapter. Here it is enough to note its intimate connection, according to social teaching, with authentic human development and the common good.

Finally, it should be clear by now that pursuit of the common good always implies the social virtue of solidarity, otherwise known as civil friendship.[10] Without this, civil society and the political community built upon it degenerates into a system in which each person obeys the law (more or less) in the selfish pursuit of personal goals. Then all that is left is a hollow shell of what social teaching understands by the political community.

Political authority

Political authority has its origin in God. This is because human society is founded upon the natural inclination in man—part of his human nature—to live in society. Since human nature comes from God and, therefore, so does the inclination to live in society, the idea of society also comes from God. This is not very surprising when we remember we are created in the image of a God that is a communion of divine Persons! Furthermore, all societies need authority if they are to avoid chaos; if they are chaotic they are harmful rather than helpful, especially to the weak. So, in conclusion we can say: just as society comes from God so does political authority; and this authority is for the benefit of all those who are part of the society:

> God has created men social by nature, and a society cannot 'hold together unless someone is in command to give effective direction and unity of purpose. Hence every civilized community must have a ruling authority, and this authority, no less than society itself, has its source in nature, and consequently has God for its author.'[11]

In this way of conceiving things, God, as the author of human nature, is the author of political authority in the same way that, as author of marriage, He is the author of parental authority. Neither authority is dependent on the will of man but flows from human nature, and in this way from God.[12] Of course, the truth of political authority coming from God is supported by revelation, since Christ himself reminds Pilate that his authority was 'given from above' (Jn 19:11).

Rejecting the idea that God is the author of political authority, as is common today, has many negative consequences. First, there is likely to be a loss of respect for civil authority, because if it is not from God then it is only from man, and there is no natural reason why one man should be subject to another.[13] This is a particularly pernicious tendency in democracies where, if social agreement is seen as the sole basis of authority, citizens who disagree with this or that law can feel that it has no power to command their obedience other than the fear of coercion. When it is accepted that political authority comes from God, obedience to the ruler can be understood as obedience to God; then men are not demeaned by civil obedience but ennobled.[14] Leo XIII makes this point in *Diuturnum Illud*, when he says:

> Now, a society can neither exist nor be conceived in which there is no one to govern the wills of individuals, in such a way as to make, as it were, one will out of many, and to impel them rightly and orderly to the common good; therefore, God has willed that in a civil society there should be some to rule the multitude. And this also is a powerful argument that those by whose authority the State is administered must be able so to compel the citizens to obedience that it is clearly a sin in the latter not to obey. But no man has in himself or of himself the power of constraining the free will of others by fetters of authority of this kind. This power resides solely in God, the Creator and Legislator of all things; and it is necessary that those who exercise it should do it as having received it from God.[15]

Second, if the ultimate source of authority is the people, then experience shows that the people become the arbitrator of the truth and the good. Practically, it is then the majority or the powerful who determine the moral code of the society, including or excluding different groups, and different human rights, according to their preference. The basis of society is thereby undermined. Third, when God is not affirmed as the author of political authority, there is a tendency to exclude God from the civil realm, as if He had no interest in it, and as if He was not the ultimate end of society. When God is excluded from the public square, so to speak, society no longer has the compass it needs to guide it on its way. As Pope Benedict XVI tells us, 'without God man neither knows which way to go, nor even understands who he is.'[16]

Finally, on this point, it is worth noting that religion and the Church are not rivals for political authority, as some claim who would like to exclude the Church from having an active role in society. On the contrary, the Church is political authority's greatest champion because, by pointing

The Political Community

to the divine origin of political authority, it gives this authority its only true and firm foundation. In *Diuturnum Illud*, Leo XIII notes that some governments in his time have resorted to violence and threats to impose their authority. He points out that fear is a weak foundation for obedience, and goes on to say:

> It is therefore necessary to seek a higher and more reliable reason for obedience, and to say explicitly that legal severity cannot be efficacious unless men are led on by duty, and moved by the salutary fear of God. But this is what religion can best ask of them, religion which by its power enters into the souls and bends the very wills of men causing them not only to render obedience to their rulers, but also to show their affection and good will, which is in every society of men the best guardian of safety.[17]

While God is the author of political authority, the people are the first subject of this authority. The idea is that they first receive power from God and then transfer this authority to individuals to govern them. This notion, it has to be said, is not expressed with any detail in social teaching. The most explicit statement is in the Compendium, which states:

> The subject of political authority is the people considered in its entirety as those who have sovereignty. In various forms, this people transfers the exercise of sovereignty to those whom it freely elects as its representatives.[18]

Correctly understood, this theory seems to be compatible with the statements made on this issue by Leo XIII in his encyclical *Diuturnum Illud*. There, wanting to emphasis the divine origin of political power, he denies the thesis that 'all power comes from the people, that those who exercise it in the State do so not as their own but as delegated to them by the people,' and says that when the people choose a ruler 'by this choice, in truth, the ruler is designated, but the rights of ruling are not thereby conferred.'[19] The right to rule can ultimately come only from God as the origin of political power; but this does not preclude the people, as the first recipients of this power, determining who should practically exercise it. The political power the people have themselves received (rather than created) is neither delegated nor conferred, but rather transferred to an individual or small group, to rule. It is not said to be delegated because this implies that the people are not wholly under the political authority of the appointed ruler, and it is not said to be conferred because this implies that the people are the author of the authority.

It is important to point out that this notion of how power comes to the ruler from God via the people is different from both 'the divine right of kings' and the theory of the 'social contract'. In the theory of the divine right of kings, the power comes to the ruler directly with no meditation on the part of the people whatsoever. The difference between the Catholic position and the theory of social contract is more subtle, but no less profound. While both agree that the people are the first subject of power, the Catholic position emphasizes more that this subject has received this power (from God), and so political power is not a human institution or convention. Moreover, social teaching stresses the social nature of the human being and, therefore, that the political community and political authority are natural and, furthermore, mandatory. There is a moral imperative for men to form societies and then to transfer power to a smaller group to govern the society. Again, and perhaps most importantly, when power is transferred it is not merely delegated as if the governors became no more than functionaries following every whim of the people and likely as not to have power taken back from them at any moment. Rather, there is a radical transfer of power and, even if some time limit is place on this transfer, the people are then obliged to obey their rulers in all things that are not immoral.

Political authority and the moral order

As we have just seen, a distinct element of the Catholic understanding of political authority is that, coming from God, it has the power to demand the obedience of citizens; but this exists only as long as the political authority stays within the moral order. To put all this another way: if political authorities demand from citizens things which are immoral, their power to demand obedience evaporates.

God's law, of which morality is part, is not arbitrary. It is given to us so that we might flourish as human beings and ultimately so that we might have communion with Him. His authority over us, expressed in part by the moral code of conduct He gives us, is like that of a Father over his child, since it is for the good of the child and aims to guide the child towards maturity. Since political power comes from God, we can understand it as a share in God's authority; and if it shares in His authority it shares in the purpose or goal of his authority. Therefore, for a political authority to command something contrary to the moral law laid down by God is to undermine the very purpose of this authority and accordingly to corrupt it.

Concretely, what we are saying is that citizens are not obliged to obey the immoral laws and commands of political authorities.[20] In the words of St Augustine, when the State commands or encourages its citizens to act immorally it becomes nothing more than a 'band of robbers.'[21] John XXIII reminds us that:

> [L]aws and decrees passed in contravention of the moral order, and hence of the divine will, can have no binding force in conscience, since 'it is right to obey God rather than men' (Ac 5:29) ... 'a law which is at variance with reason is to that extent unjust and has no longer the rationale of law. It is rather an act of violence.'[22]

When a law or command is immoral—such as a law permitting abortion or pornography—citizens are not only under no obligation to submit to them, they may also be called upon to actively resist them, by lobbying, protesting, and even obstructing the carrying out of the law. If the moral law is seriously and repeatedly violated by a Government, even armed resistance could be licit. Since, as we have seen, unjust laws are not true law but are really violence, resisting them becomes a matter of self-defence.[23]

Self-defence, civil resistance, and rebellion

Civil resistance to unjust laws is part of the legitimate defence of individuals (and of citizens in general) to the violence that is inherent in such legislation. In certain circumstances, this right to self-defence can even justify rebellion.

When someone has a right, he also has a right to uphold it and enforce it. If a person could not act so as to uphold his right, then he could hardly be said to have a right. So, if a person truly has a right to life and a right to property, for example, he must also have certain rights to uphold these rights, in some cases even to the extent of using force.

Accordingly, when an attack is made on the life, health, property, or good name of an individual, a person is within his rights to defend himself. He may even have a duty to defend himself. For example, a father may have a duty to defend his life against an assailant so he can care for his family. A husband may have a duty to defend his good name if its loss would shame his wife.

Several criteria must be verified if a person is to be sure that his self-defence is legitimate. First, the attack must be unjust and unprovoked. To put this another way, the aggressor must be in the wrong. The corollary to this is that a criminal does not have the right to defend himself against the reasonable aggression of a police officer seeking to apprehend him. Second, the aggression must be certain. It is not necessary that the first blow has been made by the aggressor, but there must be moral certainty that he intends to attack and has actually done something to prepare for this. So, for example, to legitimately defend oneself against a would-be-robber, the aggressor need not have broken down the door of your house, but he must have picked up the crow-bar in order to do so. Third, the use of physical force should be a last resort. All other ways to dissuade the aggressor or repel him must either be impractical or have proved to be ineffective. Fourth, an appropriate level of force should be used to repel the aggressor. This means that if the harm suffered is light, then the force used to repel the aggressor can, likewise, only be light. You cannot shoot a child who has come into your garden to steal an apple from your orchard. Sometimes, however, lethal force can be used, namely when only this would prevent a person suffering serious harm, such as loss of life or being raped. If the aggressor is seeking to steal a significant amount of property such as would cause real hardship to the owner, and lethal force alone could prevent this, then it might be used. Fifth, if force is going to be used to repel the aggressor, there should be some chance of success. This prevents the useless multiplication of violence. This criterion also excludes vengeance, understood as violence against the aggressor after the attack has taken place.

Later, these criteria will be applied to the question of a just war, that is, to the legitimate defence by a nation against the attack of another. Here, let us see how they might be applied to the defence of citizens against an unjust and violent government.

In principle, just as one individual has the right to forcibly defend himself against another, so citizens and individuals may forcibly defend themselves against unjust laws and actions on the part of the government, when the laws and actions bring about serious injury. A citizen could forcibly resist a forced sterilization or abortion, for example. This is something different from the case of government measures that are unpopular, perhaps even unwise, but not strictly unjust, such as a moderately excessive rate of taxation. In these cases, the citizens should obey the laws, though of course they can campaign for a change.

However, not every injustice on the part of the government would warrant seeking to overthrow it, since not every injustice undermines its authority to the degree that one can say it has forfeited its right to govern or is of such gravity that the legitimate self-defence of the citizens would warrant the destruction of the government. Therefore, we must make a distinction between, on the one hand, resisting (even forcibly) individual laws and actions of the government and, on the other, seeking to overthrow the government itself. Leo XIII, addressing Catholics in France who opposed the government of that time, saying that was 'animated by such anti-Christian sentiments that honest men, Catholics particularly, could not conscientiously accept it,' reminded them that the 'distinction between constituted power and legislation had ... [to be] carefully kept in view.'[24] Laws may be bad, but the government as such may still be legitimate.

However, the point can be reached where government violence is so widespread and persistent that the citizens are justified in using lethal force against the government itself in order to defend themselves. By lethal force we mean destroying the government by rebellion. Another way of looking at this would be to say that the point can be reached where the government has clearly abandoned the pursuit of the common good, which is its raison d'être and, thereby, has forfeited its authority as such.

Let us assume, for example, that a government is guilty of serious, widespread, and prolonged violation of human rights such as the unjust imprisonment, torture, and murder of citizens. In this scenario, how does the fivefold criterion for self-defence apply?

In this case, we can suppose that the first and second criteria are verified. The aggression is unjust and certain. The third criterion would mean that the citizens must have tried other methods of stopping the violence, say by protesting, lobbying, organizing general strikes, or have rightly judged that these methods, or others, would not be effective because, for example, protesters are routinely imprisoned or otherwise silenced. The fourth criterion would determine what kind of force can be used against the government. Since we are assuming the harm suffered by the citizens is very grave (death, torture, and unjust imprisonment), the citizens could rightly seek to oust the government even using lethal force if ultimately necessary. The fifth criterion would call for a prudential judgment as to whether the rebellion can be successful and not end up producing a situation in which more violence and disorder results. This is always a danger with any revolution or rebellion. In *Quod Apostolici Muneris*, Leo XIII cautions against hasty rebellion 'lest public order be only the more disturbed, and lest society take greater hurt therefrom.'[25]

Sometimes the violence of the State is aimed at a minority with the collusion or support of the majority. This is the case, for example, in societies where abortion is legalized. In such situations, the likelihood of a rebellion succeeding is slim and this would probably preclude the use of violent force as a means of self-defence or overthrowing the government.

Cooperating with evil

The Compendium tells us that 'it is a grave duty of conscience not to cooperate ... in practices which, although permitted by civil legislation, are contrary to the Law of God.'[26] Cooperation, as it is referred to here, is an action, licit in itself, by which one person helps another to act immorally. Formal cooperation occurs when a person helps another and at the same time concurs with the evildoer in, at least minimally, willing this evil action. An example of this would be when the father of a pregnant woman helps her to acquire an abortion, say by arranging the appointment with the doctor, and at the same time wills her to have the abortion. Compare this to her friend who drives her to the abortion clinic but does not want her to go through with the abortion and even tries to dissuade her. The friend's action might not be justified, but it is not formal cooperation.

Material cooperation occurs when a person, doing something in itself licit, helps another to perform an evil action but does not in any way concur with him in willing this evil action. An example of this would be the work of a hospital cleaner who cleans, and hence prepares, the operating theatre where an abortion is to take place, but in no sense wills the abortion and perhaps even finds it repugnant that abortions are carried out (along with other operations) in that place.

Nonetheless, the fact that cooperation is only material does not necessarily excuse it. The principle of double effect must be applied. In the pursuit of some good goal, a person might sometimes be excused in helping an evildoer. The co-operator must not intend the evil of the evildoer, his own act must be itself good or indifferent, and there must be a just proportion between the good the co-operator is pursuing and the evil he foresees but does not intend, namely the evil of the evildoer. So, if we take again the example of the hospital cleaner, her work of cleaning is itself indifferent or good. Furthermore, she is pursuing a very important goal, namely earning a living for herself and her family. In such a case, her material cooperation would probably be excused.

Proximity can also be an important factor in evaluating material cooperation. A nurse working in an operating theatre during an abortion may not want the child to be killed and she may only be handing the doctor the instruments he needs when he requests them, so she is not directly killing the child. Nonetheless, this is immediate cooperation with a very evil action. The cleaner's work is much less immediately associated with the evil and so while she may be excused, the nurse's cooperation cannot, even if her job is at stake.

Other factors must also be taken into consideration in judging when material cooperation is permitted. These include the likelihood of scandal and the possibility that the co-operator will be desensitized to evil and even led into sin. There is no mathematical formula to be applied here! In some cases, only a person with a developed virtue of prudence can make the correct judgment as to whether material cooperation in a given situation is licit.

The general principle is that material cooperation should be avoided as much as possible, but can be tolerated in some circumstances. Sometimes it is very hard to avoid, for example in the case of paying taxes, some of which will go towards supporting evil actions (such as abortions).

The possibility of immoral laws raises the question of conscientious objection. This is the right not to participate in practices that a person believes are morally wrong. In his encyclical *Evangelium Vitae,* John Paul II, thinking no doubt of doctors and nurses who refuse to become involved in anti-life practices such as abortion, says that:

> [T]hose who have recourse to conscientious objection must be protected not only from legal penalties but also from any negative effects on the legal, disciplinary, financial and professional plane.[27]

Obviously, whether there is really a case for conscientious objection will depend on the nature of the laws being objected to. Practically, when the State recognizes the right to conscientious objection, one of several situations exists. There could be a tacit admission on the part of the authorities that the law might be wrong, such as seems to be the case in the exemption given in some countries to doctors not to perform abortions as part of the medical care of their patients. Or, while the practice might be licit in itself, it is recognized that there are moral dangers involved in carrying out what is absolutely speaking right, for example fighting in a just war. Since the soldier, in carrying out his duties, could easily be put in a situation where he cannot know for sure if lethal force can morally be used against the enemy, or whether collateral damage can be tolerated, the option is given for persons to serve their country in another way. Finally, there are situations where, for reasons of religion and conscience, individuals are exempt from regulations because, in respecting the person's right to self-determination, the exemption does not compromise the common good of the society. An example of this would be laws protecting workers who refuse to work on Sundays, even when Sunday trading is generally permitted. If the common good of society were really at stake, then there is no ground for an exemption. No one is exempt from paying reasonable taxes simply on the basis of conscience, since such an exemption would undermine the common good.

Political authority and punishment of criminals

If the purpose of the State is to ensure the common good of the society, the State must have, as a last resort, the power to coerce citizens and punish criminals for the sake of the common good.[28] So, for example, if a citizen refuses to pay reasonable taxes—money needed to bring about the common good of the society in which he lives—the State must have, ultimately, the right to force this citizen to pay or even to take the money by force. Of course, there is also the matter of regulating the relations between individual citizens: if one citizen wrongs another, say by taking his belongings, the State has the task of punishing this crime.

There are several purposes of punishment. First of all, there is the protection of the society from criminals. In this way, the State acts in self-defence when it punishes, and especially incarcerates, criminals. It is protecting the raison d'être of the State itself, namely the common good, which is undermined by criminal activity. The State is also defending itself when the punishment of criminals is used to deter others from following their example. In addition to the motives of self-defence and deterrence, punishment, in the words of the Catechism, 'has a medicinal scope,' since 'as far as possible it should contribute to the correction of the offender.'[29] Finally, punishment has a retributive character. This points to the fact that it is a kind of 'cosmic law' that punishment is due for wrong-doing apart from whether it will protect society, deter others, or heal the criminal.[30]

When social teaching speaks of punishment, it is thinking first of all about imprisonment and fines. Nonetheless, the ultimate punishment, the death penalty, is not absolutely excluded. Even when capital punishment is not part of the law of a country, in theory the State always retains the right to impose this penalty as the ultimate means of self-defence and as the ultimate form of retribution. However, in the modern age, the goals of punishment can normally be achieved by other means. For example, unlike in days gone by, criminals can be humanly but securely incarcerated (for life if necessary) and in this way the safety of society is ensured.

From the perspective of safeguarding society, John Paul II argues that today the cases where capital punishment is needed 'are very rare, if not practically non-existent.'[31] For this reason, the Church lauds those States that have removed this penalty from their statutes (though it remains a latent power).[32] John Paul II clearly felt that the use of the death penalty was a hindrance to the establishment of a culture of life. Removing this form of punishment was, therefore, a testament to the supreme value of human life. It is for this reason that the most extended discussion of capital punishment is found in his encyclical on the culture of life, *Evangelium Vitae*.[33] A practical reason against capital punishment is, of course, that miscarriages of justice are, obviously, not repairable when the death penalty is applied.

Regarding now corporal (physical) punishment, the Church has traditionally not spoken against it and Scripture seems to allow for it (e.g. Pr 13:24, 19:18). However, it appears harsher than some other forms of punishment and a new (positive) sensitivity to human dignity shies away from it. On the other hand, torture, understood as the use of humiliating moral or physical violence seeking to coerce the will, is absolutely prohibited. The only clear case in Scripture where some moral evaluation is offered on torture is the death of the seven brothers in the Second Book of Maccabees (2 M 7). The narrative greatly praises the bravery of the brothers and condemns utterly the cruelty of their tormenters. The prohibition is absolute: torture may not be used in any situation whatsoever. The Catechism tells us:

> Torture, which uses physical or moral violence to extract confessions, punish the guilty, frighten opponents, or satisfy hatred, is contrary to respect for the human person and for human dignity. [34]

It is noteworthy that the Catechism gives a list of possible motives for torture, all of which are rejected. The question asked sometimes today is whether torture might be legitimate when used to gain potentially lifesaving information from captured terrorists. While there is no statement of the Church expressly condemning this particular motivation, it seems impossible to reconcile this with the emphatic stance of John Paul II against torture:

> The memory of Jesus—stripped, flogged, and derided right up until the sufferings of his final agony—should always make him [the believer] resolve never to see analogous torments inflicted on any one of his brothers in humanity. Spontaneously, the disciple of Christ rejects every recourse to such methods, which nothing could justify.[35]

Also of note is Benedict XVI's Message for the World Day of Peace in 2006. While condemning terrorism unreservedly, he says:

> The Fathers of the Second Vatican Ecumenical Council, in the Pastoral Constitution *Gaudium et Spes*, pointed out that 'not everything automatically becomes permissible between hostile parties once war has regrettably commenced.' As a means of limiting the devastating consequences of war as much as possible, especially for civilians, the inter-

national community has created an international humanitarian law. In a variety of situations and in different settings, the Holy See has expressed its support for this humanitarian law, and has called for it to be respected and promptly implemented, out of the conviction that the truth of peace exists even in the midst of war. International humanitarian law ought to be considered as one of the finest and most effective expressions of the intrinsic demands of the truth of peace. Precisely for this reason, respect for that law must be considered binding on all peoples.

Of course, this requires considerable restraint and moral fibre on the part of authorities and peoples threatened by terrorism, but it should be remembered that while torture is contrary to the dignity of the victim, even more it debases the one who inflicts it. Including torture, without any qualification, among a list of other evils, the Fathers of Vatican II said that 'all these things and others of the same sort are truly disgraceful, and while they poison human civilization, they debase the perpetrators more than the victims and utterly contradict the honour due to the Creator.'[36]

Forms of government

In considering different forms of government, it is usual to make distinctions between monarchies, aristocracies, and democracies. As the etymology of monarchy suggests, this system of government is when power is ultimately lodged with one person. While monarchy is, therefore, the 'rule of one person,' the word aristocracy means the 'rule of the most excellent' or 'the rule of the best.' Democracy means literally the 'rule of the people.' It is common to make a further distinction between direct democracy, where everyone is directly involved in decision-making, either by assembling together or by referendum, and representational democracy, where the people select representatives to make the important decisions.

Despite these definitions, concretely it is not always so simple to clearly differentiate between these three systems. For example, monarchy does not necessarily imply that the position of leadership is inherited. The Holy Roman Emperor was a monarch, but he was elected by a group of nobles. The same was true in the Polish-Lithuanian Commonwealth of the sixteenth, seventeen, and eighteen centuries. As recently as the twentieth century, there has been an elected monarch in Norway, Haakon VII, who was chosen by plebiscite. Of course, if monarchs are elected, then immediately the political system has an element of aristocracy (if the election is by the few) or democracy (if the election is by all the people). Normally, even elected monarchs hold office for life, but this feature is arguably not part and parcel of monarchy as such, since its essence is 'the rule of one,' and not how the authority is passed on or how long power is held. In that sense, despite commonly being thought of as democracies, the presidential system of the United States of America and the prime-ministerial system of Russia have elements of monarchical rule because so much power is invested in one person.

The point is that, at closer inspection, terms like monarchy and democracy are rather elastic or loosely defined. What we call democracy today is commonly quite a mixed system that includes elements of monarchy and aristocracy as well. The United Kingdom is a particular example of this. It, like Sweden, Spain, Denmark, Thailand, Morocco, and others, is a constitutional monarchy (where ultimate power is nominally invested in one person), yet it has a parliament made up of two houses, one appointed (the House of Lords) and one elected (the House of Commons). There are, therefore, elements of monarchy, aristocracy, and democracy in the political system of the United Kingdom.

Such a mixed system of government is actually the one favoured by St Thomas.[37] He favoured it because it has the possibility of the combining the positive elements of each of the three alternatives. Monarchy has the advantage that it brings order and unity, since in any organization (a family, a business, or even a football team) the many are brought together in the pursuit of a common goal by a single ultimate authority or head. Furthermore, monarchy mirrors the divinely established order: just as there is one God ruling the universe, so there might be one leader ruling a country.[38] Aristocracy has the advantage that it gives the most talented members of society a special influence in the political community. Democracy is good in that it produces a government that is more likely to be acceptable to all, and this is conducive to peace. St Thomas also notes that this mixed system is the divinely established order given by God to Israel when He led them out of Egypt. Moses was like a king, but under him were seventy-two wise men chosen by the people.[39] A mixed system also guards against the corruption of the political order: it hinders monarchy from falling into tyranny, aristocracy into oligarchy, and democracy into mob rule.[40]

In the next section, we shall focus on democracy because it is the most common form of government in the modern world. However, it is important to note that while in recent times the Church has made positive statements about democracy—and we shall presently see why this is so—the Church approves of various forms of government. The aim of government, as we have seen, is the common good, and any form of government that attains this is acceptable. Conversely, any form of government that does not promote the common good is unacceptable, no matter what name it gives itself, even democracy. On this account, anarchy alone is to be utterly rejected, since it necessarily undermines the common good.

The clearest magisterial statement indicating that various political arrangements are acceptable comes from Leo XIII's encyclical *Au Milieu des Sollicitudes* (1892). There, addressing the Catholics in France, he says:

> Various political governments have succeeded one another in France during the last century, each having its own distinctive form: the Empire, the Monarchy, and the Republic. By giving one's self up to abstractions, one could at length conclude which is the best of these forms, considered in themselves; and in all truth it may be affirmed that each of them is good, provided it lead straight to its end—that is to say, to the common good for which social authority is constituted; and finally, it may be added that, from a relative point of view, such and such a form of government may be preferable because of being better adapted to the character and customs of such or such a nation. In this order of speculative ideas, Catholics, like all other citizens, are free to prefer one form of government to another precisely because no one of these social forms is, in itself, opposed to the principles of sound reason nor to the maxims of Christian doctrine.[41]

There is sometimes a perception that the Church has moved from favouring monarchies to favouring democracies. This is debatable. We need to distinguish between what the Church has actually said about these systems themselves and what she has said, or how she has acted, towards individual instance of these systems. The above statement from Leo XIII makes it clear that neither monarchy nor democracy as such is preferred. However, the types of democracy and republicanism that sprang up at the end of the eighteenth century and during the nineteenth century in Europe were often violently opposed to the Church. In light of that, the Church then sometimes favoured as a concrete alternative a monarchical system, but this cannot be read to mean that monarchy as such is preferred. For example, the welcome given by Pope Leo XII to the restoration of the French monarchy after the revolution (the Bourbon restoration of 1814) must be seen in the light of the alternatives: a return to the violent anti-clericalism of the Republic (1792-1799) or a continuation of the bullying experienced under Napoleon.

Something similar is true about democracy in the twentieth century. Positive statements about democracy must be seen in the light of the concrete political alternatives, namely fascism and communism. Praising democracy in the light of these perverse political regimes cannot be read to mean that only democracy is now a valid system of governance and that monarchy has fallen from favour.

Democracy

In the previous section, we noted that some of the democratic movements of the eighteenth and nineteenth were hostile to the Church. In turn, the Church was wary of them.[42] Now that democratic movements and democratic States have found a more benign attitude towards the Church, She Herself has come to appreciate many good elements in democracy. Democracy allows citizens to participate in the pursuit of the common good by making political choices. In this way, it is a fitting system for human beings who, created in the image of God, are able to make choices and freely order themselves toward what is good. Men are not like animals who are only led; they have leaders but are called to actively take part in the development of the society they live in. Democracy is also the best system for holding leaders accountable, thereby better assuring that they work for the common good and not for their own advantage or the advantage of a privileged few. In this sense, it is a system that forestalls the formation of small groups who usurp the political community for their own narrow interests. Furthermore, democracy allows the peaceful transition of power from one leader and ruling group to another. Finally, from a more theoretical perspective, democracy also seems to fit very well with what we have said about how political authority comes from God via the people (as the subject of authority) to the leader. For this reason, Pius XII noted that the 'democratic form of government appears to many as a postulate of nature imposed upon reason itself.'[43] Nonetheless, in this statement, Pius XII stops short from saying that democracy is the only acceptable form of government. There may be other systems that fulfil the dual criteria of achieving the common good and respecting the dignity of the citizens. Therefore, the Catechism reminds us that:

> [I]f authority belongs to the order established by God, the choice of the political regime and the appointment of rulers are left to the free decision of the citizens. The diversity of political regimes is morally acceptable, provided they serve the legitimate good of the communities that adopt them.[44]

Great care must be taken not to impose Western-style democracy on other nations that are not ready for it or are ill-suited to accept it. John XXIII reminds us that, 'in determining the structure and operation of government which a State is to have, great weight has to be given to the circumstances of a given people, circumstances which will vary at different times and in different places.'[45]

In order to appreciate the favourable view social teaching towards democracy, it is very important to be clear about what the Church understands by democracy. Democracy is much more than a system of election; other factors are required if we are to have a true democracy. There needs to be the rule of law[46] and the division of power, that is, the separation of judicial, executive, and legislative powers.[47] Of the latter, John XXIII said that this division of power 'is in keeping with the innate demands of human nature,' because it ensures impartiality and freedom.[48] There also needs to be structures of participation. This is the role of political parties, which, together with referendums, are the main means by which the aspirations of citizens can be interpreted and hence the normal way of bringing about the participation of citizens in decision-making.[49] Finally, there needs to be the widespread dissemination of truthful information about the state of the political community. This requires especially that the means of social communication—newspapers, radio, television, and internet—are both free from political interference and dedicated to communicating the truth. Without this, it is not possible for citizens to make objective political judgments.

Beyond these structural or what we might call institutional elements of democracy, there needs to be what Pius XII called the 'spirit of democracy.'[50] On the part of politicians and public servants, this means a determined effort for service; in citizens, it means a respectful attitude to those who so serve. This is a particular issue in democracy, since the electorate put the government in power and can, for this reason, tend to look down on it. Citizens must also have generous attitude towards seeking the common good, in a word, solidarity. Where solidarity is lacking in society, by excessive individualism or tribalism, then true democracy struggles to take root or maintain itself.

Finally, but most importantly, democracy must be built on the foundation of unchangeable moral values. Democracy is said to be 'the rule of the people for the people.' If the phrase 'of the people' points to the system of election and participation, a system in which the majority determine those who will be given power, then 'for the people' indicates its orientation to the common good; but this is only possible if there are some values that cannot be changed by majority decision. Only this can prevent the majority from depriving smaller groupings in the society from their share in the common good and from their human rights. Without this foundation of moral absolutes, democracy is in danger of being perverted, of becoming mob rule and the tyranny of the majority. In the words of John Paul II, 'history demonstrates, a democracy without values easily turns into open or thinly disguised totalitarianism.'[51] Exactly the same point is behind the following admonition of Pius XII in his famous radio broadcast of Christmas 1944:

> A sound democracy, based on the immutable principles of the natural law and revealed truth, will resolutely turn its back on such corruption as gives

to the state legislature an unchecked and unlimited power, and moreover, makes of the democratic regime, notwithstanding an outward show to the contrary, purely and simply a form of absolutism.[52]

This is exactly what has started to happen when democratic states legalize abortion. In these cases, the powerful majority has deprived the weaker minority (the unborn) of a fundamental human right. Democracy is not an end in itself, but the means to good government. If it fails in this, then it fails absolutely:

> This is what is happening also at the level of politics and government: the original and inalienable right to life is questioned or denied on the basis of a parliamentary vote or the will of one part of the people—even if it is the majority. This is the sinister result of a relativism which reigns unopposed: the 'right' [to life] ceases to be such, because it is no longer firmly founded on the inviolable dignity of the person, but is made subject to the will of the stronger part. In this way democracy, contradicting its own principles, effectively moves towards a form of totalitarianism.[53]

The idea that democracy can only be built upon a solid foundation of values that are not susceptible to being altered by the majority confronts the opinion, not infrequently aired, that democracy is built on relativism: 'it is not unusual to hear the opinion expressed in the public sphere that such ethical pluralism is the very condition for democracy.'[54] Those who believe this consider anyone who holds to the possibility of knowing the truth, particularly Catholics, unsuitable to participate in the democratic process:

> Nowadays there is a tendency to claim that agnosticism and sceptical relativism are the philosophy and the basic attitude which correspond to democratic forms of political life. Those who are convinced that they know the truth and firmly adhere to it are

considered unreliable from a democratic point of view, since they do not accept that truth is determined by the majority, or that it is subject to variation according to different political trends.[55]

The truth of the matter is quite to the contrary. Relativism itself is the greatest enemy of true democracy since, by determining what is right on the basis of majority opinion (and thus opening the door for the oppression of the minority), it undermines the whole purpose of the political community, namely the common good.

From what we already know of social teaching, it will be clear to us that the Church accepts a plurality of political solutions to concrete problems; what She does not accept is a plurality of fundamental moral principles. This means that two Catholics can, in good conscience, be affiliated with opposing political parties that offer divergent solutions to social problems as long as they both affirm the fundamental principles of morality. For example, one Catholic politician might champion private medical insurance, while another might place the emphasis on State insurance. Within certain bounds, these are both legitimate solutions to the question of healthcare provision. There can be a plurality of equally valid solutions. What neither can support, for example, is the provision of abortion within these healthcare plans, since abortion opposes a fundamental human right, the right to life. Likewise, neither side could propose the exclusion of some sections of society from healthcare provision, since this would contradict the principle of the (equal) human dignity of each citizen. When it comes to moral principles, then, a plurality of positions is not possible, or at least if there is a plurality they are not equally valid. To deny the right to life of the unborn is not morally equal to upholding it! This does not contradict the principle of equality, since we can still hold that the people holding the opinions are of equal dignity, simply as human beings, while vigorously opposing the idea that the opinions they hold are equal.

Finally, to say that there must be an unchangeable foundation of moral principles on which democracy must be built is not the imposition of religion on political life, since the moral principles at stake are not religious principles, but rather principles of natural law.[56] Certainly, given the moral confusion that reigns in the modern world, the Church has become, in our day, the special guardian of these principles, but they remain moral principles that can be arrived at by reason and are the common heritage of humanity.

Indeed, it is not too much to claim that the Church is the greatest champion of democracy, not because She denies that other forms of government are legitimate, but because She in particular teaches and defends the immutable values that are the foundation of democracy, especially the dignity of the human person. Pius XII makes this point when, in his 1944 Christmas Radio Broadcast on *True and False Democracy*, he says:

> If the future is to belong to democracy, an essential part in its achievement will have to belong to the religion of Christ and to the Church, the messenger of our Redeemer's word which is to continue His mission of saving men. For she teaches and defends supernatural truths and communicates the supernatural helps of grace in order to actuate the divinely-established order of beings and ends which is the ultimate foundation and directive norm of every democracy.[57]

Moreover, as Pius XII notes in the same broadcast, true democracy requires men who are 'spiritually eminent and of strong character,' men able to overcome the temptation to use the political system for selfish advantages.[58] He dedicates that address not to a discussion of the external mechanics of democracy but to the character requirements of both citizens and leaders without which a true democracy will flounder. Again the Church makes a considerable contribution to this, not only through Her moral teaching but also because She 'communicates the supernatural helps of grace,' on the basis of which the requisite moral character can be formed.

The relationship of Church and State

In considering the relationship between the Church and the State, it is useful to consider briefly the most important statements from the Magisterium on the matter.[59] However, the starting point must be those words of Jesus concerning the duty of paying taxes, namely that one is 'to give to Caesar what is Caesar's and give to God what is God's' (Mt 22:21). A basic conclusion to be drawn from these words is that the State and the Church are not the same and hence a conflagration of the two is wrong. These words of Christ are actually quite revolutionary because for both the Romans and the Jews the political order and the sacred order were hardly distinct. Indeed, the death of the early martyrs was often occasioned by the fact that these early Christians would not give their religious allegiance to the State: they would not follow the State religion nor recognize Caesar as a god. The distinction of religion from the State is in some ways a Christian concept. Islam, for example, does not have such a dualist notion.

The next important statement on the relationship between Church and State comes from Pope Gelasius I (492-496). In a letter to Emperor Anastasius, *Duo Sunt*, Gelasius describes the divinely ordered separation of the offices of king and priest. This means that there are two powers in the world: the State, whose main concern is the temporal well-being of its citizens, and the Church, whose main concern is the eternal well-being of mankind. The two powers are supreme in their own realm, and there ought to be a mutual submission—the priest should obey the king in civil matters, the king ought to obey the priest in religious matters. Ultimately, however, the priestly office is weightier, since it relates to the final goal of life, namely salvation.

One of the most important statements concerning the relationship of Church and State is from Boniface VIII's Bull *Unam Sanctam* (1302). This Bull was part of the Pope's response to what he saw as King Phillip IV of France's attempts to subject the French Church to his own power. The main aim of the Bull was to point out that to be in the Church one must be subject to the authority of the pope, not the king. Also in that document, Boniface claims that the Church wields not only supreme spiritual power on earth but, ultimately, also has supreme temporal authority. This claim is supported by an interpretation of Jesus' exchange with St Peter in the Garden of Olives on the night Christ was arrested (Lk 22:38; Mt 26:52). There, Peter tells Jesus that he has two swords, to which Jesus replies that two is sufficient. Boniface interprets the two swords as symbols of spiritual and temporal authority, both wielded by Peter, and so also by his successors. The idea is that Peter represents Christ on earth and Christ is the supreme authority above all other authorities, temporal as well as spiritual (Mt 28:18). But, Boniface notes, just as Christ chose not to exercise temporal power directly, nor does the pope. He points out that Jesus commands Peter to put one sword back in its sheath (Mt 26:52) but not to rid himself of it. The conclusion to this interpretation, then, is that the pope as the Vicar of Christ is the ultimate temporal authority on earth but that he does not exercise this directly. Rather, temporal rulers are left to rule but they do so 'at the will and sufferance of the priest [the spiritual authority in the Church].' Put plainly, 'one sword ought to be under the other sword, and so the temporal authority is to be subject to the spiritual authority.'[60]

In more recent times, the most significant statements on the relationship of Church and State come from Leo XIII. In *Immortale Dei* (1885), he restates the key principles of a distinction between the spheres of authority and the hierarchical order between them. Of the distinction of authority he says:

> The Almighty, therefore, has given the charge of the human race to two powers, the ecclesiastical and the civil, the one being set over divine, and the other over human, things. Each in its kind is supreme, each has fixed limits within which it is contained ... One of the two has for its proximate and chief object the well-being of this mortal life; the other, the everlasting joys of heaven. Whatever, therefore in things human is of a sacred character, whatever belongs either of its own nature or by reason of the end to which it is referred, to the salvation of souls, or to the worship of God, is subject to the power and judgment of the Church. Whatever is to be ranged under the civil and political order is rightly subject to the civil authority. Jesus Christ has Himself given command that what is Caesar's is to be rendered to Caesar, and that what belongs to God is to be rendered to God.[61]

Expressing the hierarchical relationship between the two powers, Leo XIII uses the comparison of the relationship between the body and the soul. He says there 'exist between these two powers a certain orderly connection, which may be compared to the union of the soul and body in man.'[62] This analogy of body and soul implies something more than mutual autonomy; it points to a profound cooperation between the two powers:

> In matters, however, of mixed jurisdiction, it is in the highest degree consonant to nature, as also to the designs of God, that so far from one of the powers separating itself from the other, or still less coming into conflict with it, complete harmony, such as is suited to the end for which each power exists, should be preserved between them.[63]

In another encyclical, *Libertas Praestantissimum* (1888), Leo XIII expresses this idea of 'harmony' and 'orderly connection' between Church and State in the idea of, where possible, the State recognizing the special status of the

Catholic Church as the true religion with a special mission on earth.[64]

At Vatican II, statements about the relationship between the Church and State are made in *Dignitatis Humanae* and *Gaudium et Spes*. In the latter, the Council Fathers restate that 'in their proper spheres, the political community and the Church are mutually independent and self-governing.'[65] This being the case, in *Dignitatis Humanae*, the Council Fathers claim for the Church 'the independence which is necessary for the fulfilment of her divine mission.'[66] This independence—the complement to the State's 'legitimate autonomy of temporal affairs'[67]—includes the right of the Church to organize Herself, select Her own ministers, form associations and educational establishments, own property, teach and evangelize, worship in public, and comment on the moral rectitude of different solutions to social questions.[68]

As well as asserting the rights of the Church and the rights of the State, like Leo XIII, the Constitution *Gaudium et Spes* has something to say about the cooperation between the two:

> [B]oth [Church and State], under different titles, are devoted to the personal and social vocation of the same men. The more that both foster sounder cooperation between themselves with due consideration for the circumstances of time and place, the more effective will their service be exercised for the good of all.[69]

It is to bring about this cooperation as much as to ensure the freedom of the Church that the Church has often entered into treaties (called a concordat) with different States.[70]

Dignitatis Humanae says two more things pertinent to the question of the relationship of the Church and State. It says that the perennial teaching of the Church concerning the duty of the State towards the Church remains (see Leo XIII, above) and it allows for the Church be given special constitutional recognition by the State, as long as other religions are also given appropriate freedoms.[71] So, in a predominantly Catholic country, for example, the Church could be given a special legal or social status, such as privileges in starting schools or an advisory role in the formation of laws, just as Anglican bishops in the United Kingdom have by their appointment to the lower house of Parliament.

Before moving on, it would be worth trying to clarify the main points to be garnered from all these different sources. It seems fair to say that there are three. First, each party (the Church and the State) has its own special realm of activity and along with this comes a certain autonomy. Second, there is a hierarchy between the two realms, in which the Church is ultimately superior to the State just as the spiritual goal of human life is superior to earthly goal. To put this another way, the temporal well-being of man is ordered to his spiritual well-being, and it is for this reason that the State could and, if conditions allow, should give a special recognition to the Church because of Her special and higher mission. Third, while both realms enjoy some autonomy, they are both concerned with the good of the same subject, namely man. Accordingly, the relationship between the Church and State should be marked not by antagonism and suspicion, but by a note of cooperation.

More recently, Benedict XVI has spoken positively of the distinction of Church and State as it is constitutionally arranged in France. On his return from a pastoral visit to Paris and Lourdes (2008), he said that in French history 'the need developed for a healthy distinction between the political and religious spheres in accordance with Jesus' famous words: "Render to Caesar the things that are Caesar's, and to God the things that are God's" (Mk 12:17).'[72] This separation in France, he points out, was necessary for freedom. Here he is thinking of a legitimate religious freedom that makes membership of the Church—unlike membership of the State—wholly a matter of choice.

What Benedict says here, cannot be taken to mean that special constitutional recognition of the Church is always wrong.[73] Benedict XVI is addressing the situation in France. He points out that it is precisely because Christianity was historically so strong in France that the tendency to blur the distinction of Church and State was a particular danger in that country. One might add that since French history shows that establishment of the Church normally meant the gradual subjugation of the Church to the State, disestablishment also ensures the freedom of the Church. Establishment of the Church almost invariably leads to the State claiming rights over the Church, such as the appointment of bishops.

Nonetheless, and this is of great importance, Benedict XVI warned that 'genuine secularism does not mean ... leaving the spiritual dimension out of consideration.' He made the same point more strongly in an address to the British Parliament in a State visit to the United Kingdom in 2010. In that speech, he points out that although the moral norms that are the foundation of any political community can be known by reason—since they are part of natural law—they often are not adequately grasped and, therefore, the Church is indispensable in 'correcting' reason in its search for these norms and their application. This being so, he understandably laments the privatisation of religion in modern societies: the banishing of 'religion ... [from] the public square.'[74] The result of this privatisation of religion is that, once the moral compass of society is marginalized, moral norms are determined and applied only on the basis of majority opinion. In this way, the door is opened for the oppression of the minority and the weak, for example the legalization of abortion and embryo experimentation. Furthermore, when the Church is squeezed out of public life, not only is there no longer a moral authority in society, but the State tends to fill the vacuum left by the Church, thereby becoming the only authority and hence totalitarian.

In conclusion, then, it seems true to say that if by disestablishment is meant that each power—the Church and the State—is given the space it needs to fulfil its proper function, then this is good. But, if by disestablishment is meant the privatisation of religion and an exaggerated autonomy of the temporal from the spiritual, then this is bad. It might be better to speak of a distinction of Church and State rather than a separation. On the one hand, history shows that this distinction is necessary for the religious freedom of citizens as well as for the freedom of the Church to carry out Her mission. On the other hand, when religion is privatised and the Church marginalized, freedom is undermined because the moral foundations of the State are compromised as the State slips into totalitarianism.[75]

Religious Freedom

In modern times, the question of the relationship between the Church and State has become in particular a question of religious freedom. This was prompted by the experience of the Church in Communist countries during the twentieth century where the Catholic Church (along with other Christian denominations) was vigorously persecuted. In response to this persecution, the Second Vatican Council promulgated the Declaration on Religious Freedom, *Dignitatis Humanae*. In that declaration, the Church proclaimed the right to religious freedom. This is the right of individuals and groups not to be coerced by the State or any other group in matters of religious worship, whether by being forced to worship against their conscience, or prevented from worshiping according to their conscience both in private and in public:

> This freedom means that all men are to be immune from coercion on the part of individuals or of social groups and of any human power, in such wise that no one is to be forced to act in a manner contrary to his own beliefs, whether privately or publicly,

whether alone or in association with others, within due limits.[76]

This right ought to be part of the law of every country and can only be restricted for serious reasons when the exercise of it would be contrary to the common good, for example because the practice of this right would lead to immoral activities, such as polygamy, or the incitement to violence.

The basis of this right is the dignity of the human person who is called upon to direct himself freely towards the truth. It is, therefore, contrary to human dignity for him to be prevented in doing this or coerced to act contrary to his conscience in religious matters. This right, like all rights, comes also with a duty: the duty to search and hold fast to the truth. Accordingly, the Fathers of the Council state:

> The right to religious freedom has its foundation in the very dignity of the human person ... [and] it is in accordance with their dignity as persons—that is, beings endowed with reason and free will and therefore privileged to bear personal responsibility—that all men should be at once impelled by nature and also bound by a moral obligation to seek the truth, especially religious truth. They are also bound to adhere to the truth, once it is known, and to order their whole lives in accord with the demands of truth.[77]

In addition, the right to religious freedom is founded on the truth about truth, since truth is not something that can be imposed upon someone by force, but must impose itself by virtue of its own credibility. The Council Fathers tell us that 'the truth cannot impose itself except by virtue of its own truth, as it makes its entrance into the mind at once quietly and with power.'[78] Jesus Himself sets us an example in the sense that He never forced anyone to accept the message of the Gospel, but offered it freely to all.

Dignitatis Humanae claims the Church has a special mission in the world but does not, on the basis of this, make any concrete demands on the State to formally recognize

Her unique status, but only to afford Her the freedom necessary to fulfil Her mission.[79]

It would be impossible to mention the Declaration *Dignitatis Humanae* without briefly addressing the question of development of doctrine. There is no doubt that the expression of the right of religious freedom found in *Dignitatis Humanae* is an authentic example of such development. This is a complex issue and here it is only necessary to touch on some of the main points.

If one reads Pius IX's *Quanta Cura* or Leo XIII's *Immortale Dei* and *Libertas Praestantissimum*, one is struck that the idea of religious liberty expressed in those encyclicals is more restrictive and limited. Furthermore, on the basis that the State has a responsibility towards the common good including the promotion of truth and the suppression of error, there are bolder statements about the duty of the State to the true religion and, accordingly, to recognize the unique status of the Catholic Church.

It is clear that Council Fathers did not wish to reject this older teaching on religious freedom because at the beginning of *Dignitatis Humanae* we read that the declaration wishes to 'leave untouched traditional Catholic doctrine on the moral duty of men and societies towards the true religion and towards the one true Church.'[80] On the other hand, it also seems true that the Council Fathers were aware that they were developing the doctrine because the opening paragraph tells us that the Council seeks to bring 'forth new things that are in harmony with the things that are old.'[81]

There is no doubt that over the years separating Pius IX and Leo XIII from the Council several important developments had occurred. First, within society and within the Church a greater sensitivity to the dignity of the human conscience had developed. This led to the conclusion that while error itself has no right to be propagated, those in error (human beings) have rights not to be coerced. Second, the historical situation had changed from a militant liberal secularism in the nineteenth century to militant atheism in the twentieth century. If in the mid and late nineteenth century the popes needed to protect the flock from excessive demands of liberalism with regard to freedom of speech, in the twentieth century the Church was called upon to be the champion of freedom in the face of atheistic Communism. Third, there was the emergence of the ecumenical movement and a new appreciation of what was good in other Christian denominations and, to a much lesser degree, even in other religions; the so-called 'seeds of the Word.'[82] Lastly, there is the question of the mission of the Church. In the modern age, the Church seems to have concluded that Her mission is better achieved by a greater separation from the State, seeing as most States are now thoroughly secular in mentality. Accordingly, *Gaudium et Spes*, without repudiating the special status of the Church, states:

> For her part [the Church], does not place her trust in the privileges offered by civil authority. She will even give up the exercise of certain rights which have been legitimately acquired, if it becomes clear that their use will cast doubt on the sincerity of her witness or that new ways of life demand new methods.[83]

In the modern world, the Church is unlikely to receive any benefit from the State in furthering Her evangelical mission as, perhaps, She did in the past. The Council reminded the laity that, in our age, the faith will be spread from the bottom up and not from the top down.[84]

In conclusion, in renewal and reform something always changes while something stays the same; whereas in revolution everything changes! In the case of the Church's teaching on religious liberty, the doctrinal principles have remained constant. These are that unique character of Jesus Christ and the Church He founded, the duty to seek religious truth, and the dignity of the human person. Undoubtedly, these principles have been considered afresh and allowed to illuminate each other in such away that, along with some very significant changes in the historical context, a new presentation of the Church's perennial understanding of religious freedom has been articulated.

Notes

1. His death is recorded by Eusebius in *The Martyrdom of Polycarp*.
2. Cf. Pius XI, *Quas Primas*.
3. Vatican II, *Gaudium et Spes*, 74.
4. Pius XII, *True and False Democracy*, (Christmas Radio Broadcast, 1944), 9.
5. John XXIII, *Pacem in Terris*, 93–97.
6. Nationality does not confer a right to sovereignty because the State is formed by the consent (implicit or explicit) of the citizens and these may be of many nationalities. Furthermore, nationality is not precise: who exactly are the English or the Welsh? Furthermore, many disputes would likely arise from basing statehood directly on nationality and this is contrary to the common good. Cf. Thomas Higgins, *Man as Man*, (Rockford, IL: Tan Books, 1992), 532.
7. John XXIII, *Pacem in Terris*, 97.
8. *Ibid.*, 55.
9. *CSDC*, 388.
10. *CSDC*, 390.
11. John XXIII, *Pacem in Terris*, 46, quoting Leo XIII, *Immortale Dei*, 3; cf. *CSDC*, 393.
12. This articulation of the origin of authority is to be distinguished from that offered by the theory of the 'social contract,' first proposed by Jacques Rousseau. The theory of the social contact claims that man is not naturally a social creature. Rather, God allows men to do what seems best and it seemed best that men freely give up some autonomy to be protected in a State; and so authority is from God in this remote way, as condoning what man considered a suitable arrangement. See Jean-Jacques Rousseau, *The Social Contract*, trans. H. J. Tozer (Ware: Wordsworth's Edition, 1998), Book I, Chapter 6, 14–16.
13. John XXIII, *Pacem in Terris*, 48.
14. *Ibid.*, 50.
15. Leo XIII, *Diuturnum Illud*, 11.

16 Benedict XVI, *Caritas in Veritate*, 78.
17 Leo XIII, *Diuturnum Illud*, 24.
18 *CSDC*, 395.
19 Leo XIII, *Diuturnum Illud*, 6; cf. Pius X, *Notre Charge Apostolique*.
20 *CSDC*, 397.
21 St Augustine, *City of God*, Book IV, chapters 4–5.
22 John XXIII, *Pacem in Terris*, 51 (quoting St Thomas, *Summa Theologiae*, I II, q. 93. a.3 ad 2).
23 *CSDC*, 401.
24 Leo XIII, *Au Milieu des Sollicitudes*, 21.
25 Leo XIII, *Quod Apostolici Muneris*, 7.
26 *CSDC*, 399.
27 John Paul II, *Evangelium Vitae*, 74.
28 *CSDC*, 402.
29 *CCC*, 2266.
30 St Thomas, *Summa Theologiae*, I II, q.87 a.1.
31 John Paul II, *Evangelium Vitae*, 56; cf. *CCC*, 2267.
32 *CSDC*, 405.
33 John Paul II, *Evangelium Vitae*, 27, 40, 56.
34 *CCC*, 2297; *CSDC*, 404.
35 John Paul II, *Address to the International Red Cross* (Geneva, 15 June 1982), 5.
36 Vatican II, *Gaudium et Spes*, 27.
37 St Thomas Aquinas, *Summa Theologiae*, I II, q.95 a.4, 105.1.
38 *Ibid.*, I II, q.105 a.1 obj. 2.
39 *Ibid.*, I II, q.105 a.1.
40 *Ibid.*, I II, q.105 a.1 ad2.
41 Leo XIII, *Au Milieu des Sollicitudes*, 14.
42 Cf. Gregory XVI, *Mirari Vos*; Pius IX, *Quanta Cura* and the *Syllabus of Errors*.
43 Pius XII, *True and False Democracy* (Christmas Radio Broadcast, 1944), 8.
44 *CCC*, 1901.

The Political Community

45 John XXIII, *Pacem in Terris*, 68.
46 John Paul II, *Ecclesia in America*, 56.
47 John Paul II, *Centesimus Annus*, 44.
48 John XIII, *Pacem in Terris*, 68.
49 *CSDC*, 413.
50 Pius XII, *True and False Democracy* (Christmas Radio Broadcast, 1944), 12, 19.
51 John Paul II, *Centesimus Annus*, 46.
52 Pius XII, *True and False Democracy* (Christmas Radio Broadcast, 1944), 17.
53 John Paul II, *Evangelium Vitae*, 20.
54 Congregation for the Doctrine of the Faith, *Doctrinal Note on Some Questions Regarding the Participation of Catholics in Political Life*, 2.
55 John Paul II, *Centesimus Annus*, 46; cf. *CSDC*, 407.
56 Congregation for the Doctrine of the Faith, *Doctrinal Note on Some Questions Regarding the Participation of Catholics in Political Life*, 5–6.
57 Pius XII, *True and False Democracy* (Christmas Radio Broadcast, 1944), 28.
58 *Ibid.*, 15.
59 For a more detailed presentation of the relationship between Church and State see Paul Haffner, *The Mystery of the Church* (Leominster: Gracewing, 2010), 231-260.
60 Boniface VIII, *Unam Sanctam*.
61 Leo XIII, *Immortale Dei*, 13–14.
62 *Ibid.*, 14.
63 Leo XIII, *Immortale Dei*, 35.
64 Leo XIII, *Libertas Praestantissimum*, 21.
65 Vatican II, *Gaudium et Spes*, 76; cf. *CSDC*, 424.
66 Vatican II, *Dignitatis Humanae*, 13.
67 Vatican II, *Gaudium et Spes*, 36.
68 *CSDC*, 426.
69 Vatican II, *Gaudium et Spes*, 76.
70 *CSDC*, 427.

[71] Vatican II, *Dignitatis Humanae*, 1, 6.
[72] Benedict XVI, General Audience: *Reflections of Recent Apostolic Journey to France* (17 September 2008).
[73] Cf. Vatican II, *Dignitatis Humanae*, 6.
[74] Benedict XVI, *Address to British Parliament* (17 September 2010).
[75] Joseph Ratzinger, *Church, Ecumenism and Politics: New Endeavors in Ecclesiology* (San Francisco: Ignatius Press, 2008), 155–157.
[76] Vatican II, *Dignitatis Humanae*, 2.
[77] Vatican II, *Dignitatis Humanae*, 2.
[78] *Ibid.*, 1.
[79] *Ibid.*, 13.
[80] *Ibid.*, 1.
[81] *Ibid.*
[82] Vatican II, *Ad Gentes*, 11.
[83] Vatican II, *Gaudium et Spes*, 76.
[84] Vatican II, *Apostolicam Actuositatem*, 2.

7

Human Rights

There is no doubt that the modern age is marked by sensitivity to human rights. After the Second World War, and in light of the atrocities committed by the National Socialists, the newly formed United Nations Organization adopted the *Universal Declaration of Human Rights* on 10 December 1948. The Church views very positively the attention paid to human rights; according to John Paul II, the Universal Declaration is 'a true milestone on the path of humanity's moral progress.'[1] Moreover, this modern sensibility to the question of human rights has been reflected in the social teaching of the Church beginning especially with John XXIII's encyclical *Pacem in Terris*. Human rights were a major theme of the pontificate of John Paul II, who addressed them in his first encyclical, *Redemptor Hominis*, in a section entitled, 'Human rights: letter or spirit.'[2]

It would be wrong, however, to imagine that the Church suddenly became interested in human rights only after the mass violation of these rights during World War II, or in the 1960s when racial equality emerged as a global issue. This would be wrong for a number of reasons. First, while the use of the term 'human rights' is of recent vintage in social teaching documents, the idea of justice and giving others what is due to them is an age-old concern of the Church.[3] Human rights are a modern way of speaking about what is due to some person or some group out of justice. Second, already in Leo XIII's *Rerum Novarum* (1891), the central issue is a particular group of human rights, namely the rights of workers. Third, by proclaiming and defending the ultimate basis of human rights, namely the dignity of the human person created in the image of God, the Church is the true and perennial champion of human rights. Furthermore, by courageously opposing the totalitarian regimes of the twentieth century, She stood against the main perpetrators of human rights violations. In the light of this, it is better to say that *Pacem in Terris* is the first time there is a detailed consideration of human rights as such, as opposed to this or that right, a consideration using the modern rights language.

The basis, characteristics, and aim of human rights

The concept of a right is not easy to define, since there is no more fundamental concept from which to start. Therefore, it is more helpful to describe what we mean by a right, and this is done by exploring the basis, characteristics, and goal of human rights.

In *Pacem in Terris*, John XXIII says of human rights that they 'derive directly from [man's] dignity as a human person, and ... are therefore universal, inviolable and inalienable.'[4] These ideas are now expanded.

All rights follow on from the status of the thing said to have a right; for example, adults have a right to vote, parents have a right to educate their children, British citizens have a right to live in Britain. In each case, the right flows from the status. In the same way, human rights follow on from the status of being human, which comes with a special dignity. This dignity can be known by reason alone insofar as it is evident that there is something special about mankind in relation to other animals. Nevertheless, the profundity of this dignity is only reached by revelation, namely the manifestation that man is created in the image of God (Gn 1:26). Man has a special relationship with God and this gives him a special dignity. Furthermore, the realization that God became man and that this man, Jesus

Christ, died for the salvation of all men, dramatically exalts human dignity. In the words of Vatican II: 'since human nature as He assumed it was not annulled, by that very fact it has been raised up to a sublime dignity in our respect too.'[5] To say that human rights 'derive directly from [man's] dignity as a human person' is to point out that they are innate—inborn—and not earned or conferred by any human authority. They come rather from the author of human nature, God Himself.

In the quotation from *Pacem in Terris* above, we can see that John XXIII notes three characteristics of human rights. He says they are universal, inviolable, and inalienable. To this we should also add that they are indivisible.[6] Universal means that human beings without exception have them since, as we have just said, they come with human nature and are not conferred by any human authority, such as the State. They are said to be inviolable because they can never be violated under any pretext. For example, the right to found a family cannot be taken away from a person because of concerns about population growth. Inalienable means that human rights, as a whole or individually, cannot be taken away from anyone or any group such as happens when abortion is legalized. Inalienable equally means that human rights cannot be rejected by the possessor of the right, such as happens in the case of one who consents to be killed by assisted suicide. Indivisible means that they come 'as a package' and only make sense as a coherent set, since taken all together they express the dignity of the human person. Only promoting a sub-set of human rights would be to fail to protect and promote human dignity. It is not possible to claim to respect human dignity because all citizens are accorded the right to life but not the right to religious liberty or freedom from unjust imprisonment.

Having considered something of the character of human rights, we should say something about the content of human rights. The point is that man has a calling to flourish as a human being and this includes many elements. He needs to be able to support his bodily life and the life of those dependent on him. He needs to live in a family and civil society. He needs to pass life on. He needs to develop intellectually and spiritually. Each of these elements of human flourishing is the basis of a right in the sense that human rights have as a goal nothing less than human flourishing. Without attempting to be exhaustive, John Paul II gives a list of these rights in *Centesimus Annus*:

> [T]he right to life, an integral part of which is the right of the child to develop in the mother's womb from the moment of conception; the right to live in a united family and in a moral environment conducive to the growth of the child's personality; the right to develop one's intelligence and freedom in seeking and knowing the truth; the right to share in the work which makes wise use of the earth's material resources, and to derive from that work the means to support oneself and one's dependents; and the right freely to establish a family, to have and to rear children through the responsible exercise of one's sexuality.[7]

Within this package of rights it is possible to discern some order or hierarchy. As a foundation there is the right to life, since this is the prerequisite for the enjoyment of all other rights, such as the right to work, the right to own property, and the right to an education. As the crown there is the right to religious liberty, since this right promotes the final goal of human life, namely communion with God. Without this right, the other rights lose their meaning, as life without God loses its meaning.[8]

The relationship between rights and duties

A correct articulation of the relationship between rights and duties is of great importance. A right is a moral power to coerce the will of another. This means that by having a right there is a correlative duty placed on others to respect this right. For example, if you have a right to life, this implies I have a duty—a moral obligation—to act in such a way that I respect and uphold this right.[9] John XXIII notes that a mentality can arise in which rights are claimed but duties are shirked. This, he points out, is disastrous for human rights, since a refusal to fulfil our duties to others undermines the rights we are so keen to claim: 'to claim one's rights and ignore one's duties, or only half fulfil them, is like building a house with one hand and tearing it down with the other.'[10]

Again, and perhaps even more importantly, there exists a relationship between right and duty within the same person; this means that my right to life implies for me a duty to protect my life.[11] John XXIII makes this point when he says:

> [T]he right to life involves the duty to preserve one's life; the right to a decent standard of living, the duty to live in a becoming fashion; the right to be free to seek out the truth, the duty to devote oneself to an ever deeper and wider search for it.[12]

What is most important to see here is that the right is in some way built upon the duty. The duty is, in a sense, the foundation of the right and not vice versa! This means that a right can only exist when there is a corresponding duty. In *Caritas in Veritate*, Benedict XVI says that 'it is important to call for a renewed reflection on how rights presuppose duties, if they are not to become mere licence.'[13] His point is that the idea of 'duty first' is a very useful test for the authenticity and extension of a right, especially in an age where, at least in the Western world, all sorts of rights are claimed that have no basis in natural law. For example, the right to marry is based on a duty for humanity to propagate and educate offspring. This shows us that a right to same-sex 'marriage' is fictitious because it does not seek to respond to this duty, since it cannot. Or again, in the light of the duty to protect one's life, on the basis of what duty might we found a right to euthanasia?

Alongside this emergence of new 'rights' there is a kind of 'rights gap' opening up in which new rights are being invented in the rich and decadent West, while in the Third World fundamental rights, such as right to a basic education and healthcare, are not respected. In *Caritas in Veritate*, Pope Benedict notes:

> On the one hand, appeals are made to alleged rights, arbitrary and non-essential in nature [such as the right to homosexual marriage], accompanied by the demand that they be recognized and promoted by public structures, while, on the other hand, elementary and basic rights remain unacknowledged and are violated in much of the world [such as the right to a human standard to living].[14]

It is instructive to note that this rights gap is the product of relativism. In the one case (the Third World), relativism fails to impose the same basic standard of rights on all (the rich and the poor); in the other case (the decadent West), it fails to found human rights in the truth of the human person because it denies there is such a truth! Thus, any conception of human rights that takes relativism as its point of departure is bound to fail.

Human rights and the common good

In the chapter on the political community, we discussed what John XXIII meant when he said 'it is generally accepted today that the common good is best safeguarded when personal rights and duties are guaranteed'.[15] The truth of this statement lies in the fact that, as we have just said, human rights aim at human flourishing. When the rights of all are respected and everyone fulfils his duties (to both himself and others) the society itself will flourish.

As well as being a way to achieve the common good, this same common good can sometimes place limits on the extension of individual human rights. Most dramatically, as we have seen, the State has the right to punish very serious offences with death, and often with imprisonment. In such cases, the right to life or the right to freedom of movement is subordinated to the common good. Much less dramatically, the right to employment is also limited by the needs of the common good. A person cannot demand employment from society when there is no need for this work. Likewise, while all persons have a right to an elementary education, higher education should be more restrictive, being reserved for those who, because of their talents, would contribute more to the common good by further studies. Lastly, there is sometimes a need for whole societies to voluntarily limit the exercise of our personal rights for the good of others. For example, the rich countries may have to forego some of their economic rights for the sake of the poor:

> In teaching us charity, the Gospel instructs us in the preferential respect due to the poor and the special situation they have in society: the more fortunate should renounce some of their rights so as to place their goods more generously at the service of others.[16]

As we have already said, this might mean, for example, allowing poor countries to export their goods without demanding reciprocal access to their markets. This is an example of what John Paul II means when he speaks of justice needing to be 'corrected' by mercy.[17]

Notes

[1] John Paul II, *Address to the 34th General Assembly of the United Nations* (2 October 1979), 7; cf. John Paul II, *Address to the 50th General Assembly of the United Nations* (5 October 1995).

[2] John Paul II, *Redemptor Hominis*, 17.

[3] For a more detailed overview of the evolution of rights language in social teaching, see Thomas D. Williams, *Who Is My Neighbour: Personalism and the Foundations of Human Rights* (Washington, DC: The Catholic University of America Press, 2005), 31–47.

4   John XXIII, *Pacem in Terris*, 145.
5   Vatican II, *Gaudium et Spes*, 22.
6   *CSDC*, 154.
7   John Paul II, *Centesimus Annus*, 47.
8   *CSDC*, 155.
9   John XXIII, *Pacem in Terris*, 30.
10 *Ibid.*, 30.
11 A practical implication of this would be that one is not at liberty to refuse hydration even in a state of terminal illness, unless the administration of it is excessively burdensome (cf. Congregation for the Doctrine of the Faith, *Reponses to Certain Questions of the United States Conference of Catholic Bishops Concerning Artificial Nutrition and Hydration* [1 August 2007]).
12 John XXIII, *Pacem in Terris*, 29.
13 Benedict XVI, *Caritas in Veritate*, 43.
14 *Ibid.*, 43.
15 John XXIII, *Pacem in Terris*, 60.
16 Paul VI, *Octogesima Adveniens*, 23; cf. *CSDC*, 158.
17 John Paul II, *Dives in Misericordia*, 14.

8

The International Community

Like human rights, the Church is positive about the progress that has been made in recent decades to form an International Community, a community of nations. She is positive because She sees this community as the outworking of an important reality—the unity of the human race—that can be a powerful force for the good of all men. Accordingly, in addressing the United Nations General Assembly, John Paul II is able to say that the Church, because She is 'concerned for the integral good of every human being, has supported the ideals and goals of the United Nations Organization from the very beginning.'[1] Elsewhere, he stated that the same organization 'has made a notable contribution to the promotion of respect for human dignity, the freedom of peoples and the requirements of development, thus preparing the cultural and institutional soil for the building of peace.'[2]

Clearly then, the Church views the International Community not as an artificial construction of modern times but, on the contrary, the fulfilment on a global scale of man's social nature. According to Christian revelation, all human beings are of one race. This means something more than that they share a common nature; it means that they share common parents! We are all one family! From the book of Genesis, we can see that the profound unity of the beginning was shattered by sin, as brother turned against brother (Gn 4:1-16). If there is an experience of disharmony in the human race, then this is to be traced back to the reality of sin that always divides, as love unites. This being so, the unity of the human race has been re-established by Jesus Christ, since He came to deal with sin. Dying for all men, He has 'broken down the wall' (Ep 2:14) that separated individuals and peoples. Finally, He calls us all, every man, woman, and child, into the ultimate and most profound of all unities, that of the communion of saints.[3] When the Church contemplates how much the unity of human peoples is part of the mission of Christ, it cannot but look upon the International Community—despite its imperfections—as a positive development.

Before we turn to consider the International Community in more detail, we ought to very briefly consider the place the Catholic Church has in bringing about the unity of the human race. The Catholic Church, since Her members come from every people of the world, is also an expression of this profound unity among men. John XXIIII says that 'the Church by divine right pertains to all nations. This is confirmed by the fact that She already is everywhere on earth and strives to embrace all peoples.'[4] As Catholics, we should not be afraid of supra-national organizations—we are part of one! According to Vatican II's *Lumen Gentium*, the 'Church is in Christ like a sacrament or as a sign and instrument both of a very closely knit union with God and of the unity of the whole human race.'[5] As a sacrament, the Church is more than a mere sign of the unity of the human race; She is also the cause of this unity, since by teaching the moral law and offering grace She helps to break down divisions caused by sin and to establish concord between all men and all nations.[6] This has great significance in the modern world, where more and more nations are made up of citizens from diverse ethic backgrounds. The Catholic faith, universal in its appeal and able to be accepted by every culture, can be a real source of unity even within nations, as much as between nations.

The purpose of the International Community

If the foundation of the International Community is the unity of mankind, its raison d'être is the international common good. The international common good or goods are those good things that the citizens of each nation need to live well but that can only be had by the nations working together, since they are the sort of things that cannot now be secured without international cooperation. The Catechism tells us that 'human interdependence is increasing and gradually spreading throughout the world. The unity of the human family, embracing people who enjoy equal natural dignity, implies a universal common good.'[7] Just as the individual citizen can only attain by collaboration with others some goods he needs to flourish, so also today the nations must collaborate on a global scale if they and their members are to flourish. In both cases, a political authority is needed if the common good is going to be achieved. The conclusion is that just as the national government is the political authority responsible for the national common good, so likewise the International Community needs a political authority to ensure the international common good.

The question that now arises is what precisely are these international common goods? Without excluding others, three predominate: peace, development, and the environment. It was the question of peace that brought the International Community to centre stage of Catholic social teaching, while the environment has, in more recent times, consolidated its place.

In the modern age, peace can normally only be achieved and ensured by recourse to the International Community, because the interrelation of nations and the power of modern weapons mean that disputes between countries tend to spill over into regional and even world conflicts. Bi-lateral treaties—for centuries the instrument for keeping peace between nations—are no longer sufficient. With regard to the environment, it has become evident that abuse of the environment in one country, say through the emission of noxious gases or the pollution of water reserves, usually has ramifications for many other countries, and even the whole world. Again, as we have already discussed in some detail, in the era of globalization, a holistic and universal development is a good beyond the power of any single nation to achieve. The community of nations alone can bring about the structural changes needed to make this a reality.

In all three areas—peace, the environment, and development—three factors are behind the emergence of International Community as one of the key social issues in the last fifty years. The first is the increased power of man. Mankind, in contrast to former times, is able to make weapons (nuclear and biological) that, if used, would have negative implications for the whole world. Again, mankind is able to mine and use fuels to such an extent that the impact is felt not just on a local or even national scale, but on a global scale. The second factor is the increased political and economic interrelation of nation states, such that their destinies are now inextricably bound together. Financial and political upheaval in one country sends its shock waves around the world. The good of each nation is now tied more or less to the good of all the other nations. The third factor is, paradoxically, the decreasing importance of the nation state which goes hand in hand with the process of globalization. Nation states on their own can no longer effectively control the economic activity of companies that increasingly operate on a global scale.

The structure of the International Community

The relationship between individual States and the International Community is a mirror of the relationship between the individual and the State. Accordingly, many of the same—and by now familiar—principles of social teaching apply. For example, we can speak of the 'rights of nations,' as we speak of rights of individuals.[8] So, just as each citizen has the right to life, so each nation has a right to existence, and just as citizens have a right to self-defence and self-determination, so does every nation.[9]

Since with rights come duties, for each nation there is a duty to act justly in relation to other nations and an obligation to seek the international common good. This, for example, would preclude a nation seeking to develop itself without due consideration to the good of other nations, by aggression, or even by the excessive use of common resources or unconstrained pollution of the environment.

The principles of subsidiarity and solidarity also apply and are of paramount importance for the correct structuring of the International Community.[10] Explicitly making the parallel between citizens and the State on the one hand, and the individual State and the International Community on the other, John XXIII observes:

> The same principle of subsidiarity which governs the relations between public authorities and individuals, families and intermediate societies in a single State, must also apply to the relations between the public authority of the world community and the public authorities of each political community.[11]

The principle of subsidiarity means that the International Community must not take away from individual nations the tasks they are capable of doing themselves, or at least capable of doing with the assistance of the International Community, such as organizing healthcare and education, facilitating the creation of jobs, and feeding their citizens. John XXIII states:

> The public authority of the world community is not intended to limit the sphere of action of the public authority of the individual political community, much less to take its place. On the contrary, its purpose is to create, on a world basis, an environment in which the public authorities of each political community, their citizens and intermediate associa-

> tions can carry out their tasks, fulfil their duties and exercise their rights with greater security.[12]

On the other hand, to prevent a self-centred nationalism, the principle, or rather virtue, of international solidarity must be at the heart of the international order and must be fostered by each nation and government. International solidarity is a determination on the part of each nation that all the other nations might share in the goods of peace, development, and an environment fit for mankind.

The International Community is formed on the basis of nations giving up some sovereignty for the sake of participating in the international common goods. Sovereignty is what makes a nation a subject or actor in the world, but it is not as absolute. Like all political realities, it is for the sake of the common good and, therefore, can be modified in order to attain the common good.[13] An example of this is the creation of the European Union, the genesis of which can be traced back to the creation of the European Coal and Steel Community in 1952. That organization was inspired by the French (Catholic) foreign minister Robert Schuman who proposed that, for the sake of peace, France and West Germany ought to place control of coal and steel production into the hands of a supranational organization. To give another example: today, for the sake of the environment, individual nations might choose to give up some control over environmental policies, and hence give up some of their sovereignty, in order to achieve agreements and regulations that will benefit them and others. However, no nation should be forced to join the International Community or an international organization. The Compendium says that 'it is essential that such an authority arise from mutual agreement and that it not be imposed.'[14] Nonetheless, it is perhaps possible to argue that there is a moral obligation on the part of the leaders of a nation to join the International Community, since the good of their own citizens and of the world can now hardly be achieved without universal membership. In one of his Messages for the World Day of Peace, John Paul II asks, 'Is this not the time for all to work together for a new constitutional organization of the human family, truly capable of ensuring peace and harmony between peoples?'[15] Nonetheless, this should not be interpreted as if social teaching proposes a 'super-state.' This is explicitly denied by John Paul II in the same message when he says:

> [L]et there be no misunderstanding. This does not mean writing the constitution of a global super-State. Rather, it means continuing and deepening processes already in place to meet the almost universal demand for participatory ways of exercising political authority, even international political authority.[16]

As we have already seen, the political fact must follow on from the social fact, and the reality is that the world is not culturally speaking one people and so one political authority does not, at least in our time, naturally arise from it.

While rejecting the idea of a super-state, the International Community—formed by the consent of the nations—is a true political community created for the sake of achieving an international common good. Therefore, like all political communities, there must be a corresponding political authority or power able to regulate and ultimately coerce individual nations so that this common good is realized. There must, therefore, be international law and some international power to enforce these laws. These laws can have no other foundation than natural law, since only this law (common as it is to all human beings, since it is written on their hearts) is universal enough to encompass all nations. Here, again, we can see the inherent limitations of relativism; it cannot possibly be the foundation for the International Community, since it fails to offer any solid basis for agreement or for mutual interaction.

Finally, let us note that in some ways there is, actually, a difference between the relationship of citizens to the State, on the one hand, and the relationship of States to the International Community, on the other. Individual citizens cannot really opt out of being members of the State, whereas individual States can withdraw from the International Community or simply not enter. Furthermore, while the International Community must have real authority this does not make it into a super-state because the breath of the authority enjoyed by the International Community is much more limited than that of a State, being restricted, at this time, to a limited number of issues, such as trade and the environment.

The current state of the International Community

The International Community is realized first and foremost through the United Nations Organization that was formed after the Second World War, on 24 October 1945, with fifty-one members. Today it has over one hundred and ninety member States, which constitutes nearly all the countries of the world. Only three sovereign states are not in the United Nations as member states, namely Taiwan, Kosovo, and the Holy See.

The main organs of the United Nations are: the General Assembly, the main deliberative body; the Security Council, which debates and makes resolutions in regard to conflicts; the Economic and Social Council, which seeks to promote cooperation in economic and social matters; the Secretariat, which makes studies and gathers information; and the International Court of Justice, which decides cases between member States when there is a dispute, for example over territory. In addition there are various agencies that carry out specific tasks. The most famous are the World Health Organization (WHO), the World Food Programme (WFP), the United Nations Children's Fund (UNICEF), United Nations Educational, Scientific and Cultural Organization (UNESCO), International Atomic Energy Agency (IAEA), and the World Bank. From this very brief description of the structure of the United Nations, it is clear that there is a particularly emphasis on peace and development.

The International Community

The Catholic Church herself is not a 'member State' of the United Nations but has—in Her capacity as a sovereign State (the Holy See)—the status of a 'permanent observer.' As a sovereign State, the Holy See also holds diplomatic relations with more than one hundred and seventy countries. What all this means is that the Church is a political actor on the international stage, and this is something very positive, since it allows the Church to promote Her social teaching in a truly international way.

Now, while the Church is for the most part positive about the work of the United Nations and the International Community in general, She is not unaware, nor silent, about some of the aberrations that have occurred in the work of the International Community.

One major concern of the Church vis-à-vis the International Community is the tendency for the more powerful nations to use it for their own selfish ends. In theory, each nation is an equal member of the International Community regardless of its size, power, or economic development, just as each citizen is equal within each State. In practice, however, more powerful nations, alone or in groups, in both economic and political matters, have sometimes yielded to the temptation of using the International Community to create situations most favourable to them, and less favourable to the weaker nations. Aware of this reality, in *Caritas in Veritate*, Benedict XVI says:

> In the face of the unrelenting growth of global interdependence, there is a strongly felt need, even in the midst of a global recession, for a reform of the United Nations Organization, and likewise of economic institutions and international finance, so that the concept of the family of nations can acquire real teeth. One also senses the urgent need to find innovative ways ... of giving poorer nations an effective voice in shared decision-making.[17]

The second major reservation on the part of the Church relates to the activities of some of the United Nations agencies, especially as they have come under the influence of some non-governmental organizations with social agendas that contradict social teaching. This concern about (and at times criticism of) the United Nations agencies is most evident in two letters written by John Paul II to the chairmen of two important conferences sponsored by the United Nations in the 1990s. The first was in preparation for the International Conference on Population and Development (1994), the so-called Cairo conference. The second was for the United Nations conference on women held in Beijing the following year.

In his letter to Nafis Sadik, chairman of the Cairo conference, John Paul II warns against using development as a cover for introducing rights of contraception, sterilization and abortion, or, according to the euphemism often used in such conferences, 'reproductive rights':

> Development has been and remains the proper context for the international community's consideration of population issues. Within such discussions there naturally arise questions relating to the transmission and nurturing of human life. But to formulate population issues in terms of individual 'sexual and reproductive rights,' or even in terms of 'women's rights,' is to change the focus which should be the proper concern of governments and international agencies.[18]

He also warned against the disturbing tendency to undermine the place of the family as the basic unit of society, or otherwise drastically redefine the family in such a way as to ignore the special place of marriage, something that he notes is contrary to the United Nations' very own Declaration on Human Rights:

> Moreover, questions involving the transmission of life and its subsequent nurturing cannot be adequately dealt with except in relation to the good of the family: that communion of persons established by the marriage of husband and wife, which is— as

> the Universal Declaration of Human Rights affirms—'the natural and fundamental group unit of society' (art. 16.3) ... [a]t this moment in history, when so many powerful forces are arrayed against the family, it is more important than ever that the Conference on Population and Development should respond to the challenge implicit in the United Nation's designation of 1994 as the 'International Year of the Family' by doing everything within its power to ensure that the family receives from 'society and the State' that protection to which the same Universal Declaration says it is 'entitled.' Anything less would be a betrayal of the noblest ideals of the United Nations.[19]

Finally, he laments the ominous and almost sinister exclusion from the preparatory material for the Cairo conference of any reference to the protection of the unborn child, something that had been explicitly stated as the wish of the member States at a previous conference:

> [t]he international consensus of the 1984 Mexico City International Conference on Population that 'in no case should abortion be promoted as a method of family planning' is completely ignored in the draft document. Indeed, there is a tendency to promote an internationally recognized right to access to abortion on demand, without any restriction, with no regard to the rights of the unborn, in a manner which goes beyond what even now is unfortunately accepted by the laws of some nations. The vision of sexuality which inspires the document is individualistic. Marriage is ignored, as if it were something of the past. An institution as natural, universal and fundamental as the family cannot be manipulated without causing serious damage to the fabric and stability of society.[20]

Many of the same concerns, namely family, sexuality, abortion, and population control, surface again in John Paul II's letter to Gertrude Mongella, chairman of the Beijing conference. He warns:

> In order to respect this natural order of things, it is necessary to counter the misconception that the role of motherhood is oppressive to women, and that a commitment to her family, particularly to her children, prevents a woman from reaching personal fulfilment, and women as a whole from having an influence in society. It is a disservice not only to children, but also to women and society itself, when a woman is made to feel guilty for wanting to remain in the home and nurture and care for her children.[21]

In concluding his letter, he says that 'we must hope that the Conference will set a course that avoids the reefs of exaggerated individualism, with its accompanying moral relativism.'[22]

Perhaps the most stinging of critiques concerning these aspects of the work of the United Nations comes from the Pontifical Council for the Family, which is most intimately involved in the Holy See's participation in such conferences. In its document, *Declaration on the Decrease of Fertility in the World*, it says:

> Indeed, for 30 years, the conferences sponsored by this organization have provoked and nurtured unfounded fears about demography, especially in the southern countries. On this alarmist basis, different agencies of the UN have invested and continue to invest huge financial resources in order to compel many countries to institute Malthusian policies. It has been proven that these programs, always imported from abroad, usually involve coercive measures of fertility control. In the same way, international aid for development is regularly granted on the condition of establishing programs of population control which include forced sterilizations, or sterilizations performed without proper informed consent. Local governments are also adopting such Malthusian policies, and non-governmental organizations—of which the most important is the well-known International Planned Parenthood Federation—are actively fostering these policies.[23]

In recent years, the tendency towards undermining the family and marriage has accelerated and evolved into the assertion of 'sexual orientation' rights, practically meaning the equating of homosexual partnerships with marriage. In this respect, the Holy See has opposed the proposed United Nations *Declaration on Sexual Orientation and Gender Identity* (2008).[24]

The International Community and development

We said at the beginning of this chapter that the reason for the International Community is to achieve international common goods, and we mentioned three that stand out, namely development, peace, and the environment. The next two chapters will be dedicated to the topics of peace and the environment respectively, but before concluding this chapter something should be said about development.

In the chapter on economic life, it was explained what social teaching understands by the word 'development,' namely, that it must be holistic—seeking not just economic prosperity but also a moral, cultural, and spiritual enrichment—and that it must be universal, that is, it ought to be enjoyed by everyone; in the words of Pope Paul VI, 'it has to promote the good of every man and of the whole man.'[25] The second major point social teaching makes about development is that it is a right. This right flows from the principle of the Universal Destination of Goods (UDG) and the equality of all men and all nations. Paul VI reminds us:

> Now if the earth truly was created to provide man with the necessities of life and the tools for his own progress, it follows that every man has the right to glean what he needs from the earth. All other rights, whatever they may be, including the rights of property and free trade, are to be subordinated to this principle. They should in no way hinder it; in fact, they should actively facilitate its implementation.[26]

Remember, all rights have a correlative duty, so this means that the right of each nation to development places on all other nations—on the International Community—a duty to help poor nations develop. John Paul II tells us that 'collaboration in the development of the whole person and of every human being is in fact a duty of all towards all, and must be shared by the four parts of the world: East and West, North and South.'[27]

If we turn first of all to the economic component of development, while foreign financial and technical aid are important helps, social teaching states that trade is the best way for poor countries to achieve development. In *Centesimus Annus*, John Paul II notes that those countries that have economically isolated themselves from the world market are those which have suffered stagnation, whereas those that have succeeded in taking part in it have developed. In conclusion, he says:

> It seems therefore that the chief problem is that of gaining fair access to the international market, based not on the unilateral principle of the exploitation of the natural resources of these countries but on the proper use of human resources.[28]

It should be noted that John Paul II says that the key is gaining 'fair access' to the world market. The point is that fair trade is not the same as free trade:

> It is evident that the principle of free trade, by itself, is no longer adequate for regulating international agreements. It certainly can work when both parties are about equal economically; in such cases it stimulates progress and rewards effort. That is why industrially developed nations see an element of justice in this principle ... But the case is quite different when the nations involved are far from equal. Market prices that are freely agreed upon can turn out to be most unfair. It must be avowed openly that, in this case, the fundamental tenet of liberalism (as it is called), as the norm for market dealings, is open to serious question.[29]

Paul VI concludes that trade can only be called fair when it is structured so that every nation is given the chance to share in prosperity: 'free trade can be called just only when it conforms to the demands of social justice.'[30] For poor countries, this goal almost certainly cannot initially be achieved through free trade, understood as the mutual liberalization of restrictions on importing and exporting goods. Such an agreement is only fair between nations of equal economic power. If poor countries lift restrictions designed to protect their weak economies, receiving in return open access to the markets of rich counties, then there will be only one winner—the rich countries. Producers from rich countries can often produce goods at lower costs and certainly of higher quality, with the help of subsidies (this is especially true of agricultural goods), economies of scale, modern public infrastructure, higher levels of educated and skilled workers, or they can temporarily deflate prices, absorbing short term losses, in order to corner markets. Producers in poor countries simply must sell their goods in order to survive, they have no subsidies, nor can they afford to sell goods at a loss.

Given this state of affairs, social teaching calls on rich countries to go beyond the strict bounds of justice—a so-called level playing field—and accept conditions of trade that favour the poor. Rich countries ought to generously open up their markets to the poor, while not demanding straight away strictly equivalent rights of access to the markets of the poor countries.[31] This is a concrete application of the preferential option for the poor and what John Paul II calls the need for mercy to 'correct' justice.[32] While it is laudable that individual countries would arrange their trade with poorer countries in this 'merciful' way, the reality of economic globalization means that only the International Community can really make it effective through a global agreement on trade that especially takes into account the plight of the poor countries of the world.

The principle of preferential option for the poor must also be taken into consideration when dealing with foreign debt.[33] This is debt that governments of one country owe to foreign lenders. While the largest debts are often held by rich countries, foreign debt is a problem mostly for poorer countries, since they are less able to pay it back. The interest payments alone are often beyond them. Debt is, consequently, a significant obstacle to the economic development of poor countries. This problem was highlighted in a particular way in the millennium year (2000) because of the Jewish tradition of cancelling debts in Jubilee years. John Paul II spoke frequently about this. In his Apostolic Letter for the preparation of the Jubilee year, *Tertio Millennio Adveniente*, he says:

> Christians will have to raise their voice on behalf of all the poor of the world, proposing the Jubilee as an appropriate time to give thought, among other things, to reducing substantially, if not cancelling outright, the international debt which seriously threatens the future of many nations.[34]

Normally, it obviously pertains to justice to pay back debts. In the case of foreign debt, however, the situation is often complicated because the money was sometimes lent irresponsibly and to governments who were not honest custodians of the common good of their citizens. Sometimes the money lent was 'tied' in such a way that the borrowing country must use it to buy goods from the lending country, in this way perpetuating colonial links. When all is said and done, the principle of justice must be upheld, but again 'corrected' by mercy. The poor themselves are not responsible for the situation, but they are the ones who suffer most as a result.

Notes

1. John Paul II, *Address to the General Assembly of the United Nations Organization* (5 October 1995), 1.
2. John Paul II, *Message for 2004 World Day of Peace*, 7.
3. Cf. *CSDC*, 428-31.
4. John XXIII, *Mater et Magistra*, 178.
5. Vatican II, *Lumen Gentium*, 1.
6. Cf. Vatican II, *Gaudium et Spes*, 89, 92.
7. *CCC*, 1911; cf. *CSDC*, 433.
8. John XXIII, *Pacem in Terris*, 80.
9. *Ibid.*, 92; cf. *CSDC*, 437.
10. *CSDC*, 441.
11. John XXIII, *Pacem in Terris*, 140.
12. *Ibid.*, 141.
13. John Paul II, *Sollicitudo Rei Socialis*, 15.
14. *CSDC*, 441.
15. John Paul II, *Message for 2003 World Day of Peace*, 6.
16. *Ibid.*
17. Benedict XVI, *Caritas in Veritate*, 67.
18. John Paul II, *Message to Nafis Sadik, Secretary General of the 1994 International Conference on Population and Development* (18 March 1994).
19. *Ibid.*
20. *Ibid.*
21. John Paul II, *Message to Gertrude Mongella, Secretary General of the United Nations Fourth World Conference on Women* (26 May 1995), 3.
22. *Ibid.*, 8.
23. Pontifical Council for the Family, *Declaration on the Decrease of Fertility in the World*, 2.
24. Statement of the Holy See Delegation at the 63rd Session of the General Assembly of the United Nations on the Declaration on Human Rights, *Sexual Orientation and Gender Identity* (18 December 2008).
25. Paul VI, *Populorum Progressio*, 14.

[26] *Ibid.*, 22; *CSDC*, 446.
[27] John Paul II, *Sollicitudo Rei Socialis*, 32.
[28] John Paul II, *Centesimus Annus*, 33.
[29] Paul VI, *Populorum Progressio*, 58.
[30] *Ibid.*, 59.
[31] *Ibid.*, 61; cf. *CSDC*, 364.
[32] John Paul II, *Dives in Misericordia*, 14.
[33] *CSDC*, 450.
[34] John Paul II, *Tertio Millennio Adveniente*, 51.

9

Peace

Peace, of course, is more than 'freedom from or cessation of war.'[1] St Augustine offers a more positive definition when he says that 'the peace of all things is the tranquillity of order.'[2] By order he means that everything is in its proper place in regard to everything else. So the peace of the family, for example, is the tranquillity that comes about from the children loving each other and obeying their parents, and the parents loving each other and lovingly governing their children. In fact, this definition of peace, offered by St Augustine, is very versatile because it can even be applied to what we might call 'peace of mind,' or personal peace, since a man is said to be a peace with himself when all his desires are well ordered and in harmony with each other.

The social encyclical that deals most directly with the theme of peace is John XXIII's *Pacem in Terris*, which means 'Peace on Earth.' Pope John does not quote St Augustine's definition of peace, but the connection of order to peace is very clearly the cornerstone of the encyclical which starts with the following statement:

> Peace on Earth—which man throughout the ages has so longed for and sought after—can never be established, never guaranteed, except by the diligent observance of the divinely established order.[3]

The relationship between peace and order is also clearly reflected in the structure of *Pacem in Terris* because the main point of the encyclical is to describe the proper order that ought to exist between: citizens and the State; one State and another; and, finally, each State and the International Community, all with a view to achieving peace.

There is a very important corollary to this intimate connection between peace and order. It makes it clear that lack of peace is fundamentally the result of disorder. When citizens are not rightly ordered to each other (which is to say they are being unjust to each other and are not treating each other like human beings), then there is lack of civic peace. Likewise, when the government does not have an attitude of service towards its citizens but oppresses them like serfs, the result is civic strife. When children do not obey their parents, and parents do not love each other and lovingly govern their children, then domestic peace is shattered. When an individual man wills at one level something and at another level the opposite, there is no personal peace (peace of mind). In all these situations of disorder, there is also conflict. But, one might ask, what is the cause of all this disorder and consequently this lack of peace?

The answer, of course, is sin! Original sin, personal sin, and structures of sin! It is original sin that lies behind the conflicting desires in each individual. It is personal sin that shatters the relationships in families and between neighbours. It is structures of sin—itself the result of personal sin—that sets up disordered relationships between the State and citizens and between one State and another. This simple observation has some very important consequences. It means that there can be no peace without a solution to sin, and this means that peace cannot be brought about merely by structural reforms and technology. In *Caritas in Veritate*, Benedict XVI notes that in our day 'even peace can run the risk of being considered a technical product, merely the outcome of agreements between governments or of initiatives aimed at ensuring effective economic aid.'[4] In truth, peace can only be brought about by dealing with sin at a very personal level: by conversion! As John Paul II reminded us in his 1984 Message for the World Day of

Peace, 'from a new heart, peace is born,' whereas, 'war is born from the sinful heart of man.'[5] Ultimately, then, peace is a gift from God, 'a peace the world cannot give' (Jn 14:27), because He alone can root out the cause of conflict, namely sin, and give us new hearts.[6] Recognizing our dependence on God for the establishment of true peace, John XXIII finished his encyclical on peace by reminding 'all men of good will' that:

> So magnificent, so exalted is this aim [of worldwide peace] that human resources alone, even though inspired by the most praiseworthy goodwill, cannot hope to achieve it. God Himself must come to man's aid with His heavenly assistance, if human society is to bear the closest possible resemblance to the kingdom of God ... [t]he very order of things therefore, demands that ... we pray earnestly to Him who by His bitter passion and death washed away men's sins, which are the fountainhead of discord, misery and inequality.[7]

Before moving on, let us note two more consequences of this connection between sin and conflict.

First, Christianity and particularly the Church has a vital role to play in bringing about peace, because it has the solution to sin and because it has an exalted vision of the dignity of the human person. In this sense, peace is part of the mission of the Church. In the words of John Paul II, the Church is a 'sacrament or sign and instrument of peace in the world and for the world.'[8] The Church manifests to the world the possibility of having a society of men and women drawn from every nation of the earth and who, 'reconciled and at peace through the grace of Christ,' live in harmony with each other. She is, therefore, 'a gift and leaven of peace offered by God to the whole of the human race.'[9] Accordingly, it is totally contrary to the truth to claim (as some do) that religion is detrimental to peace in society and that humanism or agnosticism is the way to achieve civic peace. Humanism will never bring peace as it will never be able to deal with sin, nor does it offer any secure foundation for the dignity of the human person:

> Let men make all the technical and economic progress they can, there will be no peace nor justice in the world until they return to a sense of their dignity as creatures and sons of God, who is the first and final cause of all created being. Separated from God a man is but a monster, in himself and toward others; for the right ordering of human society presupposes the right ordering of man's conscience with God, who is Himself the source of all justice, truth and love.[10]

In a message entitled 'Religious Freedom: Condition for Peace,' contrasting religious faith with a modern 'faith in technology', John Paul II notes that 'faith brings people together and unites them, makes them see others as their brothers and sisters; it makes them more attentive, more responsible, more generous in their commitment to the common good,'[11] all factors that promote peace in society.

Second, the relationship between sin and conflict reveals that perfect peace is an eschatological reality, a reality that can never be achieved completely on this earth, because only at the end of time will sin be utterly done away with. This should not, of course, make us less fervent in our efforts for peace here and now, but it should make us realistic about what can be achieved, and guard us against despondency.

The relationship of peace to justice and charity

The two social values most intimately connected with peace are justice and charity. It is not by chance that the organization in the Church responsible for the dissemination of Catholic social doctrine is the Pontifical Council for Justice and Peace. Justice, as we have seen, is the virtue that inclines us to give to others what is due to them. When people are not given what is due to them, such as respect, food, education, religious freedom, rightful autonomy, then violence is done to them and there is no peace; and of course, there is the constant danger that they will respond to injustice with violent retaliation. The respect for human rights and a just distribution of the goods of this earth are, therefore, a prerequisite, sine qua non, for peace.[12] It is for this reason that Paul VI can say that development is 'the new name for peace,' since 'extreme disparity between nations in economic, social and educational levels provokes jealousy and discord, often putting peace in jeopardy.'[13] Justice, therefore, clears the way for peace but, from all we have said above, it should be clear that peace is properly the fruit of charity:

> True and lasting peace is more a matter of love than of justice, ... [because] the function of justice is merely to do away with obstacles to peace: the injury done or the damage caused. Peace itself, however, is an act and results only from love.[14]

Charity is usually defined as 'willing the good of the other.' It is, therefore, the virtue that puts our will into harmony with the will of our spouses, friends, and neighbours. In the words of St Thomas, it brings about concord: oneness of heart. From this oneness of heart flows the tranquillity that we call peace. Consequently, St Thomas can say that 'peace is the "work of justice" indirectly, insofar as justice removes the obstacles to peace: but it is the work of charity directly, since charity, according to its very nature, causes peace. For love is "a unitive force."'[15] Pius XI sums all this up in *Quadragesimo Anno*, when he states:

> [T]he law of charity, 'which is the bond of perfection' (Col 3:14), must always take a leading role. How completely deceived, therefore, are those rash reformers who concern themselves with the enforcement of justice alone ... even supposing that everyone should finally receive all that is due him, the widest field for charity will always remain open. For justice alone can, if faithfully observed, remove the causes of social conflict but can never bring about

union of minds and hearts. If this bond [of charity] is lacking, the best of regulations come to naught, as we have learned by too frequent experience.[16]

The consequence of this primacy of charity is that peace in a society can no more be imposed 'from above'—by the government or by mere structural change—than can the virtue of charity. Rather, the peace of a society is the flowering of the peace that reigns in the heart of each citizen and particularly in the family, as the first cell of society. It is, ultimately, a bottom-up process: 'it is absolutely necessary that peace begin to take root as a value rooted deep within the heart of every person. In this way it can spread to families and to the different associations within society until the whole of the political community is involved.'[17]

War and the failure of peace

Catholic social doctrine recognizes that there are extraordinary circumstances in which a country can and even ought to use military force, namely in the case of self-defence or the defence of innocent victims of aggression. This is no more than the application to the State of an individual person's right of self-defence.[18] A war of aggression is, however, always illicit and it is never considered as a suitable means for countries to resolve problems that arise between them. This prohibition also precludes war for the sake of honour or to punish another nation. It is easy to find quote after quote from the popes lamenting the tendency of nations to try and solve their disputes by war. Famous among them is Paul VI's impassioned plea to the nations of the world in his speech to the General Assembly of the United Nations Organization in October 1965 when he said, 'Never again war, never again war! It is peace, peace which ought to guide the destiny of people and all humanity,'[19] and the warning of Pius XII on the eve of the outbreak of World War II, that 'nothing is lost by peace; everything may be lost by war.'[20] In more recent times, John Paul II, in a speech to the diplomatic staff of the Holy See, said: 'war is not always inevitable. It is always a defeat for humanity.'[21]

This general attitude of extreme caution has been strengthened in the light of two modern phenomena. First, the increasingly powerful and destructive nature of modern weapons and, second, the greater interrelation between countries, which means that it is very difficult to stop conflicts between two nations from drawing in others, and indeed engulfing the entire regions of the world.[22] Because of this new situation, Vatican II says that 'these considerations compel us to undertake an evaluation of war with an entirely new attitude.'[23] This is the clear message that runs throughout John XXIII's encyclical *Pacem in Terris*, penned only a few months after the Cuban missile crisis of October 1962, a crisis that brought the USA and the USSR to the brink of war. In that encyclical he observes:

> Men nowadays are becoming more and more convinced that any disputes which may arise between nations must be resolved by negotiation and agreement, and not by recourse to arms ... this conviction owes its origin chiefly to the terrifying destructive force of modern weapons. It arises from fear of the ghastly and catastrophic consequences of their use. Thus, in this age which boasts of its atomic power, it no longer makes sense to maintain that war is a fit instrument with which to repair the violation of justice.[24]

In summary, then, while there always remains a right to self-defence and sometimes a duty to combat aggression, because of the essentially lamentable character of war, this right must be exercised according to stringent criteria. We have already discussed the criteria for a just self-defence in chapter six, when we considered the right of citizens to defend themselves against unjust laws, even to the extent of rebelling against the government. These criteria are now recalled and applied concretely to the question of military action.[25]

The criteria are as follows: First, the attack of the enemy is unjustified, that is to say, the enemy is the aggressor. Second, the damage that has been, or will be, inflicted on a country is grave, is certain (if it has not yet occurred), and is lasting. This would obviously preclude war in cases when territorial water or air space was infringed, since this is not a lasting or grave violation of sovereignty. Third, all other means to resolve the problem have been found to be ineffective, or are impractical. Such means would include economic and political sanctions, dialogue, and mediation. Fourth, there is a serious prospect of success. This precludes the useless multiplication of violence. It does not, however, preclude heroic efforts to defend one's own country against the odds, but means that those in charge of the common good cannot demand from citizens that they act in futile ways in order to defend their country. Fifth, the use of military force as a means of defence cannot produce evils and disorder greater than that which they seek to eliminate.

It is very important to remember that these are only criteria which would legitimise defence in general. Further to this, in the carrying out of military action, each act must also be morally evaluated. Vatican II reminds us that 'the mere fact that war has unfortunately broken out [does not] mean that all is fair between the warring parties.'[26] Applying this, we might conclude that during the Second World War, while the Allies had a right and even a duty to defend themselves and others against the aggression of Nazi Germany, this does not legitimise all the military action they took, for example the indiscriminate bombing of German cities.

The issue at stake here is the protection of civilian lives. The only legitimate target of military action is combatants. Included in this category are all members of the armed forces and anyone who gives them immediate help. Of course, it is not always easy to draw a line between immediate and more remote help. People working in transportation of military equipment and the production of military equipment seem to render immediate help. On the other hand, persons working in agriculture and the production of foodstuffs part of which will, undoubtedly, be used by soldiers, seem to render remote help. When only remote help is being given, then seeking to kill such persons is not proportionate to the 'violence' they are inflicting upon you. Of course, the reality is that military and civilian targets are often in close proximity. The principle of double-effect can be invoked: foreseen but unintended civilian casualties can be tolerated if the intention is solely to destroy the military target and the execution of the operation takes reasonable precautions to minimize civilian deaths.

In the carrying out of military action, individual soldiers must take personal responsibility and cannot hide behind the immoral orders of superiors.[27] The Catechism reminds us that 'actions deliberately contrary to the law of nations and to its universal principles are crimes, as are the orders that command such actions. Blind obedience does not suffice to excuse those who carry them out.'[28] When doubt arises about the morality of the actions commanded, soldiers can normally give the benefit of the doubt to their superiors. Nonetheless, conscientious objectors must to not be forced to fight, but ought to accept other forms of service. *Gaudium et Spes* states that 'laws should make humane provision for the case of conscientious objectors who refuse to carry arms, provided they accept some other form of community service.'[29] This right of objection rests upon the real possibility of being placed in situations where it is difficult to determine the morally best course of action and where the action taking place is of the highest gravity, namely killing another person. The right to conscientiously object recognizes that someone has a right not to be placed in such situations. It is not a recognition that it is wrong to kill a person in self-defence.

The 'just war theory' does not absolutely preclude a 'pre-emptive' strike on the part of a nation that is threatened by another but that is not, as yet, physically attacked.

Nonetheless, social teaching is extremely cautious about this and recommends that such military action be done through the International Community, given the difficulty of making an objective assessment of how concrete the threat really is.[30]

Given that wars of aggression are ruled out, the military capacity of a country can only be proportioned to the right of defence. This determines the quantity and type of armaments it may legitimately acquire.[31] It also has implications for the type of weapons that can be manufactured in the first place. Here is another sector of the economy where the market cannot be given free rein:

> Weapons cannot be considered as any other good exchanged on the global, regional or national market. Their possession, production and trade have deep ethical and social implications and they must be regulated by paying due attention to specific principles of the moral and legal order. Among the principles there is the principle of sufficiency, which allows States to possess only the means necessary to guarantee the legitimate protection of their people.[32]

Some types of weapon are excluded outright, such as biological and chemical weapons, because of their indiscriminate and particularly injurious nature. They fall foul to the condemnation of the Vatican II which stated: 'Any act of war aimed indiscriminately at the destruction of entire cities or extensive areas along with their population is a crime against God and man himself. It merits unequivocal and unhesitating condemnation.'[33]

The other type of weapon explicitly condemned by the Church is anti-personal mines. In his message for the 1999 World Day of Peace, John Paul II condemned those still producing and using these weapons 'with disregard for the clearly expressed will of governments and peoples to put a final end to the use of such an insidious weapon.'[34]

Catholic social doctrine provides a nuanced position on the retention of nuclear weapons. It does not suggest unilateral disarmament, and to this extent permits nations to hang on to these weapons as a deterrent. One might say nuclear weapons are tolerated but not promoted. They are tolerated because the unilateral elimination of them might, in the current situation, lead to a greater evil than retaining them, such as invasion and domination. These weapons could only ever be used against military targets and there can be no intention—even an implicit or conditional intention—for these weapons to be used on civilian targets (hence they cannot licitly be programmed and set up ready for an indiscriminate strike on centres of population). Deterrence, then, means that an enemy country is held back from military action because the nuclear weapons of its adversary might be used against its armies. The fact that the enemy worries that in the heat of war its adversary might act immorally and use these weapons on its civilians (perhaps part of the dynamic of deterrence) does not make it immoral for a country to hold these weapons with the intention of using them only on military targets.

Nonetheless, social teaching clearly states that deterrence is not a means to peace, and ought not to be considered as a permanent solution. *Gaudium et Spes* notes that the arms race prepares the way for a nuclear Armageddon, breeds mistrust (the antithesis to peace), pulls other nations into rearmament, and diverts resources from addressing the root causes of tension such as poverty and underdevelopment.[35] The Cold War arms race—the context of the statement from *Gaudium et Spes*—involved the stockpiling of huge nuclear arsenals by the world's superpowers, absorbing significant material and intellectual resources.

The East-West conflict has, at least temporarily, passed (or is less intense) but there has now emerged a new arms race where previously non-nuclear nations seek to develop atomic weapons. This brings with it the same real danger of a nuclear holocaust. Catholic social teaching urges mutual and controlled disarmament and that the effort to prevent the spread of nuclear military capability among the nations of the world (non-proliferation), must be matched by efforts on the part of those countries with these weapons to disarm. The mandatory goal is the complete elimination of the presence of these weapons in the world. John Paul II summarizes the position of the Church when he says:

> [T]he Holy See is of the opinion that, in the sphere of nuclear weapons, the banning of tests and of the further development of these weapons, disarmament and non-proliferation are closely linked and must be achieved as quickly as possible under effective international controls. These are steps towards a general and total disarmament which the international community as a whole should accomplish without delay.[36]

Terrorism

A working definition might describe terrorism as organized violence aimed at non-military targets in order to create fear with the aim of gaining some political goals, or of punishing a group or a country. While violence has existed since the beginning of the human race (as the story of Cain and Abel reveals), and the French Revolution witnessed the so-called 'Reign of Terror,' terrorist groups are a relatively modern phenomenon emerging particularly in the 1970s. Terrorism seems also to be an evolving reality, and the twenty-first century has witnessed various 'new things' in the world of terrorism. More recently, it has become highly organized and financed, sometimes State-sponsored, global in organization and impact, and not uncommonly connected to religious groups. In many ways, terrorism has replaced the Cold War as the major threat to world peace.

From a moral point of view, terrorism is always to be condemned because of its careless attitude to human life. Terrorists seek to use people as a means to gain some political end. Because of this, the condemnation is absolute:

> The absolute unacceptability of terrorism lies precisely in the fact that it uses innocent people as means to obtain its ends, thus showing contempt and utter disregard for human life and dignity.[37]

Implied in this condemnation is the right of nations to protect themselves against terrorism even by military force, according to the criteria for self-defence outlined above:

> There exists therefore a right to defend oneself against terrorism, a right which, as always, must be exercised with respect for moral and legal limits in the choice of ends and means. The guilty must be correctly identified, since criminal culpability is always personal and cannot be extended to the nation, ethnic group or religion to which the terrorists may belong.[38]

One important consideration in the fight against terrorism is the need to avoid encroaching upon the human rights of those suspected or convicted of terrorism (say by recourse to torture) or of the population itself under the pretext of safeguarding it (say by unwarranted powers of surveillance or detention given to security forces). This would be to play into the hand of the terrorists whom are rightfully opposed because of their disregard for human rights.[39]

Combating terrorism cannot be only a matter of policing and military force. The roots of terrorism must also be addressed. This means addressing poverty and injustice, especially the scandalous disproportion between the rich and poor countries of the world:

> International cooperation in the fight against terrorist activities must also include a courageous and resolute political, diplomatic and economic commitment to relieving situations of oppression and marginalization which facilitate the designs of terrorists. The recruitment of terrorists in fact is easier in situations where rights are trampled upon and injustices tolerated over a long period of time.[40]

Of course, there are also ideological as well as material factors behind terrorism. Pope Benedict says that 'in analysing the causes of the contemporary phenomenon of terrorism, consideration should be given, not only to its political and social causes, but also to its deeper cultural, religious and ideological motivations.'[41] He points to two particular ideologies, namely nihilism and fundamentalism. Nihilism is a total disregard for the value of life and society, while fundamentalism seeks to impose (rather than propose) personal convictions by force. The latter, of course, often has a religious dimension. It is for this reason, among others, that John Paul II and Benedict XVI have vigorously pursued inter-religious dialogue as a way to foster peace.

Notes

1. *The Concise Oxford Dictionary*, 6th edition, edited by J. B. Sykes (Oxford: Clarendon Press, 1976), 881.
2. St Augustine, *City of God*, Book XIX, chapter 13.
3. John XXIII, *Pacem in Terris*, 1.
4. Benedict XVI, *Caritas in Veritate*, 72.
5. John Paul II, *Message for 1984 World Day of Peace*, 1, 3.
6. CSDC, 492.
7. John XXIII, *Pacem in Terris*, 168-9.
8. John Paul II, *Message for 2000 World Day of Peace*, 20.
9. John Paul II, *Message for 1982 World Day of Peace*, 11.
10. John XXIII, *Pacem in Terris*, 215.
11. John Paul II, *Message for 1988 World Day of Peace*, 3; cf. Benedict XVI, *Caritas in Veritate*, 72.
12. CSDC, 494.
13. Paul VI, *Populorum Progressio*, 76; cf. John XXIII, *Mater et Magistra*, 157.
14. Pius XI, *Ubi Arcano*, 35.
15. St Thomas Aquinas, *Summa Theologiae*, II II, q.29 a.3 ad3.
16. Pius XI, *Quadragesimo Anno*, 137.

17   *CSDC*, 495.

18   *CSDC*, 504, 506.

19   Paul VI, *Address to the General Assembly of the United Nations* (4 October 1965), 5.

20   Pius XII, *Broadcast Message* (24 August 1939).

21   John Paul II, *Address to the Diplomatic Corps* (13 January 2003), 4.

22   *CSDC*, 498.

23   Vatican II, *Gaudium et Spes*, 80.

24   John XXIII, *Pacem in Terris*, 126–127.

25   *CCC*, 2309; *CSDC*, 500.

26   Vatican II, *Gaudium et Spes*, 79.

27   *CSDC*, 503.

28   *CCC*, 2213.

29   Vatican II, *Gaudium et Spes*, 79.

30   *CSDC*, 501; cf. United Nations Organization, *Charter of the United Nations Organization*, articles 39–51.

31   *CSDC*, 508.

32   Pontifical Council for Justice and Peace, *Statement by the Pontifical Council for Justice and Peace on Behalf of the Holy See Concerning the International Trade in Conventional Weapons*, 4.

33   Vatican II, *Gaudium et Spes*, 80; cf. *CSDC*, 509.

34   John Paul II, *Message for 1999 World Day of Peace*, 11.

35   Vatican II, *Gaudium et Spes*, 81; cf. *CSDC*, 508.

36   John Paul II, *Address to the Diplomatic Corps* (13 January 1996), 7

37   Archbishop Celestino Migliore, *Intervention of the Holy See at the Sixth Commission of the General Assembly of the United Nations on Measures to Eliminate International Terrorism*; cf. *CSDC*, 514-15.

38   John Paul II, *Message for 2002 World Day of Peace*, 5.

39   Archbishop Celestino Migliore, *Intervention of the Holy See at the Sixth Commission of the General Assembly of the United Nations on Measures to Eliminate International Terrorism*.

40   John Paul II, *Message for 2002 World Day of Peace*, 5; cf. John Paul II, *Message for 2004 World Day of Peace*, 8.

41   Benedict XVI, *Message for 2006 World Day of Peace*, 10.

10

The Environment

In comparison to other areas of Catholic social doctrine, the environment has received, as yet, little attention. This is not surprising if we remember that it is a relatively new issue, having emerged in the last thirty or so years, and that social teaching tends to be reflective rather than proscriptive. Social teaching, as we have seen, reflects on emerging situations in society and on the solutions that have already been proposed in regard to them. Paul VI touched on environmental issues in various speeches, but more sustained treatment had to wait until the pontificate of John Paul II, who raised it even in his inaugural encyclical *Redemptor Hominis*.[1] The most important contribution of his pontificate is, however, his message for the World Day of Peace for 1990, entitled, 'Peace with God the Creator, Peace with all Creation.' Pope Benedict mentioned the environmental crisis in his inaugural homily and it was a major theme in his first social encyclical, *Caritas in Veritate* (2009). There is also a chapter on the environment in the Compendium, and an interesting consideration of the issues by the International Theological Commission in a document called *Communion and Stewardship*.

The Hermeneutic of Stewardship

The attitude of social teaching towards the environment is formed on the basis of the biblical account of creation. According to the book of Genesis, God created the universe and placed man at its head. This is expressed by the fact that man is created last, and he alone is created in the image and likeness of God (Gn 1:26). Moreover, God brings all the animals to him to name, which is a sign of his power over them (Gn 2:19). Perhaps most importantly, God commands man to 'subdue the earth' (Gn 1:28) and tells him that all the creatures may be used for his benefit (Gn 1:29). Since scripture also tells us that God 'put him [man] in the garden of Eden to work it and keep it' (Gn 2:15) we see that the gift of creation comes with responsibilities.

In the light of this revelation, the basic principle of social doctrine in regard to the environment is the concept of stewardship. This principle, or hermeneutic, states that man, created in the image and likeness of God, shares in the divine task of ruling over creation and caring for it. Creation is seen as a gift from God to mankind as a whole. As a gift, while making man the lord of the created world, it comes with the responsibility to use creation wisely and for the common good. Man can use all the other creatures for his benefit, but they remain God's handiwork and, as gifts to man, are to be treasured as manifestations of God's wisdom, power and love. Ultimately, creation has a sacramental dimension, meaning it reveals God the Creator to man. St. Paul tells us that 'since the creation of the world God's invisible qualities—his eternal power and divine nature—have been clearly seen, being understood from what has been made' (Rm 1:20). This is a powerful motive for respect.[2]

In some mysterious way, Creation will also share in the redemption won by Christ. Scripture speaks of 'a new heaven and a new earth' (Rev 21:1), and says that 'creation waits with eager longing for the revealing of the sons of God ... because the creation itself will be set free from its bondage to decay' (Rm 8:19, 21). In truth, we do not know what this renewal of creation entails, only that God's redemption encompasses all of creation with an utterly unique place for mankind. The Catechism states that the

The Environment

universe will be transformed, 'so that the world itself, restored to its original state, facing no further obstacles, should be at the service of the just,'[3] but, it adds, 'we know neither the moment of the consummation of the earth and of man, nor the way in which the universe will be transformed.'[4] Despite this obscurity, the inclusion of creation in redemption is another powerful motive for Christians to respect creation.

Since, according to the stewardship model, creation is for the benefit of man, social teaching is generally positive about technological and scientific advances, as it is about material prosperity. This is because they are a manifestation of man's share in God's creative power, by which he brings to greater perfection what is latent in the gift of creation. As the Fathers of Vatican II note:

> Far from thinking that works produced by man's own talent and energy are in opposition to God's power, and that the rational creature exists as a kind of rival to the Creator, Christians are convinced that the triumphs of the human race are a sign of God's grace and the flowering of His own mysterious design.[5]

Moreover, such advances, which include for example new strains of crops resistant to pests and droughts, can be a real help in the fight against poverty. Nonetheless, such scientific advances are not self-justifying simply by being scientific! In evaluating them, it is not enough that the goal in mind — such as relief of hunger, or cheaper food — is good. As with all human actions, the circumstance of the action and the foreseeable consequences must be considered. When it is an issue of creating new strains, or of genetic modification, this consideration would include the effect of this modification in the ecosystem.

One question that is bound to arise is whether man can do anything he likes to a creature. The basic answer is that creatures are created for the good of mankind, and so as long as they are used for the true benefit of man, they have attained the goal God created them for. This means that they can be used for food and clothing, and domesticated for work and leisure. They can also be the object of scientific experimentation when the goal sought is important and good, and there is no other way to carry out the research. Nonetheless, the move away from animal experimentation, as it becomes less necessary because of alternatives, is a good thing conforming to God's plan for creation:

> It is certain that animals are at the service of man and can hence be the object of experimentation. Nevertheless, they must be treated as creatures of God which are destined to serve man's good, but not to be abused by him. Hence the diminution of experimentation on animals, which has progressively been made ever less necessary, corresponds to the plan and well-being of all creation.[6]

Inflicting suffering on animals without good reason, say for pleasure and sport, is not permissible, since it represents a failure on the part of man in his task as steward. This does not amount to a proclamation of animal rights as much as to a warning that man can degrade himself in failing to live up to the task God has given him.[7]

Today, there are some who claim that Christianity is a major obstacle to the protection of the environment because it preaches a God who places man above the rest of creation and orders him to subdue the earth:

> An unfortunate aspect of this new ecological awareness is that Christianity has been accused by some as in part responsible for the environmental crisis, for the very reason that it has maximized the place of human beings created in the image of God to rule of visible creation. Some critics go so far as to claim that the Christian tradition lacks the resources to field a sound ecological ethics because it regards man as essentially superior to the rest of the natural world, and that it will be necessary to turn to Asian and traditional religions to develop the needed ecological ethics.[8]

The Environment

Social teaching, obviously, refutes this and points out that only the Christian vision of creation can hold the middle ground between, on the one hand, a so-called cosmocentricism and, on the other, a consumerist vision of creation. Cosmocentricism turns creation into a museum not to be touched and makes man just another species, an attitude not uncommon in the ecological movement influence by the New Age.[9] John Paul II noted that:

> [I]t is being proposed that the ontological and axiological difference between men and other living beings be eliminated, since the biosphere is considered a biotic unity of undifferentiated value. Thus man's superior responsibility can be eliminated in favour of an egalitarian consideration of the 'dignity' of all living beings.[10]

Somewhat connected with cosmocentricism is the danger of divinizing creation in a pantheistic way. This is likewise a tendency of the New Age. It is in contradiction to the Christian doctrine of creation from nothing (*ex nihilo*), since this doctrine clearly indicates the distinction between the One who creates and what is created.

On the other hand, a technological mentality views creation in a purely materialistic way, as something with no intrinsic purpose or value but only as something for man to gain power over.[11] This vision of reality is opposed to the Christian understanding of creation. According to the Christian vision, the universe comes into being by the power of a God who creates with a purpose in mind—since it is created by the Word who is Eternal Wisdom (cf. Jn 1:1). God then places man over the earth not as a tyrant but as a steward.[12]

The hermeneutic of stewardship is closely related to principle of the Universal Destination of Goods (UDG), since both point to the truth that God gave creation to mankind for the benefit of all men. When it is a matter of the just use of resources, the principle of the Universal Destination of Goods means that it is unjust for the rich to hoard disproportionately the resources of the world and that the present generation has an obligation to ensure that coming generations have enough for a truly human existence. A good steward not only considers the present needs but also the future. This attitude should give birth to a solidarity with the generations to come, manifested in concretely modifying the way we live now.[13] John Paul II makes this connection between the Universal Destination of Goods and the environment when he says:

> [T]he earth is ultimately a common heritage, the fruits of which are for the benefit of all. In the words of the Second Vatican Council, 'God destined the earth and all it contains for the use of every individual and all peoples' (*Gaudium et Spes*, 69). This has direct consequences for the problem at hand. It is manifestly unjust that a privileged few should continue to accumulate excess goods, squandering available resources, while masses of people are living in conditions of misery at the very lowest level of subsistence. Today, the dramatic threat of ecological breakdown is teaching us the extent to which greed and selfishness—both individual and collective—are contrary to the order of creation, an order which is characterized by mutual interdependence.[14]

This way of expressing the environmental problem makes it clear that it is a moral question before it is a technical question. John Paul II noted that:

> [A]n adequate solution cannot be found [to the environmental crisis] merely in a better management or a more rational use of the earth's resources, as important as these may be. Rather, we must go to the source of the problem and face in its entirety that profound moral crisis of which the destruction of the environment is only one troubling aspect.[15]

Following in this vein, Pope Benedict noted in his inaugural homily that 'the external deserts in the world are growing because the internal deserts have become so vast.'[16] Here he is thinking of the great spiritual desert caused by materialism. The point is that an exaggerated desire for material well-being—greed and selfishness—is a potent factor in the current ecological crisis because it leads to a disproportionate use of material resources by the few. Therefore, when considering the environment, to the principle of man created in the image of God must be added the revelation concerning the fall of man, since the reality of sin has an important bearing on the environmental crisis of today. Revelation touches directly upon this when it notes that one of the consequences of the fall of man is a disruption in creation as a whole (Gn 3:16; Rm 8:20).

The demographic question

Today the question of population is often raised within the context of the environment. Therefore, we shall discuss the question of demography here.

John XXIII was the first pope to give significant attention to demographics. In *Mater et Magistra*, he paraphrases the concerns of some when he formulates the question, 'How can economic development and the supply of food keep pace with the continual rise in population?'[17] Here, then, the context of the discussion is development. Today, we would add to this the question of how the environment can be protected in the face of population increase. The answer some give to these questions is that it simply cannot, and so the single most important solution is to reduce the number of human beings. Paul VI notes—in tones much more dramatic and urgent that John XXIII—that:

> There is no denying that the accelerated rate of population growth brings many added difficulties to the problems of development where the size of the population grows more rapidly than the quantity of available resources to such a degree that things seem to have reached an impasse. In such circum-

stances people are inclined to apply drastic remedies to reduce the birth rate.[18]

In considering social teaching's response to this, let us first consider the question of development, and then of the environment.

Population and development

Social teaching opposes a crude analysis of the situation that places endue emphasis on the limiting of population growth (or even the reduction of population) as the key to development. It notes that many densely populated countries with very limited resources are, nonetheless, highly economically developed, such as Japan and the United Kingdom. This is because the ultimate resource of a nation is its people. In an increasing technological world, 'human resources' and 'human know-how' are more and more the key to development and the most limiting resource for many companies. This being the case, in *Caritas in Veritate*, Pope Benedict correctly notes that development is often related to population increase.[19] In our time, Ireland would be an example of this, since the years of the so-called Celtic Tiger (1995-2007) coincided with the baby boom of the early 1980s. One factor here is that young people bring vitality to a society, another of course is that population increase means not only a bigger workforce but also an increased market for goods. Of course, there may well be other factors contributing the Ireland's economic miracle, but it at least shows that population increase is not opposed to development, and indeed may well favour it.

In *Mater et Magistra*, John XXIII also opposed the prophets of disaster who based their arguments on crude predictions of population growth and availability of resources. There, he notes that the availability of resources must be measured against the ingenuity of mankind to use resources more efficiently and discover new resources. John XXIII spoke of resources being nigh-infinite in the face of human intelligence.[20] Recent statements of social teaching—such as that of Paul VI quoted above—are more cautious and recognize that resources are indeed finite. John Paul II notes that:

> [W]e live in a finite world, the resources of which are indeed limited. As a result, we have a specific moral duty to use these resources wisely, taking into account not only our own present needs but also the needs of future generations.[21]

What remains clear is that underdevelopment has many factors of which population increase is only one factor to be considered. There is, in addition, the question of poor education, poor infrastructure, and wars. Above all, there is the question of whether rich nations are willing to help poor nations to develop.[22] Pointing the finger at population increase as the main hindrance to development is convenient for rich nations because it does not require them to make the sacrifices necessary for the poor to join them at the table of prosperity.

Since governments are responsible for the common good, and this includes development, they can legitimately concern themselves with the question of demographics.[23] The government might concern itself with the geographical distribution of population in the case where there is a mismatch between the location of resources and the location of people. Of course, the more controversial issue is the State's role in seeking to curb population growth. Paul VI clearly states both the right and the limit of the State in this regard:

> There is no doubt that public authorities can intervene in this matter, within the bounds of their competence. They can instruct citizens on this subject and adopt appropriate measures, so long as these are in conformity with the dictates of the moral law and the rightful freedom of married couples is preserved completely intact. When the inalienable right of marriage and of procreation is taken away, so is human dignity.[24]

As we can see from this, when it is a question of curbing population growth, the intervention of the State is very strictly defined. They can give their people objective information about the relationship of demographic trends to development, 'information concerning the condition and needs of the country.'[25] They can also educate them in means of family planning that are morally sound.[26] The promotion of immoral forms of birth control, or of abortion and sterilization are, of course, prohibited. If the State was to have recourse to such illicit means, it would no longer be promoting true development, since it would be promoting a one-sided materialistic view of development that disregards moral development and human rights.[27] Ultimately, in the words of John XXIII, we must believe that 'a provident God grants sufficient means to the human race to find a dignified solution to the problems attendant upon the transmission of human life.'[28]

At the end of the day, the decision about the number of children born belongs to the parents. It is utterly against the right order of things for the State to usurp this. If the State can take away this most fundamental decision from the parents, then parental authority is utterly void, and the State has fallen into totalitarianism. Not only does the final decision lay with the parents, the State must not penalize them for their decisions, neither financially or by socially stigmatizing them.[29] Of course, the parents must make this decision carefully. Paul VI says that:

> [f]inally, it is for parents to take a thorough look at the matter and decide upon the number of their children. This is an obligation they take upon themselves, before their children already born, and before the community to which they belong—following the dictates of their own consciences informed by God's law authentically interpreted, and bolstered by their trust in Him.[30]

Saying that the parents must, among other criteria, consider their duty before the community means that parents really might decide to limit family size for the common good. On the other hand, they might respond to the same duty by having a larger family. This might be the case in some Western countries whose population decline threatens to economically undermine them:

> [I]n the northern hemisphere the nature of this problem is reversed: here, the cause for concern is the drop in the birthrate, with repercussions on the aging of the population, unable even to renew itself biologically. In itself, this is a phenomenon capable of hindering development.[31]

Population and the environment

As we have seen, at the heart of the environmental crisis is a profound moral malaise in which there is a lack of solidarity between rich and poor and between this generation and those to come. In both cases, one group—the rich of our time—refuses to reform its lifestyles and continues to consume a disproportionate amount of the world's resources, to the great detriment of the environment. Given this diagnosis, a reduction in population is not going to solve the problem because, as rich countries prove, an increase in the consumption of resources can coincide with minimal increase in population. The focus of attention should be as much on the level of personal consumption as on the number of consumers.

In fact, both John Paul II and Benedict XVI note that an anti-life attitude—that is often part and parcel of programs to reduce population—is harmful to the environment, for two reasons. First, precisely because it tends to promote the value of 'having over being,' that is, it promotes consumerism:

> [T]he ecological question ... accompanies the problem of consumerism and ... is closely connected to it. In his desire to have and to enjoy rather than to be and to grow, man consumes the resources of

the earth and his own life in an excessive and disordered way.[32]

Second, anti-life practices such as abortion, euthanasia, and embryo experimentation sow confusion into society about the dignity of the human person. Now, if the human being, who even reason can acknowledge is the high-point of creation,[33] is not respected, there is no lasting motivation or energy to protect the rest of creation. Pope Benedict makes this point in *Caritas in Veritate*, when he says:

> In order to protect nature, it is not enough to intervene with economic incentives or deterrents; not even an apposite education is sufficient. These are important steps, but the decisive issue is the overall moral tenor of society. If there is a lack of respect for the right to life and to a natural death, if human conception, gestation and birth are made artificial, if human embryos are sacrificed to research, the conscience of society ends up losing the concept of human ecology and, along with it, that of environmental ecology. It is contradictory to insist that future generations respect the natural environment when our educational systems and laws do not help them to respect themselves.[34]

The environment, the State, and the market system

We have already seen that Catholic social teaching favours a market system of economics over a centrally-planned system. One reason for this is that the market system gives value to resources because they can be traded, and this tends to result in a better use of resources. Nonetheless, we have also seen that the environment is one of the areas—along with things like healthcare provision, education, and culture—where the market cannot be given absolute freedom. Dealing with harmful industrial by-products and emissions can be expensive. Accordingly, environmental concerns can fall by the wayside. Therefore, the State (and, in the age of globalization, the International Community) have a duty to regulate the market in this respect.

This regulation will obviously include standards and laws, but can also, to some extent, integrate market mechanisms as, for example, in the concept of carbon emission credits. This is a system by which companies would buy and sell the right to certain quantities of carbon emission. Clean companies would be able to sell their credits, thereby being rewarded for their contribution to the safeguarding of the environment, while dirty companies would have the added cost of buying extra credits, an incentive to clean up their act.

Notes

[1] John Paul II, *Redemptor Hominis*, 16. For an overview of magisterial texts on the environment see Paul Haffner, *Towards a Theology of the Environment* (Leominster: Gracewing, 2008), 107–144.

[2] *CSDC*, 487.

[3] *CCC*, 1047.

[4] *CCC*, 1048.

[5] Vatican II, *Gaudium et Spes*, 34.

[6] John Paul II, *Address to the members of the Pontifical Academy of Sciences* (23 October 1982).

[7] In this respect, UNESCO's *Universal Declaration of Animal Rights* (15 October 1978) goes too far in using the terminology of 'rights' for animals. By this, it blurs the distinction between human beings and other animals.

[8] International Theological Commission, *Communion and Stewardship*, 72.

[9] Pontifical Council for Culture and the Pontifical Council for Interreligious Dialogue, *Jesus Christ: The Bearer of the Water of Life, A Christian Reflection on the 'New Age'*, 2.3.4.1.

[10] John Paul II, *Address to participants in a convention on 'The Environment and Health'* (24 March 1997), 5.

[11] *CSDC*, 462.

[12] *CSDC*, 463.

13 *CSDC*, 459.
14 John Paul II, *Message for 1990 World Day of Peace*, 8.
15 *Ibid.*, 5.
16 Benedict XVI, *Inauguration Homily* (24 April 2005).
17 John XXIII, *Mater et Magistra*, 187.
18 Paul VI, *Populorum Progressio*, 37.
19 Benedict XVI, *Caritas in Veritate*, 44; cf. John Paul II, *Sollicitudo Rei Socialis*, 25.
20 John XXIII, *Mater et Magistra*, 189.
21 John Paul II, *Letter of His Holiness John Paul II to the Participants in the Fifth Christian-Muslim Colloquium* (20 April 1996).
22 John XXIII, *Mater et Magistra*, 190.
23 Paul VI, *Populorum Progressio*, 37.
24 *Ibid.*
25 Vatican II, *Gaudium et Spes*, 87.
26 Paul VI, *Populorum Progressio*, 37.
27 *CSDC*, 483.
28 John XXIII, *Mater et Magistra*, 199.
29 *CCC*, 2372.
30 Paul VI, *Populorum Progressio*, 37.
31 John Paul II, *Sollicitudo Rei Socialis*, 25.
32 John Paul II, *Centesimus Annus*, 37.
33 Vatican II, *Gaudium et Spes*, 12.
34 Benedict XVI, *Caritas in Veritate*, 51.

11

Liberation

In this chapter we shall briefly address the issue of freedom and liberation. It becomes a concern for Catholic social teaching because of two modern phenomena. On the one hand, there is Liberation Theology with its distinctive vision for revolution and political freedom and, on the other hand, there is individualism, which is an ideology or way of life built upon a misconception about the true character of personal freedom. Both, at least implicitly, propose a vision of society at odds with the one offered by social teaching.

A sign of the times: aspiration for liberty

There can be no doubt that the aspiration for freedom is a sign of the times and, in itself, a very positive sign. The root of this aspiration is deep within man, since, as a rational creature, he is self-determining. Therefore, the desire for freedom is innate and can never be totally extinguished.

The reason why this aspiration has, in the modern era, taken on a widespread public expression is perhaps more complex. One factor may be that the scientific revolution has gradually given man more and more power over nature and in this respect seemingly opened up the possibility for man to free himself from poverty and from the ravages of natural disasters. Somewhat historically coinciding with this scientific revolution has been the realization of certain political and social freedoms. This includes such things as wider access to education and healthcare, the abolition of slavery, broader participation of citizens (both men and women) in decision-making, and the rejection of racism. In this regard, the Congregation for the Doctrine of the Faith can say that 'by comparison with previous systems of domination, the advances of freedom and equality in many societies are undeniable.'[1]

The advent and increase in the influence of the mass media has also contributed to the aspiration for freedom principally by making those who are oppressed and poor aware of the liberties and prosperity enjoyed by others, thereby igniting in them a desire to share in these blessings. Oppressive regimes find it increasingly hard both to hide their activities from the world, and to prevent their own citizens from becoming aware of the liberties enjoyed in other countries.

Along with these factors, and in a sense before them in importance, is the influence of Christianity. It seems most true to say that 'the question for liberation and the aspiration to liberation, which are among the principle signs of the times in the modern world, have their first source in the Christian heritage.'[2] Christianity proclaims man created in the image of God and, therefore, supremely promotes his dignity. Moreover, it preaches Christ the Redeemer, the Liberator of mankind from the bond of slavery to sin and to the Devil. It takes to itself the Jewish Holy Scriptures that are full of the stories of Yahweh, the God who comes to the aid of the poor and downtrodden, leading them out of the slavery of Egypt and then Babylon.

It is precisely because of Her unique vision of the dignity of mankind that the Church commends the modern aspiration for freedom and, indeed, the achievement of some significant freedoms. However, it is clear that for many the aspirations of freedom have not been achieved, since countless people still languish in poverty and are oppressed. Moreover, new forms of servitude have arisen to replace those that have been vanquished. For example, while technology has made impressive contributions to the liberating of people from grinding poverty, in more recent times it has, in some sense, turned back on man and now threatens him, for example by way of nuclear or chemical warfare, terrorism, and the technological manipulation of human life at its conception. What greater servitude can be imagined than the phenomenon of frozen human embryos? In his inaugural encyclical, *Redemptor Hominis*, John Paul II expresses all of this when he says:

> The man of today seems ever to be under threat from what he produces, that is to say from the result of the work of his hands and, even more so, of the work of his intellect and the tendencies of his will. All too soon, and often in an unforeseeable way, what this manifold activity of man yields is not only subjected to 'alienation,' in the sense that it is simply taken away from the person who produces it, but rather it turns against man himself, at least in part, through the indirect consequences of its effects returning on himself. It is or can be directed against him. This seems to make up the main chapter of the drama of present-day human existence in its broadest and universal dimension.[3]

Hand-in-hand with the threat of technology divorced from moral constraint, there is the prevalence of individualism, which locks people into lives of loneliness and brings poverty on others by depriving them of their share in the common resources of creation. Or, again, what are we to make of the rise of totalitarian political regimes, notably those of Nazism and Communism? How did these oppressive regimes arise within a century marked by the aspiration for freedom? Certainly, they owe something of their existence to technology that allowed the State to gain such pervasive influence over its citizens, but they owe more to a corruption of the notion of freedom itself. It is this perversion of the notion of freedom that we must now consider more closely with regard to individualism and Liberation Theology.

Individualism

Writing as the Prefect for the Congregation for the Doctrine of the Faith, Cardinal Ratzinger suggests that the likely answer of the modern man to the question 'what does being free mean' would be 'a person is free when he is able to do whatever he wishes without being hindered by an exterior constraint and ...[he] enjoys complete independence.' Of course, taken in this way, other people—and especially the family and the Church (and ultimately even God Himself)—will always appear as a potential threat to freedom. The net result is that man comes to see 'atheism as the true form of emancipation and of man's liberation, whereas religion or even the recognition of the moral law constitute forms of alienation.'[4]

The main problem with this answer to the question about freedom is that it does not conform to the truth of what it means to be human. To be human—to experience fulfilment—a person needs to be in relationships with others and ultimately with God. Cutting oneself off from the will of others is not a recipe for happiness, but rather for isolation and depression. Making freedom (especially this perverted understanding of freedom) the goal in life is to put the cart before the horse, because true freedom is not a goal in itself but an opportunity to enter into truthful and respectful relationships with others:

> Far from being achieved in total self-sufficiency and an absence of relationships, freedom only truly exists where reciprocal bonds, governed by truth and justice, link people to one another. But for such bonds to be possible, each person must live in the truth. Freedom is not the liberty to do anything whatsoever. It is the freedom to do good, and in this alone happiness is to be found.[5]

All this means that true freedom is liberation from egocentricity. Now, since it is sin that lies at the root of self-centeredness and prevents us from flourishing as human beings, the most radical liberation is freedom from the power of sin over us, a liberation achieved by the great liberator of mankind, Jesus Christ.

From what we have said, it should be clear that social teaching in no sense rejects the contribution of technology and political movements towards freedom. It encourages these, but warns that there will be no authentic liberation unless the real meaning and depth of liberation is appreciated. The inability of technology and politics to deliver the freedom they seemed to promise, an inability all too evident today, is related precisely to this misconception of the meaning and value of freedom.

Finally, we should say a word about the relationship between freedom and a family-centred vision of society, in the light of the perception that institutions like the family undermine personal freedom. We have already noted that this is more than a theoretical discussion because in some countries the right of parents over their children has already been compromised, for example in the area of the parents' right to direct the education of their children. It is ironic that ignoring the parents in these ways is sometimes justified on the basis of promoting freedom—the freedom of the child. The truth is that an individualism that bypasses the family ultimately undermines freedom. When the family is bypassed, the result is one of two scenarios. Either society lapses into gross individualism which, since it is a recipe for isolation and lack of fulfilment, is the antithesis of freedom, or it tends towards a totalitarian collectivism. The reason for the latter is that when the family is removed, the bulwark against the potentially overreaching power of the State is done away with. Each individual then stands alone before the power of the State. When the family is bypassed, the State tends to step in to fill the vacuum of authority, and necessarily oversteps its legitimate authority. This undoubtedly happened in the Communist regimes of the twentieth century; in places, it seems to be happening in some Western countries in which the family is being bypassed.

Liberation Theology

To complete this consideration of 'liberty' we need to consider the phenomenon of Liberation Theology because, especially in Latin America, it has had a profound influence on the way many believers view society and social teaching. Liberation Theology can be defined as 'a theological reflection centred on the biblical theme of liberation and freedom, and on the urgency of its practical realization.'[6] This is only a very general definition, and there are many flavours of Liberation Theology. Not all, by any means, run contrary to the social teaching of the Church, and so we must be careful not to become nervous of the word 'liberation' as if it is synonymous with heterodoxy![7] It is perhaps more accurate to speak of liberation theologies.

Like many theological movements, its genesis is complex. It began after the Second Vatican Council and drew support from the second meeting of the South American Bishops' Conference (CELAM) in Medellín, Columbia, in 1968. This meeting produced a declaration on justice that was an authentic presentation of Catholic social thought, but some reflection that it inspired was not. The Peruvian priest Gustavo Gutiérez is often credited as the founder of Liberation Theology through his book *A Theology of Liberation: History, Politics, Salvation* published in 1972, though another South American theologian, the Brazilian Rubem Alves, who had penned a book called *Towards a Theology of Liberation* four years earlier, must also be credited as an important influence.

While Liberation Theology started in Latin America, its concern for the poor and oppressed had an immediate impact on the universal Church. The question of poverty and social justice was a central topic for the 1971 Synod of Bishops, which produced a document called *Justice in the World*, and the backdrop of Liberation Theology is clearly discernible in Paul VI's encyclical on evangelisation, *Evan-*

gelii Nuntiandi, the fruit of the 1974 Synod of Bishops. There he notes:

> The Church, as the bishops repeated, has the duty to proclaim the liberation of millions of human beings, many of whom are her own children—the duty of assisting the birth of this liberation, of giving witness to it, of ensuring that it is complete. This is not foreign to evangelisation.[8]

Yet, already clearly aware of the dangers of some forms of Liberation Theology, he goes on to say:

> We must not ignore the fact that many, even generous Christians who are sensitive to the dramatic questions involved in the problem of liberation, in their wish to commit the Church to the liberation effort are frequently tempted to reduce her mission to the dimensions of a simply temporal project. They would reduce her aims to a man-centred goal; the salvation of which she is the messenger would be reduced to material well-being. Her activity, forgetful of all spiritual and religious preoccupation, would become initiatives of the political or social order. But if this were so, the Church would lose her fundamental meaning. Her message of liberation would no longer have any originality and would easily be open to monopolization and manipulation by ideological systems and political parties.[9]

This statement from Pope Paul strikes at the heart of the issue. The main problem with heterodox liberation theologies is that they uncritically import some aspects of Marxism and, in so doing, foreshorten the Christian faith and impoverish the concept of freedom.

John Paul II was well aware of this danger, so when in 1979 the Latin American Bishops' conference met for the third time at Puebla, Mexico, he went there to address the Bishops. In a speech full of encouragement, he sounds the following warning about inadequate presentations of the mission of Jesus Christ and His Church:

> In other cases people purport to depict Jesus as a political activist, as a fighter against Roman domination and the authorities, and even as someone involved in the class struggle. This conception of Christ as a political figure, a revolutionary, as the subversive of Nazareth, does not tally with the Church's catechesis.[10]

The category of 'class struggle' is one of the Marxist imports that causes particular concern. In Marxist theory, class struggle is seen as a law of history in which the rich necessarily oppress the poor until the moment of revolution where the relation of domination is reversed.[11] Whatever action contributes to this reversal—this liberation—is morally acceptable. In this way, praxis does not follow on from morality, but rather creates morality![12] Since, according to this vision of reality and history, revolution is necessary, there is little appetite for reform. Indeed, the reform proposed by social teaching can end up being seen as stalling the moment of revolution and, therefore, as something negative.[13] In contrast, as we have seen, the Church is always nervous about revolutions—though they are not absolutely excluded as a way to remove a seriously unjust regime—because revolutions often entail violence and disruption that bears most heavily on the poor and involves serious violations of human rights:

> [T]hose who discredit the path of reform and favour the myth of revolution not only foster the illusion that the abolition of an evil situation is in itself sufficient to create a more humane society; they also encourage the setting up of totalitarian regimes. The fight against injustice is meaningless unless it is waged with a view to establishing a new social and political order in conformity with the demands of justice. Justice must already mark each stage of the establishment of this new order.[14]

Note that it is said to be an illusion that the 'abolition of an evil situation is in itself sufficient to create a more humane society.' The point is that Marxism (and materialistic ideologies in general) place greater emphasis on changing systems than on changing hearts, because they put the material before the spiritual. But the truth is that structures of sin will not be effectively dismantled until sin has been dealt with personally, in the heart of each individual:

> The acute need for radical reforms of the structures which conceal poverty and which are themselves forms of violence should not let us lose sight of the fact that the source of injustice is in the hearts of men. Therefore, it is only by making an appeal to the 'moral potential' of the person and to the constant need for interior conversion, that social change will be brought about which will be truly in the service of man.[15]

Since Marxism is avowedly atheist, the adoption of its world view also has a profound and perverse affect of the way Christian faith is understood.[16] Christ loses His divinity and is reduced to the status of a human revolutionary. The Kingdom of God likewise loses its supernatural character and is equated with the establishment of the rule of the proletariat. The Church is subjected to the analysis of class struggle, with the hierarchy being viewed as decidedly bourgeoisie. The Sacraments, especially the Eucharist, tend to lose their supernatural character and become celebrations of class solidarity. The Scriptures are similarly interpreted in a new way: John Paul II speaks of '"re-readings" of the Gospel that are the product of theoretical speculations rather than of authentic meditation on the word of God.'[17] The book of Exodus, in particular, is seen as a story of political liberation, despite the fact that the Israelites were led to freedom for the sake of entering into a covenant with God. Evangelisation takes a back seat or is interpreted to mean spreading the aspiration for political liberation.

As we have said before, the critique offered here by the Magisterium of the Church is not aimed at all theologies of liberation but only some. Moreover, any criticism of liberation theology should in no sense be taken as support or comfort for those who do oppress the poor. The problem of oppression is real; the point is that not all solutions are thereby acceptable, just as not every treatment brings health.

Finally, it is worth pointing out that individualism and Liberation Theology are united in a fundamental misconception about freedom. Freedom is seen as only (or at least overwhelmingly) about throwing off the shackles of external constraints and oppression. The interior dimension of freedom is then more or less overlooked. The greatest threats to freedom are, as we have seen, sin and the divorce of freedom from the truth. Sin cripples a person's interior freedom because it makes him a slave to his disordered desires. Freedom cut loose from the truth heads in the same direction. It makes of every man his own god, the arbitrator of good and evil, truth and falsehood. It this way, selfishness is reinforced and interior freedom crippled.

Notes

[1] Congregation for the Doctrine of the Faith, *Instruction on Christian Freedom and Liberation*, 8.

[2] Ibid., 5.

[3] John Paul II, *Redemptor Hominis*, 15.

[4] Congregation for the Doctrine of the Faith, *Instruction on Christian Freedom and Liberation*, 41.

[5] Ibid., 26.

[6] Congregation for the Doctrine of the Faith, *Instruction on Certain Aspects of the 'Theology of Liberation'*, III.4.

[7] Ibid., VI.8.

[8] Paul VI, *Evangelii Nuntiandi*, 29.

[9] Ibid., 32.

[10] John Paul II, *Opening Address at the Puebla Conference* (28 January 1979), I-4.

[11] Congregation for the Doctrine of the Faith, *Instruction on Certain Aspects of the 'Theology of Liberation'*, VIII.6.

12 *Ibid.*, VIII.7.
13 *Ibid.*, X.4.
14 Congregation for the Doctrine of the Faith, *Instruction on Christian Freedom and Liberation*, 78.
15 See, Congregation for the Doctrine of the Faith, *Instruction on Certain Aspects of the 'Theology of Liberation'*, XI.8.
16 See *Ibid.*, IX.1–13.
17 John Paul II, *Opening Address at the Puebla Conference* (28 January 1979), I-4.

Conclusion

In her social doctrine, the immediate purpose of the Church is to 'propose the principles and values that can sustain a society worthy of the human person.'[1] On the basis of these principles and values, there has been built, in the words of John Paul II, 'a *corpus* which enables her [the Church] to analyze social realities, to make judgments about them and to indicate directions to be taken for the just resolution of the problems involved.'[2] The aim of this book has been to present clearly, concisely, and faithfully this corpus as it comes to us from the Church.

In doing so, I have endeavoured to respond to the desire of the same Magisterium that the social doctrine of the Church would be more widely known. There are two groups of people which, in particular, need to be well-informed in this area. These are, on the one hand, priests and seminarians whose task it is (or will be) to instruct the faithful at the grassroots. On the other hand, there is the laity. In virtue of their particular vocation, the laity have a special obligation—and therefore right—to be instructed and formed in social teaching. They are called to be the 'leaven' of society and to conform the secular world to the values of the Gospel; something they cannot hope to do without knowing the Church's social teaching:

> [T]he laity, by their very vocation, seek the kingdom of God by engaging in temporal affairs and by ordering them according to the plan of God. They live in the world, that is, in each and in all of the secular professions and occupations. They live in the ordinary circumstances of family and social life, from which the very web of their existence is woven. They are called there by God that by exercising their

proper function and led by the spirit of the Gospel they may work for the sanctification of the world from within as a leaven.[3]

In his 'Post-Synodal Apostolic Exhortation on the Vocation and Mission of the Lay Faithful in the World and in the Church,' *Christifideles Laici*, speaking about the formation of the laity, John Paul II says that 'it is indispensable that they have a more exact knowledge—and this demands a more widespread and precise presentation—of the Church's social doctrine, as repeatedly stressed by the Synod Fathers in their presentations.' However, the Compendium, issued seventeen years after the 1987 Bishops' Synod on the laity, laments that this formation has mostly not been achieved. It says that 'this doctrinal patrimony is neither taught nor known sufficiently, which is part of the reason for its failure to be suitably reflected in concrete behaviour.'[4]

The Compendium emphasizes that this formation must include some familiarity with the main documents of the social teaching. It says that 'direct contact with the texts of the social encyclicals, read within an ecclesial context, enriches its reception and application.'[5] Therefore, this book is not offered as a replacement for such 'direct contact' but more to give the 'ecclesial context,' that is, help understand what the Church is saying in these documents.

Of all the social encyclicals to date, I would suggest the following as the most important for a lay person to have read: *Immortale Dei, Rerum Novarum, Quadragesimo Anno, Mater et Magistra, Pacem in Terris, Populorum Progressio, Laborem Exercens, Centesimus Annus* and *Caritas in Veritate*. If a person can only manage three then I would suggest he read *Rerum Novarum, Quadragesimo Anno,* and *Centesimus Annus*. Another way to have a kind of 'direct contact' with the encyclicals is to read a document from The Pontifical Council for Justice and Peace called *The Social Agenda*, which is a collection of quotations from social encyclicals arranged thematically. The Compendium and to a lesser extent the

Conclusion

Catechism (§1877-1948) are important resources of social teaching, since they offer good summaries, by they do not really represent 'direct contact' with the sources of the teaching.

Of course, knowing the teaching is only the first step! There is the corresponding call to action. Several points seem important here. First, the laity is called upon to take the initiative especially in regard to the implementation of social teaching. It is part of their vocation and mission and they do not need to wait for a further commissioning or encouragement from the authorities of the Church. They already have it! Vatican II tells us:

> Since the laity, in accordance with their state of life, live in the midst of the world and its concerns, they are called by God to exercise their apostolate in the world like leaven, with the ardour of the spirit of Christ ... The laity derive the right and duty to the apostolate from their union with Christ the head; incorporated into Christ's Mystical Body through Baptism and strengthened by the power of the Holy Spirit through Confirmation, they are assigned to the apostolate by the Lord Himself.[6]

Paul VI reiterates this in *Populorum Progressio* when he says that 'it belongs to the layman, without waiting passively for orders and directives, to take the initiative freely and to infuse a Christian spirit into the mentality, customs, laws and structures of the community in which they live.'[7] Of course, this does not mean that a lay person should ignore his parish priest and more importantly his bishop when they give advice or direction in conformity with the teaching of the Church, but they should not wait for either to take the initiative; the mission has already been given.

Second, in this call to action, there are two levels in which social teaching must be implemented. The first level is the implementation of social teaching in one's daily life according to the circumstances that we find ourselves in. This will mean one thing for a housewife looking after a home and another for the CEO looking after a large company, but nonetheless they are the same principles and values that need to be incarnated. The second level is becoming a protagonist—one might say an activist—in society. The lay faithful must be ready to exercise political power, whether this is simply by voting, or by lobbying, or even by being an elected representative. In each case, the aim is to infuse the social and political order with the values of the Gospel.[8]

* * *

This, then, is the final goal of social teaching: that society would be conformed to the values of the Gospel of Jesus Christ. In presenting this lofty goal to us, the Church, I believe, has consistently taught that there is only one way to achieve it. It claims that the solution to social problems, such as development and the environment, lies not so much in a structural reformation of society as in a moral and spiritual reformation. This is the golden thread that weaves its way from *Rerum Novarum* to *Caritas in Veritate*. Already in 1891, Pope Leo saw this truth in all its clarity:

> Those who rule the commonwealths should avail themselves of the laws and institutions of the country; masters and wealthy owners must be mindful of their duty; the working class, whose interests are at stake, should make every lawful and proper effort; and since religion alone, as We said at the beginning [of the encyclical], can avail to destroy the evil at its root, all men should rest persuaded that the main thing needful is to re-establish Christian morals, apart from which all the plans and devices of the wisest will prove of little avail.[9]

More than one hundred years later, in 2009, on the eve of the promulgation of his encyclical *Caritas in Veritate*, Pope Benedict reiterated the same sentiment when he said that:

> [T]he world cannot be renewed without new people. Only if there are new people will there also be a new world, a renewed and better world. In the beginning

is the renewal of the human being ... only if we ourselves become new does the world become new.[10]

The point is luminous and incisive. Disorder in society flows from disorder in the hearts of individuals. Vatican II tells us that it is from the 'internal divisions' in individuals that there flows 'so many and such great discords in society.'[11] Underdevelopment, environmental degradation, disregard for human rights, inhuman working conditions and pay; all these things come ultimately from selfishness. This being so, only personal conversion can establish a new social order.[12] Ultimately, this is why social teaching has its proper place only within the evangelical mission of the Church, because it is almost pointless to tell people—however right the message might be—how they should live, without giving them the power to change their lives and, by this, change society also; and this power comes only from Jesus Christ:

> The Church is conscious of being the bearer of the powerful word of God, the word that created the universe and which is able to recreate in the human heart and in society, at all its many levels, attitudes and conditions in which it is possible to bring about the civilization of love.[13]

Notes

1. *CSDC*, 580.
2. John Paul II, *Centesimus Annus*, 5.
3. Vatican II, *Lumen Gentium*, 31.
4. *CSDC*, 528.
5. *CSDC*, 529.
6. Vatican II, *Apostolicam Actuositatem*, 2-3.
7. Paul VI, *Populorum Progressio*, 81.
8. *CSDC*, 531.

9   Leo XIII, *Rerum Novarum*, 62.
10 Benedict XVI, *Homily at Vespers for Feast of Ss. Peter and Paul* (28 June 2009).
11 Vatican II, *Gaudium et Spes*, 10.
12 Cf. Leo XIII, *Rerum Novarum*, 62; Pius XI, *Quadragesimo Anno*, 127–137; John XXIII, *Mater et Magistra*, 212–257.
13 John Paul II, *Address to the Latin American Bishops' Conference, Puebla* (2 July 1980).

Bibliography

Cassidy, Eoin, G., (editor), *The Common Good in an Unequal World*. Dublin: Veritas, 2007.

Caldecott, Stratford, *Catholic Social Teaching: A Way In*. London: Catholic Truth Society, 2001.

Charles, Rodger, *An Introduction to Catholic Social Teaching*. Oxford: Family Publications, 1999.

Charles, Rodger, *Christian Social Witness and Teaching: Catholic Tradition from Genesis to Centesimus Annus: volume 1, From Biblical Times to the Late Nineteenth Century*. Leominister: Gracewing, 1998.

Charles, Rodger, *Christian Social Witness and Teaching: Catholic Tradition from Genesis to Centesimus Annus: volume 2, The Modern Social Teaching*. Leominister: Gracewing, 1998.

Charles, Rodger, *The Social Teaching of Vatican II*. San Francisco: Ignatius Press, 1982.

Coulter, Michael L., Stephen M. Krason, Richard S. Myers, and Joseph A. Varacalli (editors), *Encyclopedia of Catholic Social Thought, Social Science, and Social Policy*. Lanham MD: Scarecrow Press, 2007.

Curran, Charles, *Catholic Social Teaching 1891–Present: A Historical, Theological and Ethical Analysis*. Washington D.C.: Georgetown University Press, 2002.

Deberri, Edward P., James E. Hug, Peter J. Henriot, and Michael J. Schultheis, *Catholic Social Teaching: Our Best Kept Secret*. New York: Orbis, 1992.

De Salins, Antoine and Villeroy De Galhau, François, *The Modern Development of Financial Activities in the Light of the Ethical Demands of Christianity*. Vatican City: Libreria Editrice Vaticana, 1994.

Dorr, Donal, *Option for the Poor: A Hundred Years of Catholic Social Teaching*. New York: Orbis, 1992.

Dwyer, Judith A. (editor), *The New Dictionary of Catholic Social Thought*. Collegeville: The Liturgical Press, 1994.

Filibeck, Giorgio, *Human Rights in the Teaching of the Church: from John XXIII to John Paul II*. Vatican City: Libreria Editrice Vaticana, 1994.

Fimister, Alan, *Robert Schuman: Neo Scholastic Humanism and the Reunification of Europe*. Brussels: Peter Lang, 2008.

Gilson, Etienne (editor), *The Church Speaks to the Modern World: The Social Teaching of Leo XIII*. New York: Image Books, 1954.

Hadas, Edward, *The Credit Crunch: Making Moral Sense of the Financial Crisis*. London: Catholic Truth Society, 2009.

Haffner, Paul, *Towards a Theology of the Environment*. Leominster: Gracewing, 2008.

Harrison, Brian, *Religious Liberty and Contraception*. Melbourne: John XXIII Fellowship, 1988.

Herr, Theodore, *Catholic Social Teaching: A Textbook of Christian Insights*. London: New City, 1991.

Higgins, Thomas, *Man as Man*. Rockford: Tan Books, 1992.

Himes, Kenneth, R., (editor), *Modern Catholic Social Teaching: Commentaries and Interpretations*. Washington D.C.: Georgetown University Press, 2004.

Himes, Kenneth, R., *Reponses to 101 Questions on Catholic Social Teaching*. New York: Paulist Press, 2001.

Holland, Joe, *Modern Catholic Social Teaching: The Popes Confront the Industrial Age 1740–1958*. New York: Paulist Press, 2003.

Jones, David Albert, *Living Life to the Full: An Introduction to the Moral and Social Teaching of the Catholic Church*. Oxford: Family Publications, 2001.

May, William, *An Introduction to Moral Theology*. Huntington, IN: Our Sunday Visitor Publishing, 2003.

Massaro, Thomas, *Living Justice*. Franklin, Wisconsin: Sheed and Ward, 2000.

Mofid, Kamran, *Globalization for the Common Good*. London: Shepheard–Walwyn, 2002.

O'Brien, David, J., and Thomas A. Shannon, *Catholic Documents on Peace, Justice, and Liberation*. New York: Image Books, 1977.

Pontifical Council for the Family and The Acton Institute for the Study of Religion and Liberty, *Globalization, Economics, and the Family*. Vatican City: Libreria Editrice Vaticana, 2001.

Pontifical Council for Justice and Peace, *Compendium of the Social Doctrine of the Church*. Vatican City: Libreria Editrice Vaticana, 2004.

Pontifical Council for Justice and Peace, *From Stockholm to Johannesburg: An Historical Overview of the Concern of the Holy See for the Environment 1972 – 2002*. Vatican City: Libreria Editrice Vaticana, 2002.

Pontifical Council for Justice and Peace, *Towards a Better Distribution of Land: The Challenge of Agrarian Reform*. Vatican City: Libreria Editrice Vaticana, 1997.

Pontifical Council for Justice and Peace, *Work as the Key to the Social Question*. Vatican City: Libreria Editrice Vaticana, 2002.

Pontifical Council for Justice and Peace, *World Development and Economic Institutions*. Vatican City: Libreria Editrice Vaticana, 1994.

Ratzinger, Joseph, *Turning Point for Europe*. San Francisco: Ignatius Press, 1991.

Ratzinger, Joseph, *Church, Ecumenism and Politics: New Endeavors in Ecclesiology*. San Francisco: Ignatius Press, 2008.

Rourke, Thomas, R., *Democracy and Tyranny: The Catholic Understanding of the State and Politics*. London: Catholic Truth Society, 2009.

Scruton, Roger, *The West and the Rest: Globalization and the Terrorist Threat*. London: Continuum, 2002.

Shaw, Russell, *Ministry or Apostolate?* Huntington, IN: Our Sunday Visitor, 2002.

Sheed, Frank, *Society and Sanity*. London: Sheed and Ward, 1957.

Tierney, Brian, *The Crisis of Church and State 1050–1300*. Toronto: University of Toronto Press, 1964.

Weigel, George and Robert Royal (editors), *A Century of Catholic Social Thought: Essays on 'Rerum Novarum' and Nine Other Key Documents*. Washington D.C.: Ethics and Public Policy Center, 1991.

Whitehead, Kenneth D., (editor), *Marriage and the Common Good*. South Bend: St Augustine's Press, 2001.

Williams, Thomas D., *Who Is My Neighbour: Personalism and the Foundations of Human Rights*. Washington, D.C.: The Catholic University of America Press, 2005.

Wyszynski, Stefan, *All You Who Labor: Work and the Sanctification of Daily Life*. Manchester NH: Sophia Institute Press, 1994.

Index

Abortion, 8, 58, 69–70, 123, 141, 143, 145–147, 158–159, 166, 177, 192–193, 226, 228.
Ad Gentes (Vatican II), 174.
Advertising, 111, 130.
Alves, Rubem, 236.
Anarchy, 153.
Anastasius I, Byzantine Emperor, 161.
Animals,
    animal rights, 220, 229.
    different from man, 24, 27, 31, 45, 155, 176.
    experimentation on, 220, 229.
    man's dominion over, 218.
Apartheid, 25, 50.
Apostolicam Actuositatem (Vatican II), 57, 80, 174, 247.
Aquinas, St. Thomas, 14, 33, 83, 134, 152–153, 172, 205, 214.
Aristocracy, 151–153.
Atheism, 128, 169, 234, 239.
Augustine, St., 141, 172, 201, 214.
Au Milieu des Sollicitudes (Leo XIII), 153, 172.
Autonomy of earthly affairs, 6, 108.

Benedict XIV, Pope, 131.

Benedict XVI, Pope, 14–17, 41–43, 51, 54–55, 69, 71, 81, 82, 104, 107, 110, 113, 115, 123, 125–132, 138, 150, 165–166, 172, 174, 179–180, 182, 191, 199, 202, 214–215, 217, 222, 224, 227–228, 230, 246, 248.
Boniface VIII, Pope, 173.
Bureaucracy, 39, 114–115.

Capitalism, 2, 95, 115, 119.
    errors of laissez–faire capitalism, 28, 108, 110, 120.
    relationship of labour to capital, 91–93.
Caritas in Veritate (Benedict XVI), xii, 2, 15–16, 42, 51, 54–55, 82, 104, 107, 110, 112–113, 123, 125–126, 129–132, 172, 179–180, 182, 191, 199, 202, 214, 217, 224, 228, 230, 244, 246.
Catechism of the Catholic Church, 21, 23–24, 65, 87, 101, 114, 148, 150, 156, 185, 209, 218, 245.
Catholic Action, 13.
CELAM (South American Bishops' Conference), 15, 236.
    Meeting at Medellín (Columbia, 1968), 15.

Meeting at Puebla (Mexico, 1979), 15, 237, 240–241, 248.

Centesimus Annus (John Paul II), xiv–xv, 2, 14–16, 18, 45, 53–55, 119–120, 130–131, 173, 178, 182, 196, 200, 230, 244, 247.

Centrally planned economies, 113–115, 120.

Charity, 10, 29, 35, 41, 43, 49–51, 54, 65, 127, 181, 204–206.

Charles, Rodger, 18.

Charter of the Rights of the Family (The Pontifical Council for the Family), 80–81.

Children, 4–5, 22, 62, 77–80, 89, 99, 124, 176, 178, 194, 226, 235, 237.
  and de facto unions, 73–77.
  and education by parents, 38, 62, 65–73.
  parental authority over, 57–59, 201–202.
  United Nations' Convention on the Rights of the Child, 70–72.

Christifideles Laici (John Paul II), 12, 17, 244.

Church and state relations, 161–167, 173.
  disestablishment of the Church, 166–167.

Civilization of love, xiii–xv, 49, 247.

Class struggle, 36, 46, 99, 101–102, 238–239.

Code of Canon Law (1983), 17, 82.

Cohabitation, 63, 76–77.
  see also, De facto unions.

Collectivism, 22, 57, 235.

Colonialism, 128.

Common good, 3, 10, 15, 22, 37, 43, 47–48, 52, 54, 88, 91, 94, 97–98, 110–111, 115, 127, 138, 144, 148, 159, 171, 198, 204, 208, 218, 225, 227.
  and democracy, 155–157.
  and human rights, 180–181.
  and private property, 33.
  and religious freedom, 168–169.
  and the family, 69, 61, 64–65, 70, 74–77, 79.
  and the International Community, 185, 187–189.
  and the Universal Destination of Goods, 31.
  as limiting the right to strike, 101–102.
  as the purpose of the political community, 134–136, 153–155.
  definition of, 26–29.
  duty of the State to promote, 120–122.
  relation to option for the poor, 34.
  relation to solidarity, 40–42.
  relation to subsidiarity, 39–40.

Communism, xiii, 16, 28, 57, 119, 167, 233, 235.
  and private property, 32.
  and religious liberty, 134, 170.

254

example of centrally planned economy, 95, 113.
  failure of, 114.
Compendium of the Social Doctrine of the Church (Pontifical Council for Justice and Peace), xii–xiii, 15, 22, 49, 59–60, 62, 70, 88, 106, 108, 124, 126, 139, 145, 188, 217, 244.
Congregation for the Doctrine of the Faith, 15, 17, 52–54, 82–83, 96, 104, 173, 182, 232, 234, 240–241.
Conscientious objection, 147, 209.
Consumerism, xiii, 4, 20, 111, 123–124, 128, 227.
Contraception, 192.
Corporatism, 94.
  see also, Occupational Groupings.
Cosmocentricism, 221.
Criminals, 11, 50, 148–149.

David, King of Israel, 133.
Deberri, Edward, xv.
Decalogue, see Ten Commandments.
De facto unions, 16, 63, 73–77, 82–83.
Dei Verbum (Vatican II), 16.
Democracy, 14, 40, 54, 69–70, 137, 151–160, 171–173.
Demography, 194, 223.
Dies Domini (John Paul II), 86, 103.

Dignitatis Humanae (Vatican II), 14, 17, 164, 167–169, 173–174.
Disabled persons, 22.
Disarmament, 211–212.
Dissent, 9.
Diuturnum Illud (Leo XIII), 14, 138–139, 171–172.
Dives in Misericordia (John Paul II), 49, 55, 182, 200.
Divine right of kings, 140.
Divini Illius Magistri (Pius XI), 81.
Divini Redemptoris (Pius XI), 14, 48, 55.
Divorce, 25, 45–46, 63, 75, 240.
Donum Vitae (Congregation for the Doctrine of the Faith), 82.
Dulles, Avery, 17.
Duo Sunt (Gelasius I), 161.

Ecclesia in America (John Paul II), 16, 173.
Ecumenism, 174.
Education, 24, 27, 38, 58, 89, 100, 117, 121, 187, 204, 225, 228, 231, 235.
  as a human right, 178, 180–181.
  educating laity about social teaching, 243–244.
  primary role of family, 60, 62–63, 65–68, 71–74, 80–81.
  sex education, 58, 68.
Emigration, 115.
Equality, 35, 42, 159, 232.
  between nations, 127, 186–187, 195.

between races, 175.
inequality between marriage and de facto unions, 74.
of all persons, 3, 21–22.
of sexes, 23.
reasonable inequality in wealth, 30, 114–115.
Eusebius of Caesarea, 171.
Euthanasia, 51, 179, 228.
Evangelii Nuntiandi (Paul VI), 237, 240.
Evangelisation, 13, 66, 236–237, 239.
Evangelium Vitae (John Paul II), 17, 55, 69, 82–83, 147, 149, 172–173.

Fair trade, 51, 196.
Familiaris Consortio (John Paul II), 58, 62, 67, 80–82.
Family, 16, 22, 32, 37, 201, 206, 234–235.
   and the agencies of the United Nations, 191–195.
   contribution of family to society, 61–72.
   duty of State towards the family, 72–80.
   family planning, 64–65, 193, 226.
   right to found a family, 3.
Family wage, 78–80.
Fidei Catholicae (Council of Vienne), 52.
Fornication, 75, 78.
Free trade, 29, 124, 195–197.

Gaudium et Spes (Vatican II), 6–7, 14, 16, 28, 52–53, 55, 104, 125, 130, 150, 164, 170–174, 182, 199, 209, 211, 215, 222, 229–230, 248.
Gelasius I, Pope, 161.
Gender, 195, 199.
Globalization, 13, 47, 54, 93, 100, 111, 123–129, 131–132, 186, 197, 229.
Gravissimum Educationis, Declaration on Christian Education (Vatican II), 81.
Guilds, 95.
Gutiérez, Gustavo, 236.

Haakon VII, King of Norway, 152.
Haffner, Paul, 173, 229.
Healthcare, 72, 80, 116, 159, 180, 187, 228, 231.
Henriot, Peter, xv.
Higgins, Thomas, 171.
Holy See, 71, 151, 199, 207, 212, 215.
   and the United Nations, 194–195.
   relation to the International Community, 190–191.
Homosexuality, 63, 73–77, 82–83, 180, 195.
Hospitals, 27–28, 146.
Hug, James, xv.
Human dignity, 7, 95, 159, 177, 183, 225.
   and creation in God's image, 22.
   and prohibition on torture, 149–150.
   and religious liberty, 168.

and the International Community, 183.
  relation to human rights, 177.
Human embryos, 166, 228, 233.

Immortale Dei (Leo XIII), 14, 162, 169, 171, 173, 244.
Imprisonment, 149, 181.
  unjust imprisonment, 144–145, 177.
Individualism, 79, 121, 157, 194.
  as contrary to a correct notion of freedom, 231, 233–234, 235, 240.
  as contrary to the common good, 22, 28.
  as harmful to the family, 57.
Inflation, 97, 102.
Instruction on certain aspects of the 'Theology of Liberation', *Libertatis nuntius*, 1984 (Congregation for the Doctrine of the Faith), 15.
Instruction on Christian freedom and liberation, *Libertatis conscientia*, 1986 (Congregation for the Doctrine of the Faith), 15, 82, 104.
International Planned Parenthood, 194.
International Theological Commission, 217, 229.
Internet, 157.
Interreligious dialogue, 6.
Islam, xiii, 128, 161.

Jesus Christ, 4–8, 12, 14, 16, 26, 35, 42, 87–88, 106, 133–134, 137, 150, 160–163, 165, 168, 170, 176–177, 184, 203, 218, 229, 232, 235, 237–239, 245–247.
John XXIII, Pope, xi, 14, 17, 19, 31–32, 35, 43, 52–54, 97, 104, 135, 141, 156, 171–173, 175–177, 179–180, 182, 187, 199, 201, 203, 207, 214–215, 223–224, 226, 230, 248.
John Paul II, Pope, xiv–xv, 1–2, 8, 10, 12–18, 20, 25, 29, 32, 34–35, 39, 41–42, 45–47, 49–50, 52–55, 58–59, 62–64, 67, 69, 71, 78–83, 85–86, 89–90, 92–94, 96, 99–100, 102–104, 106–107, 112, 114–116, 119–120, 123–126, 128–132, 134, 147, 149–150, 157, 172–173, 175, 178, 181–183, 189, 192–193, 196–200, 202–204, 210, 212, 214–215, 217, 222, 225, 227, 229–230, 233, 237, 239–241, 243–244, 247–248.
Jubilee, 134, 198.
Justice, 3, 7, 24, 29, 43, 65, 68–69, 98, 100, 117, 123, 133, 149, 175, 207, 234.
  and a just wage, 96–97.
  and Liberation Theology, 236, 238.
  and the family wage, 80.
  and the ownership of private property, 35–37.
  as a key value of social teaching, 46–49.
  between rich and poor countries, 196–198.

of giving marriage a privileged place in society, 74, 76–77.
relation to mercy, 49–51, 181.
relation to peace, 204–205.
types of justice,
commutative justice, 37, 47–48, 65, 80.
distributive justice, 47–48, 65.
general justice, 48, 65.
social justice, 48, 80, 98, 100, 236.
Just wage, 90, 96–97, 111.
see also, Family wage.

Laborem Exercens (John Paul II), 15, 29, 52–53, 78, 83, 85, 90, 92, 94, 103–104, 244.
Labour and capital (relationship of), 90–91, 119, 124.
Laity, 57.
and their special responsibility for social teaching, 12–13, 243–245.
role in evangelization, 170.
Leo XIII, Pope, 2, 10, 13–14, 17, 30, 33, 35, 46, 53, 76, 78, 83, 85, 91, 96, 98–100, 103–104, 113, 120, 130, 138–139, 144–145, 153–154, 162–164, 169, 171–173, 175, 246, 248.
Letter to Families, *Gratissimam Sane* (John Paul II), 55, 62–64, 81, 83.
Liberation Theology, 233, 236–239.
and the preferential option for the poor, 35–36.
see also, Instruction on certain aspects of the 'Theology of Liberation', *Libertatis nuntius*.
Libertas Praestantissimum (Leo XIII), 14, 46, 53, 76, 83, 163, 169, 173, 14, 46, 77, 83, 163, 169.
Lumen Gentium (Vatican II), 12, 17, 184, 199, 247.

Magisterium, 8, 16–17, 36, 161, 239, 243.
Market based economies, 111, 113–116, 118–119, 122, 228.
Marriage, 16, 61–63, 66–76, 78, 124, 137, 179–180, 192–193, 195, 226.
Marxism, 2, 10, 20.
and private property, 30.
influence on Liberation Theology, 36, 237–239.
relationship of labour and capital, 91–93.
Marx, Karl, 91, 93.
Mater et Magistra (John XXIII), 14, 17, 31, 52–54, 104, 199, 214, 223–224, 230, 244, 248.
Materialism, 44, 93, 123, 221, 223, 226, 239.
May, William, 17.
Media, 67, 117, 232.
see also, Press.
Mercy, 3, 49–51, 181, 197–198.
Minorities, 43, 70, 145, 158–159, 166.
right to nationhood, 135–136.
Mirari Vos (Gregory XVI), 14, 172.

Index

Monarchy, 151–155.
Mongella, Gertrude, 193, 199.
Monopolies, 39–40, 68, 110–111, 122.
Motherhood, 5, 49, 69, 71, 79, 90, 178, 194.
Multinationals, 89.

Napoleon I, Emperor of France, 154.
Nationalism, 46, 188.
Nationalization, 33, 93, 115.
Natural law, 5, 58, 80, 129, 189.
  and human rights, 179.
  and right to private property, 30.
  As foundation of democracy, 157, 160.
  as foundation of social teaching, 8–9.
  Church as interpreter of, 7, 166.
  definition of, 46–47.
Nazism, 134, 208, 233.
New age, 221, 229.
Nihilism, 214.
Notre Charge Apostolique (Pius X), 172.
Nuclear Deterrence, 211.

Occupational Groupings, 94–95.
  see also, Corporatism.
Octogesima Adveniens (Paul VI), 14–15, 101–102, 104, 182.

Pacem in Terris (John XXIII), xi, 14, 35, 43, 53–54, 125, 135, 171–173, 175–177, 182, 199, 201, 207, 214–215, 244.
Parents and parenthood, 4, 64, 72–74, 78, 80, 176, 183, 201–202.
  as primary educators of their children, 65–68, 71.
  God as author of parental authority, 137.
  right to determine family size, 9, 226.
  role usurped by the State, 31–32, 57–58, 71, 226, 235.
Participation, 40.
Paul VI, Pope, xiii–ix, xv, 7, 14–16, 29, 52–53, 55, 101–102, 104, 106–107, 129, 182, 195, 197, 199–200, 205–206, 214–215, 217, 223, 225–226, 230, 236, 240, 245, 247.
Paul, St., 50, 88, 218.
Persona Humana (Congregation for the Doctrine of the Faith), 83.
Peter, St., 14, 162, 248.
Phillip IV, King of France, 162.
Pius IX, Pope, 14, 17, 169, 172.
Pius X, Pope, 52, 172.
Pius XI, Pope, 13–14, 16–17, 37–38, 48, 53, 55, 59–60, 81, 83, 91, 94–95, 99, 103–104, 109–111, 130, 134, 171, 214, 248.
Pius XII, Pope, 13–14, 54, 135, 155–157, 160, 171–173, 206, 215.
Polygamy, 73, 168.

Pontifical Academy of Sciences, 229.
Pontifical Academy of Social Sciences, 131–132.
Pontifical Council for Interreligious Dialogue, 16, 229.
Pontifical Council for Justice and Peace, xii, 15, 53, 204, 215, 244.
Pontifical Council for the Family, 15, 76, 80–83, 194, 199.
Pontius Pilate, 133, 137.
Population, 192–193, 199, 224, 227.
Populorum Progressio (Paul VI), 7, 14, 16, 52–53, 106–107, 129, 199–200, 214, 230, 244–245, 247.
Pornography, 25, 141.
Poverty, 37, 49, 70, 125–127, 211, 213, 219, 231–233, 236, 239.
Preferential option for the poor, 34–36, 181, 197–198.
Press, 174, 181, 214.
see also, Media.
Priesthood, 161–162, 236, 245.
Private property, 3, 10, 30–33, 94, 115, 119, 121.
Procreation, 62, 64, 73–74, 226.
Profit, 14, 34, 91, 106, 111, 115–116, 119.
Punishment, 11, 86–87, 148–149.
capital punishment, 11, 149.
corporal punishment, 149.

Quadragesimo Anno (Pius XI), 13–14, 17, 38, 53, 83, 91–92, 94, 103–104, 109, 130, 205, 214, 244, 248.
Quanta Cura (Pius IX), 14, 17, 169, 172.
Quas Primas (Pius XI), 16, 171.
Quod Apostolici Muneris (Leo XIII), 145, 172.

Racism, 232.
Ratzinger, Jospeh, 71, 174, 234.
Rebellion, 86, 142, 144–145.
see also, Revolution.
Redemptor Hominis (John Paul II), 175, 181, 217, 229, 233, 240.
Redemptoris Missio (John Paul II), 16.
Redistribution of wealth, 36, 39, 79, 127–128.
Referendums, 151, 156.
Relativism, 44–45, 129, 158–159, 180, 189, 194.
Religious freedom, 88, 134, 165, 167–169, 171, 204.
Remuneration, 96–97.
Rerum Novarum (Leo XIII), 2, 10, 13–14, 17, 30, 33, 35, 46, 53–54, 83, 85, 91, 93, 98–99, 101, 103–104, 107, 120, 130, 175, 244, 246, 248.
Revelation, 2–3, 23, 47, 137, 176, 183, 218, 223.
Revolution, 96, 145, 154, 170, 212, 238.
see also, Rebellion.
Rousseau, Jean-Jacques, 171.
Sabbath, 87, 111.

Sacraments, 184, 203.
Sadik, Nafis, 192, 199.
Samuel, Prophet of Israel, 133.
Saul, King of Israel, 133.
Schools, 4, 38, 68, 165.
Schultheis, Michael, xv.
Schuman, Robert, 188.
Second Vatican Council, 7, 13, 28–29, 57, 167, 222, 236, 245, 247.
see also, *Ad Gentis, Apostolicam Actuositatem, Dei Verbum, Dignitatis Humanae, Gaudium et Spes, Gravissimum Educationis, Lumen Gentium.*
Secularism, 166, 169.
Self-defence, 9, 11, 136, 142, 144–145, 148–149, 187, 206–207, 209, 213.
Shaw, Russell, 17.
Sicut Dudum (Eugene IV), 14.
Sin, 17, 20, 24–26, 41, 76–77, 83, 138, 147, 183–184, 202–204, 223, 232, 234–235, 239–240.
structures of sin, 24–25, 41, 76, 202, 239.
Slavery, 14, 44, 232.
Smith, Adam, 108, 130.
Social contract theory, 140, 171.
Socialism, 20, 120, 134, 175.
Soldiers, 147, 209.
Solidarity, 3, 10, 21, 52, 54, 65, 69, 122–123, 126–128, 136, 157, 239.
and the environment, 222, 227.
and the International Community, 187–188.
and trade unions, 98–100.
definition of, 41–43.
relation to other principles of social teaching, 26, 40, 120–121.
sin as the antithesis to solidarity, 24–25.
Sollicitudo Rei Socialis (John Paul II), xiv–xv, 1, 15–17, 25, 41, 52–55, 106–107, 114, 129–130, 199–200, 230.
Sovereignty, 77, 139, 171, 188, 208.
Sterilization, 143, 192, 194, 226.
Stewardship, 20, 218–219, 221.
Subsidiarity, 3, 26, 37–43, 52, 65, 68, 72, 120–122, 135, 187.
Suicide, 177.
Syllabus of Errors (Pius IX), 172.
Synod of Bishops, 15, 58, 236–237, 244.

Taxation, 79, 144.
Technology, 34, 124, 202, 204, 232–233, 235.
Ten Commandments, 8, 47, 129.
Terrorism, 135, 150–151, 212–215, 233.
Tertio Millennio Adveniente (John Paul II), 198, 200.
Theft, 24.
The Social Agenda (Pontifical Council for Justice and Peace), 15, 244.

Third World Debt, 51, 198.
Toleration, 77, 147–148, 209, 211, 213.
Torture, 144–145, 149–151, 213.
Totalitarianism, 16, 28, 32, 46, 57, 134, 157–158, 166–167, 176, 226, 233, 235, 238.
Tourism, 94.
Trade unions, 22, 98–99, 102.
Trent, Council of, 61.
True and false democracy (Pius XII), 14, 54, 160, 171–173.
Tyranny, 40, 153, 157, 221.

Ubi Arcano (Pius XI), 214.
Unam Sanctam (Boniface VIII), 162, 173.
Underdevelopment, 127, 129, 211, 225.
Unemployment, 39, 89, 130.
United Nations Organization, 70, 82, 175, 181, 183, 190–195, 199, 206, 215.
  agencies of the United Nations, 190.
  International Conference on Population and Development (Cairo, 1994), 192–193, 199.
  United Nations' Conference on Women (Beijing, 1995), 192.
  United Nations' Convention on the Rights of the Child, 70–71.
Universal Destination of Goods, 29–30, 32–34, 36, 96, 195, 221–222.
Usury, 14, 118–119, 131.

Utilitarianism, 124.

Vehementer Nos (Pius X), 52.
Veritatis Splendor (John Paul II), 8, 16, 47, 55.
Vix Pervenit (Benedict XIV), 14, 131.

War, 31, 70, 101, 150–151, 175, 190, 201, 203, 206–212.
  just war theory, 143, 147, 209.
Wealth, 34, 36, 91, 106–110, 112–113, 118, 121, 126–128, 130.
Weapons, 9, 11, 185–186, 207, 210–212, 215.
  biological weapons, 186, 210.
  chemical weapons, 11, 210, 233.
  nuclear weapons, 9, 11, 186, 211, 233.
Welfare State, 11, 31, 38–39, 116.
  nanny State, 32, 38, 121.
  social assistance State, 39.
Williams, Thomas, 181.
Women,
  attitude of United Nations conferences to, 192, 194, 199.
  complementarity to men, 23, 52.
  discrimination against, 25.
  equality with men, 21–22.
  right to remuneration for raising children, 79.
  right to work, 89–90.

www.ingramcontent.com/pod-product-compliance
Lightning Source LLC
Chambersburg PA
CBHW022108150426
43195CB00008B/317